Style as Motivated Choice

Linguistic Approaches to Literature (LAL)

ISSN 1569-3112

Linguistic Approaches to Literature (LAL) provides an international forum for researchers who believe that the application of linguistic methods leads to a deeper and more far-reaching understanding of many aspects of literature. The emphasis will be on pragmatic approaches intersecting with areas such as experimental psychology, psycholinguistics, computational linguistics, cognitive linguistics, stylistics, discourse analysis, sociolinguistics, rhetoric, and philosophy.

For an overview of all books published in this series, please see
benjamins.com/catalog/lal

Editors

Volume 44

Style as Motivated Choice. In memory of Peter Verdonk (1934-2021)
Edited by Michael Burke and Joanna Gavins

Style as Motivated Choice

In memory of Peter Verdonk (1934-2021)

Edited by

Michael Burke
University College Roosevelt

Joanna Gavins
University of Sheffield

John Benjamins Publishing Company

Amsterdam / Philadelphia

The paper used in this publication meets the minimum requirements of
the American National Standard for Information Sciences – Permanence
of Paper for Printed Library Materials, ANSI z39.48-1984.

DOI 10.1075/lal.44

Cataloging-in-Publication Data available from Library of Congress:
LCCN 2025007604 (PRINT) / 2025007605 (E-BOOK)

ISBN 978 90 272 2038 7 (HB)
ISBN 978 90 272 4484 0 (E-BOOK)

John Benjamins Publishing Company · https://benjamins.com

Table of contents

Marking the stylist from the style
The influential scholarly work of Peter Verdonk

Michael Burke
University College Roosevelt

This edited volume of stylistic scholarship and the chapters within it are dedicated to the memory of one of the kindest and most inspirational stylistics scholars of the late 20th century, Peter Verdonk. Peter was Professor of Stylistics at the University of Amsterdam and later Emeritus Professor of Stylistics. He died in November 2021 and this volume has been in the making since that time. Many of Peter's past colleagues attended his funeral in Amsterdam in November 2021 and scores of colleagues from the Poetics and Linguistics Association (PALA) attended an online service after the funeral in January 2022. That service included readings and shared anecdotal experiences from many of the scholars who have written chapters for this edited volume: Cathy Emmott, Joanna Gavins, Lesley Jeffries, Daniel McIntyre, Mick Short, Peter Stockwell, Michael Toolan, Katie Wales, and Sonia Zyngier. Shortly after these two services, I wrote two obituaries which appeared in PALA's own newsletter for the membership, and in PALA's flagship journal *Language and Literature* (published by Sage), for a wider audience.

Peter Verdonk (1934) was born in the town of Velsen, close to Amsterdam. After the war, Peter finished his schooling and began working as a marine lawyer in Amsterdam. But his passion for teaching drew him to the world of academia, and he returned to school to retrain. His teaching career began at a local grammar school until he was hired to teach in the University of Amsterdam's (UvA) Department of English Language and Literature. His doctoral thesis, entitled *How Can We Know the Dancer from the Dance: Literary Stylistic Studies of English Poetry* (also an inspiration for the title of this introduction), was written at the UvA. For the duration of his academic career, he would teach grammar, Old English, Middle English, and his cherished stylistics at his beloved University of Amsterdam. For almost three decades, he imparted knowledge teaching on three fundamental stylistics modules that he had developed himself: "Stylistics in Poetry", "Stylistics in Prose", and "Advanced Stylistics". These courses were taken by thousands of UvA English undergraduate students, all of whom benefited greatly from them,

https://doi.org/10.1075/lal.44.intro

including the author of this introduction, who also benefitted from Peter's vast expertise as a PhD supervisor.

After moving up the departmental ladder in Amsterdam, Peter eventually became the Chair of the English Department. It was around this time that he also became a full professor with the title "Professor of Stylistics", the first person to hold this title in the Netherlands. His professorial inaugural address, entitled "The Liberated Icon: From Classical Rhetoric to Cognitive Stylistics", was given in the university's grand auditorium (the Old Lutheran Church on the Singel canal in Amsterdam) to a packed house of current and former students and colleagues. Later, upon his retirement, a *Festschrift* was compiled for him. It was filled with contributions by academics both from the Netherlands and across the world. It was entitled *Contextualized Stylistics: In Honour of Peter Verdonk* (2000) and was edited by Tony Bex, Peter Stockwell and myself.

Peter Verdonk was not only a superb educator and a just and competent university administrator, but he was also a prolific writer and stylistics researcher. In the 1990s, he wrote, co-authored, and edited several influential publications on stylistics. These include *Twentieth-Century Poetry: From Text to Context* (Verdonk 1993); *Twentieth-Century Prose: From Text to Context* (Verdonk and Weber 1995) and *Exploring the Language of Drama: From Text to Context* (Culpeper, Short and Verdonk 1998). In 2002, his much-lauded book *Stylistics* was published by Oxford University Press. Peter wrote brilliant stylistic analyses in articles and chapters on many great modern English poets, many of which appeared in important journals in the field, including the PALA flagship journal, *Language and Literature*. His subjects included Owen, Auden, Heaney, Hughes and, of course, his much-beloved Philip Larkin, whom Peter would cite enthusiastically, and often.

In 2013, Bloomsbury Press published a book of Peter's entitled *The Stylistics of Poetry: Context, Cognition, Discourse, History,* which appeared in the *Advances in Stylistics* series. It contained republished works of some of Verdonk's most inspiring articles and chapters from across his extensive and prolific academic career. Peter could speak learnedly on topics ranging from the classical rhetorical works of Cicero and Quintilian to the cutting edge 21st-century theories of cognitive stylistics and indeed anything and almost everything that lay in between: be it grammatical, phonetic, historical, morphological or semantic. He was an expert on the language of (and in) Beowulf, Chaucer, Shakespeare, Milton, Dickens and any 20th-century British or Irish poet you could mention. One article in that 2013 Bloomsbury Press volume that stands out is his entry on "Style" that first appeared in 2006 in the second edition of the *Elsevier's Encyclopaedia of Language and Linguistics* (edited by K. Brown). This succinct fourteen-page entry has become a standard work and a "must-read" for any student of stylistics and style in language, as it provides a person with almost everything one needs to know about style in language.

Peter was dedicated to the Poetics and Linguistics Association (PALA) for more than four decades. He was one of its founders in the late 1970s/early 1980s and he served on the executive board for two terms as its Secretary in the 1990s. He was also a regular keynote speaker at the annual PALA conference, the last one being at the PALA 2009 conference that took place in Middelburg, The Netherlands. Together with his partner, Johanna (Joke) Bijleveld, Peter attended numerous PALA conferences, even long after retirement when he was no longer presenting his own research. He loved to talk to people, and especially to share his knowledge and wisdom with younger colleagues and early career researcher of all ages. Dozens of PALA colleagues and friends will no doubt have several treasured memories of conversations with Peter's and his calm, empathetic and thoughtful intelligence and advice.

The chapters in this volume are all inspired by the theories and ideas of Peter Verdonk's stylistic scholarship. We, the editors, approached Peter's literary linguistic colleagues from across the world, some of whom knew Peter for more than forty years and were with him when they founded the Poetics and Linguistics Association (PALA) together in the late 1970s.

In the opening chapter of the volume, on the notion of context and the poetry of John Donne, Peter Stockwell highlights how Verdonk was perhaps the first stylistics scholar to acknowledge the importance, and indeed the complexity, of context. Stockwell also shows how Verdonk remained contextually sensitive throughout his entire writing and publishing career. In the chapter that follows, written by Cathy Emmott on memory, bereaved mind styles and plot manipulation, the author leans heavily on Verdonk's theoretical idea of "style as motivated choice". In the third chapter Lesley Jeffries writes on motivation and textual meaning in poetry. Here, she follows Verdonk in demonstrating the importance, and indeed the value, of a rigorous linguistic and stylistic approach to exploring how poems make meaning. The study that follows is by Mick Short, one of the co-founders of the Poetics and Linguistics Association, along with Verdonk. As was the case in the earlier chapter by Emmott, Short focusses on Verdonk's idea of "style as motivated choice" and also on the important role that all aspects of context play in meaning making. Short analyses a poem by Seamus Heaney, one of Verdonk's favourite poets, whose work Verdonk analysed frequently and meticulously. A chapter by Daniel McIntyre follows, considering the concepts of style, structure and tone. Taking as his starting point Verdonk's well-known analysis of Auden's poem "*Musée des Beaux Arts*", McIntyre examines the nature of "truth" through stylistic-linguistic analysis, as indeed Verdonk had done in his own analysis many years earlier, albeit from a different angle. The seventh chapter in this volume is by Katie Wales. Like Short, Wales too is a founding member of PALA and worked with Peter on many occasions going back almost five decades. In her chapter, Wales focusses on how to make stylistic sense of Edward Lear's books of *Nonsense*. Following in Verdonk's footsteps, in her analysis she passionately promotes the "inseparability of form and meaning" in poetry. The study that follows by Paul Simpson is on dialogue, humour and style. In his study Simpson returns to the subject matter of the Irish TV comedy Series *Father Ted,* the subject of his chapter some twenty years earlier for the book celebrating Peter's retirement, edited by Bex, Burke and Stockwell (2000). The ninth chapter of this volume, written by Joanna Gavins, one of the co-editors of this book is entitled "Cognition and the creative interplay of word and image in Apollinaire's '*Il Pleut*'". In her chapter, Gavins successfully honours two of Peter Verdonk's long-standing scholarly interests, namely, the role of cognition in literary style and the association between word and image in verse. The tenth chapter by Michael Toolan explores the poetry of Philip Larkin, something Peter Verdonk did throughout his entire professional career. In this study, Toolan takes the same path as Verdonk, seeing literature as "world-representing" rather than "world-referencing". The final study in this volume written by Gerard Steen is on the topic of Bob Dylan's world of words. Steen too returns to Verdonk's idea of "style as motivated choice", this time from a corpus-linguistic perspective. The volume concludes with a fitting Afterword, a warm and heartfelt tribute to Peter Verdonk written by yet another of his long-standing colleagues and friends, Sonia Zyngier.

It was never my intention to make this introduction long, but instead to let the chapter contributions speak for themselves of the legacy of the man they seek to praise. Therefore, I will draw the introduction to this volume to a conclusion and wish the reader much reading pleasure in the chapters that are to come. However, I would like to leave you with one last thought: When marking the stylist from the style, we should also mark the humanist from the human, for Peter Verdonk was far more than an eminent stylistician and great scholar of the language of literature. He was an impeccably decent, deeply caring, and thoroughly humane man. What he has taught us is that great scholarship without kindness towards those who are lower down on the career ladder is not worth a jot. May this volume help build on Verdonk's scholarly and human tradition. A "stylistics of kindness" is as fitting a tribute as anyone might wish for.

References

 Bex, T., Burke, M. & Stockwell, P. (Eds.). 2000. *Contextualized Stylistics: In Honour of Peter Verdonk.* Atlanta: Rodopi.

Verdonk, P. 1988. *How Can We Know the Dancer from the Dance: Some Literary Stylistic Studies of English Poetry*. PhD Dissertation, University of Amsterdam.

Verdonk, P. (ed.). 1993. *Twentieth Century Poetry: From Text to Context*. London: Routledge.

Verdonk, P. & Weber, J. J. (eds.) 1995. *Twentieth Century Fiction: From Text to Context*. London: Routledge.

Culpeper, J. Short, M. & Verdonk, P. (eds). 1998. *Exploring the Language of Drama: From Text to Context*. London: Routledge.

Verdonk, P. 2002. *Stylistics*. Oxford: Oxford University Press.

Verdonk, P. 2006. Style. in K. Brown (Ed.), *Encyclopedia of Language and Linguistics* Volume 12 (Second Edition), 196–210. Oxford: Elsevier.

Verdonk, P. 2013. *Stylistics of Poetry: Context, Cognition, Discourse, History*. London: Bloomsbury.

CHAPTER 1

Style in its contexts
The case of John Donne

Peter Stockwell
University of Nottingham

Peter Verdonk's stylistics was contextually-sensitive throughout all of his
published work. As a scholar of both language and literature, he understood
that "context" meant more than a simple historicising and unidirectional
reading across from the moment of creative production. Context involves all
of the different moments of history in which a literary text is conceived,
created, published, read, and re-read by new generations through time. It
also involves contextualising that goes beyond the simply historical: cultural
repositioning, intertextual connections, and personal resonance, for
example. Crucially, these are all matters of language, if language is
understood properly to encompass the social and the cognitive.

In this chapter, I explore the origins, readings and positioning of John
Donne's "No man is an island" text from *Meditation XVII, from Devotions
upon Emergent Occasions* (1624), treating it as a case-study for a fully
contextualised stylistics. The text has been given a very wide range of
significances as a result of repeated and variable contextualisations both
diachronically and synchronically. In the spirit of Verdonk's contextualised
stylistics, I trace some of these patterns in order to show that style and
context are inseparable, and that their literary motivation can (only) be
studied from a rich stylistic perspective.

Keywords: cognitive poetics, context, historicism, John Donne, mind-
modelling, situatedness, style

No man is an island

No text is an island, with meanings held entirely within itself. Any text's significance and impact is a matter of its inherent patterning, but those patterns are situated in a set of contexts including history and biography, politics and belief, and
the associations of the textual patterns with other texts. Though neither of the
precursors of stylistics (Russian Formalism and American New Criticism) were
ever truly as purely formalist as their detractors suggested, the emphasis of early

https://doi.org/10.1075/lal.44.01sto

stylistics was very much on a fairly narrow definition of linguistics that would only turn much later on to pragmatics, text-linguistics, discourse analysis, sociolinguistics and cognitive poetics (see the comments, at a pivotal moment in the development of stylistics, in the introduction to Sell and Verdonk 1994: 9–26).

The division between text and context might once have been analytically convenient in order to set aside the messy business of socioculture, psychology and experience, but it is a false and unsustainably limited scoping of linguistics. Language is unanalysable without its "contexts", to the point at which it makes no sense to describe context as if it were non-linguistic. As Peter Verdonk noted, the style of a text is always situated.

> If one thing has become obvious [...], it is the fact that conscious or unconscious choices of expression which create a particular style are always motivated, inspired, or induced by contextual circumstances in which both writers and readers [...] are in various ways involved. (Verdonk 2002: 7)

Style is a motivated choice that generates effects. Since style is always situated, stylistic analysis must rest on a definition of language and linguistics that treats "context" as a central, rather than appended feature of language. Throughout his stylistics work, Peter Verdonk recognised that interdisciplinarity and a direct and encompassing analysis of text and context were essential (see, for example, Verdonk 1993, Verdonk and Weber 1995, Culpeper, Short and Verdonk 1995, and the anthology of his work in Verdonk 2013). He practised a "contextualised stylistics" (see Bex, Burke and Stockwell 2000).

In this chapter, I explore how text and context cannot properly be separated, by discussing the origins, readings and positioning of John Donne's "No man is an island" text from *Meditation XVII, from Devotions upon Emergent Occasions* (1623), treating it as a case-study for a fully contextualised stylistics.

> No man is an Iland,
> Intire of itselfe;
> Every man is a peece of the Continent,
> A part of the maine.
>
> If a Clod bee washed away by the Sea,
> Europe is the lesse,
> As well as if a Promontorie were:
> As well as if a Manor of thy friends
> Or of thine owne were.
>
> Any mans death diminishes me,
> Because I am involved in Mankinde.
> And therefore never send to know for whom the bell tolls;
> It tolls for thee.   John Donne (1623: 415–16)

Never send to know

The first step in a fully integrated analysis remains the textual patterning, which is available to all readers but is systematically identifiable with a little stylistic awareness and knowledge. In this first step, there is no need to go searching for biographical or contemporary historical information: the stylistician can simply draw on our common language capacities to note the craftedness of the text.

For example, most readers would be able to notice the sets of syntactic pairs, based on balance and parallelism, across the text. These pairs are linked to each other in a variety of meaningful semantic relations (spelling modernised):

> No man is an island / entire of itself (second phrase specifies the relevant property of an island)
> Every man is a piece of the continent / a part of the main (apposition)
> If a clod be washed away... / Europe is the less (conditionality and consequence)
> Any man's death diminishes me / because I am involved (causality and analogy).

There are even parallelisms embedded within parallels:

> As well as if a promontory were / as well as if a manor [...] were.

Here, the comparative metaphor marker "as if" sets up "promontory" and "manor" as analogous equivalents to each other, as well as analogies with the "clod/Europe" pair in the two lines preceding. The last of these ("manor of thy friends") is also paired up with the alternativity of "or of thine own", further embedding the embedding.

Second, almost all readers (based on my classroom evidence, at least) notice the negational tone in the text, framed by the emphatic negative particles at the beginning ("No man") and the end ("never send"). Aside from this syntactic negation, the text is also prominently semantically negative in tone: "piece, part, clod, washed away, the less, death, diminishes".

Third, there is an obvious switch in addressivity, from the generic opening and the general, third person references across the first half, to the second half of the text where the writer involves the reader in a direct second person address: "thy friends", "thine own". This switch from generic to personal is continued as the first person pronouns appear from the writer ("me ... I am"), and continue to the end with the imperative, second person "never send to know" and the final direct address "for thee".

Fourth, there are sound-patterns in the text that reinforce and make prominent its meanings. For example, there are echoic /m/ and /n/ repetitions across the entire text, especially in close proximity and on key words: "no man is an island ... man ... main ... promontory ... manor ... thine own ... any man's ...

diminishes me … am involved in mankind .. never send to know". There are also subtle internal rhymes, alliterations and assonances: "man … an … island", "Intire of itself", "piece … part", "man … main", "clod be … by the sea", "washed … sea … less", "death diminishes". Most strikingly, perhaps, is the iambic hexameter with which the text closes. This sits in a line on its own, with its conclusive and portentous nature set up by the finality of the previous end-stopped line, by the initial "And" and by the preparatory conclusive "therefore":

> And <u>therefore</u> <u>never</u> <u>send</u> to <u>know</u> for <u>whom</u> the <u>bell</u>

The iambic hexameter, of course, has an added, heavily stressed syllable (a *hyper-catalexis*); brilliantly, it is on the word "tolls". Just to underline the iconicity of this tolling of the bell, the final line ("It tolls for thee") repeats the heavy iambic stress on "tolls" and "thee", and the short line suggests an iconic parallel with the life cut off half-completed.

Last, it is difficult to miss the central analogy that is set up in the opening metaphor: "No man is an island". This is a neat mapping that defeats many traditional definitions of metaphor in that it is literally true. However, no one reads this as being a banal statement about the literal non-island properties of people. (It serves to demonstrate that a metaphor is a necessarily integrated readerly process of interpretation as well as a feature with textual patterning). Instead, the clause is treated as a generic sentence with a proverbial, universal flavour. This metaphor is then extended to become almost allegorical, in which people are geography. The trope governs the overall structure of the text, with an open, expansive and public first half, leading to a more personal, direct and intimate second half. The extended metaphor that dominates two-thirds of the text is characterised by the mapping of the abstract idea of an integrated holistic complexity onto concrete and familiar concepts such as islands, cliffs, houses and friends. The proverbial nature of the first stanza is carried not only by the obvious metaphoricality of the meaning, but also by the universalising simple present tense. The middle stanza is more indirect in its alternativity, with the present tense in the subjunctive mood ("If a clod be washed", "as if a promontory were"). The final stanza returns to a simple present, and reinvokes the flavour of a parable or final moral consequence.

The brief analysis above represents the bare bones of a text-focused stylistic account of the poem. But of course, I have in fact been rather mischievous here, in referring to lines, metrical patterns, stanzas and presenting the text as a poem, and I have alternated the original historical spellings with modernised forms. In fact, the famous text is not a poem at all, but is an excerpt from a prose work published in 1623. It is the seventeenth in a series of "Meditations", in *Devotions upon Emergent Occasions, and Severall Steps in my Sicknes*, by John Donne. This 630-page book is divided into three parts: "Meditations upon our humane condition", "Expostulations, and debatements with God", and "Prayers, upon the sever-all occasions, to him". The book is small: 12mo, duodecimo size, which at 18.7cm x 12.7cm makes it possible to read in the hand and carry around. Each page of close-type ends with the first word of the following page indented, so that some-one reading out loud would not need to pause to turn the page.

The full "Meditation XVII" runs to 730 words, and it sets up the tolling bell trope at the very beginning:

> "Meditation XVII"
> *Nunc lento sonitu dicunt, morieris.*
> [Now with the slow bell ringing they say, you will die]
>
> Perchance he for whom this bell tolls may be so ill as that he knows not it tolls for him; and perchance I may think myself so much better than I am, as that they who are about me and see my state may have caused it to toll for me, and I know not that. The church is catholic, universal, so are all her actions; all that she does belongs to all. When she baptizes a child, that action concerns me; for that child is thereby connected to that head which is my head too, and ingrafted into the body whereof I am a member. And when she buries a man, that action concerns me: all mankind is of one author and is one volume; when one man dies, one chapter is not torn out of the book, but translated into a better language; and every chapter must be so translated. God employs several translators; some pieces are translated by age, some by sickness, some by war, some by justice; but God's hand is in every translation, and his hand shall bind up all our scattered leaves again for that library where every book shall lie open to one another. As therefore the bell that rings a sermon calls not upon the preacher only, but upon the congregation to come, so this bell calls us all; but how much more me, who am brought so near the door by this sickness.   (Donne 1623: 411–12)

The full text mainly concerns the notion of the universal church, and clearly elab-orates a theme set out by St Paul, though Donne does not mention this source directly. Donne, who was Dean of St Paul's in London, is perhaps likely meditating on the extended biblical analogy in 1 Cor. 12: 12–31 and the more succinct Romans 12: 4–5 ("For as in one body we have many members, and all the members do not have the same function, so we, though many, are one body in Christ, and individ-ually members one of another").

The key, celebrated passage is not particularly prominent, occurring just over halfway through the Meditation; it is not even graphologically distinct, since there are no paragraph breaks in the original. And of course the original text features the "long s" (ſ) in words like "itſelfe", "waſhed" and "leſſe" and the "rounded v" (ʋ) as in "eʋery" and "neʋer". In its original form, then, the text presents itself very differently compared with the way we are used to seeing it today.

Indeed, the reformatting of the excerpt in the form of a poem is widespread. If you search online for the phrase "No man is an island", you will find many dozens of verse-layouts, with several variations in spelling, line-endings, and stanzification. For example, the layout I used for the text at the beginning of this chapter is based on that used by the *All Poetry* website (at <https://allpoetry.com /No-man-is-an-island>). *Your Daily Poem* has the text without stanza breaks; they also split the final two lines and alter the wording to "Therefore, send not to know / For whom the bell tolls, / It tolls for thee" (<https://www.yourdailypoem .com/>). The layout used by Dalhousie University for favourite poems (at <https://web.cs.dal.ca/~johnston/poetry/island.html>) also renders the text as a single block without stanzas, though still set out as a poem, and yet with different line-breaks. They also (inaccurately) present some of the older spellings as an "Olde English Version", though with modern letter-forms. The popular website *Poemhunter* (at <https://www.poemhunter.com/poem/no-man-is-an-island/>) has the text as a single block, but centrally-aligned and with the stereotypical poetic capital letters for the beginning of each line. There are very many similar modern variants: see, most popularly, <https://www.oatridge.co .uk/poems/j/john-donne-no-man-is-an-island.php>, <https://www.mensaforkids .org/read/a-year-of-living-poetically/donne-no-man-is-an-island/>, <https:// poemanalysis.com/john-donne/for-whom-the-bell-tolls/>, <http://www.poems withoutfrontiers.com/No_Man_Is_an_Island.html> and the numerous renditions on video sites such as *YouTube*. The vast majority of non-scholarly online sources (of around 1.3 million examples on a simple, crude google search) treat the text as a poem. It has remained a popular text for exactly 400 years, constantly in print in different forms. The book was so popular on publication that it was first reprinted as soon as a year later, in 1624.

For whom the bell tolls

It should be apparent from the foregoing account that even a focused stylistic analysis impinges into matters which might not narrowly be regarded as purely linguistic. The ascription of poetic creative cleverness in the iconicity of the metrics to emphasise the tolling bell, the interpretative parallelism of meanings that are structured by syntactic parallelism, the identification, character, and significance that might be construed in the extended metaphor, the intertextual allusion to a New Testament trope of the early Christian church — all of these are issues that might be regarded as contextual matters. However, my argument in this chapter is that these sorts of situated knowledge are fundamentally matters of linguistic practice, and cannot be carved off as if they were separate. It would make as much sense to decide that a knowledge of denotational word-meanings was not purely linguistic because these are drawn from memory and experience. There has been, of course, a major tradition in linguistics that has regarded structure as being the only area of interest, to the exclusion even of semantics, let alone pragmatics, cognitive psychology, and sociolinguistics. This impoverished view of language must be rejected in general, and certainly for any possibility of stylistic exploration. More importantly, these *uses* of language are essentially what language is. In this section, I will briefly address different sorts of context, in order to show firstly how they can in fact also involve a stylistic account and secondly how they can each only render a perspective that is partial and unsatisfactory.

The most significant context in current literary criticism is historicisation. Texts such as Donne's "Meditation XVII" are explored for what they can tell us about the contemporary moment of production, the culture and society that gave rise to it, the imagined poetic and ideological enterprise of the author, and occasionally the nature of how the work was received. Much of the literary criticism around Donne is biographical in orientation (following Walton 1658, see Sugg 2007, Fetzer 2013, Guibbory 2006, 2015). The *Devotions upon Emergent Occasions, and Severall Steps in my Sicknes* were written when Donne was very ill, probably from typhus (according to Motion 1999). He had recently (1621) been appointed Dean of St Paul's cathedral, and several of his sermons and the *Devotions* explore the notion that sickness is a divine visitation. Donne had been born into a Catholic family at a time (1573) when the practice was punishable. He did not get his degree after studying at Cambridge because — as a Catholic — he refused to take the oath of supremacy to the monarch. Instead, from 1591, he trained as a lawyer and was admitted to Lincoln's Inn as a barrister in London. In the years that followed, Donne amassed a great wealth as a lawyer and as a soldier: he fought alongside Essex and Raleigh against the Spanish at Cadiz (1596) and in the Azores (1597), and his service allayed any anti-Catholic perceptions of him that others might have had. He travelled extensively in this time across the Italian states and France.

Returning to England, Donne was appointed as secretary to Sir Thomas Egerton, but in 1601 he secretly married Egerton's niece, Anne More, without her father's permission. Egerton and Sir George More had him thrown into Fleet Prison for several weeks and he was dismissed from his appointment. Though his father-in-law eventually relented and paid his daughter's dowry, Donne's government career was over, and he pursued a career in the church and as the member of parliament for Taunton.

By 1610, he had changed his mind as a recusant Catholic, and argued in a pamphlet, *Pseudo-Martyr*, that it was morally possible to swear a political oath of allegiance to King James while still retaining a religious loyalty to the Pope (see Gallagher 2017). Perhaps his decision was swayed by the capture, torture and death in prison by plague of his brother for harbouring a priest, and the priest's subsequent torture and disembowelment.

It is possible, even from these bare details, to read off elements of Donne's writing as biographically driven (see Docherty 1987). The logical structures, parallelisms, universalising and consequential patterns in "Meditation XVII" appear to align with such a legally-trained background, for example. Donne himself was certainly known for inserting himself into his work, and wittily crossing the lines between imaginative writing and his life. His biographer, Walton (1658: 86–8) recounts that Donne carved the graffiti "John Donne, Anne Donne, Undone" on the door of his prison cell after his secret marriage, though the story might not be entirely accurate (see Sugg 2007, Sullivan 2016). And his poem, "A Hymn to God the Father" includes the pun on "Donne/More":

> Wilt Thou forgive that sin which I have won
>   Others to sin, and made my sin their door?
>   Wilt Thou forgive that sin which I did shun
>   A year or two, but wallowed in a score?
> When Thou hast done, Thou hast not done,
>   For I have more.   Donne (composed 1623, published 1633)

This was written around the same time as "Meditation XVII". The excerpt and the framing text also show other historicised influences building on the biographical. For example, we might consider the broader political context and wonder whether Donne's European experience is contributing a veiled politics in the text. The analogy sweeps across "Europe", but why so expansive and foreign? Why not the newly created Kingdom of Britain, for the analogy? Or even just England itself? It seems that Donne might be reaching abroad for ideas that might have been considered more dangerously seditious a decade or so earlier. In the same vein, the "peece of the Continent" can certainly be read as "peace" as well as "piece", especially read aloud in the manner for which the book was designed. Is this a subtle repudiation of England's wars over the last few decades? The historical pan across the text begins with the widest European scope, but zooms in to the promontory, a friend's manor, to your house. And the progression "No man … every man … any man" seems to be inclusive of all humanity, perhaps even foreign enemies?

The religious context in its European setting might also be considered significant, of course. As the Latin epigraph at the beginning of "Meditation XVII" invokes, a funeral bell was first rung at the time for the sick and dying, not so much after death. This was a particular tradition at the Inns of Court, when a fellow of one of the chambers was dying. Other offices would send to know who was ill. Donne would almost certainly have been aware of this tradition. Furthermore within the religious context, Donne's argument in this "Meditation" and others in the book sets out his belief that the self – personal identity – consists of the interdependence of both body and soul. Though the soul can survive, the body cannot, and this leaves the question of whether personal identity persists after death (see Arshagouni 1991, Targoff 2008, Horn 2010). By allegorising the religious context within a European frame, Donne is also subtly drawing together Catholic and Protestant theology, and finding common cause with the Christian community beyond England's shores (see Guibbory 2015: 13 for Donne's defence of the Church of England's ceremonies in the wider Christian context, and Stubbs 2008).

These historicised framings are of course available to the reader of the wider text around the celebrated "No man is an island" excerpt, and to the wider reader of Donne's other prose works, and to Donne scholars; they are more difficult for a current, modern reader to derive solely from the famous passage alone. A problem with the way historicism is currently paradigmatic in literary criticism is that it tends to historicise only the chronological moment of production, largely neglecting all of the other historical moments that constitute different contextualisations and uses of the literary work – including the current moment. Historicism historicises everything but its own practice. The issue remains as to whether historically contextual knowledge, once gained, must also *then* be regarded as part of linguistic knowledge. In the same manner as the denotational and connotational knowledge of vocabulary items is mentally schematic, I would argue that it must be.

Sometimes, such schematic knowledge is required simply for the text to be readable at all (perhaps comparable to the fact that a knowledge of Latin would be required to make any contentful sense of the Meditation epigraph). For example, Donne's poem "The Extasie" (which appeared first in the second, revised edition of his *Poems* published posthumously in 1635, within a section called *Songs and Sonets*, see McCarthy 2020) contains the lines:

> Our eye-beames twisted, and did thred
> Our eyes, upon one double string.

This makes more sense if you know that it was a widespread view (prior to Newtonian optics in the later 17th century) that sight was effected by the eye sending out a beam that hit the object being looked at. Contemporary drawings show people looking at objects with lines emerging from their eyes (actually quite similarly to 20th century Superman comic panels). In this sense, it could be argued that what begins as distinct historical context becomes essentially linguistic knowledge of propositional meaning, once it has been mentally assimilated.

Of course, there are other framing contexts that might be regarded as nonhistorical. One interpretation that has proven significant for my students arises from a broadly feminist reading of the "No man is an island" passage. Although, of course, "man" and "mankind" were generic terms for *people* at this point in history, there is also no doubt that male people were regarded as the default humans. The negation, "no man", in the opening begs an implicit but unrealised possibility that a woman could be an island, but this is not manifest in the rest of the text, I think. Although the phrase is always taken to mean "no person is an island", the exclusion of women from the passage is structural rather than simply lexical: the rest of the text is about property and a (male) friend's property, about ownership. The text avoids third person pronouns altogether (*he/she*), which is quite a feat, if you re-read it. Instead, the implicit narrative persona (the meditating "Donne") is male, and the second-person pronouns (*thy/thine/thee*) are also men: "thy friend" and "thine" are immediately underlined by "Any man". The text could have all the male lexical items replaced by "one" or "person", but there would be a poetic alteration in the loss of the echoic "main" and "manor", identified previously. The structurally patriarchal nature of the text continues in its core ideology: would a court bell be tolled for a woman? Altogether, it is not just gender being encoded here, but also property, wealth, the command of servants who are sent to enquire about the bell, social position, and also class as well.

The negations throughout the text, identified in my brief initial stylistic account, now become rhetorically significant for a feminist framing of the passage in which the female experience is notably an absence. Indeed, the rhetorical context itself is worth exploring. The passage has a persuasive, argumentative function that is realised in the form of a progression from proposition to analogy to final statement. The initial proposition ("No man is an island") is restated across the text, with the internal elements of the metaphorical mapping teased out. This opening phrase has a complex metaphorical structure. As previously mentioned, it can be read entirely on the surface as being literally true: in this sense, it is a visible metaphor rendered apparently non-metaphorical by negation (a *visible metaphor* is defined as an expression in which both of the two mapped domains are realised on the surface of the text: see Stockwell 2020:121). However, almost everyone reads the entire proposition as being an expression of an invisible metaphor in which *people are interconnected*, and thus the phrase in practice is treated as a metaphorical mapping PEOPLE ARE LAND. This complexity sets up an allegorical extension in which people are not islands but part of the mainland, in which people are clods of earth on the landmass of Europe, in which people are headlands on that coastline, or landed estates, or houses. The embedded progression of these concepts ensures that the focus remains stylistically on these elements, of course, profiling the extended metaphor so that a reader is not encouraged to ask about the agency of the sea, or who the sea represents.

The rhetorical argument proceeds, then, analogically, and by repetition of the central premise. It seems to wind up in a strongly logical consequence, signalled first by the evocation of causality ("because I am") and then by the signalling "and" that the conclusive point is coming, and then with the word "therefore". Of course, upon reflection, the switch from the extended allegorical PEOPLE ARE LAND to the tolling of a bell is not a logical operator at all, but a theological one.

It tolls for thee

It is clear from the popular existence of Donne's text in the form of a poem that the historical and biographical contexts, and even the contemporaneous social and religious ideological contexts are being set aside by many — perhaps even most — readers. This leaves a disjunction between scholarly and civilian readers that seems to me ethically and culturally undesirable. Throughout my brief account of these contexts, I have inescapably implicated language patterns in the discussion, and I do think that a drawing on linguistics in its broadest sense offers a proper, rigorous way forward without falling into biographism or a mere privileging of a moment in history.

In the 400 years between the text's composition and now, the "No man is an island" passage has been repurposed in a large variety of usages. It featured in the title of a 1940 novel by Ernest Hemingway, *For Whom the Bell Tolls*, set in the Spanish civil war; *It Tolls for Thee* is a book about bereavement by Tom Morton (2021); *No Man is an Island* is the title of a set of spiritual essays by Thomas Merton (1983). Aside from the many versions set out like a poem, phrases from the passage appear in song lyrics by the Bee Gees, Metallica, and Pig (Raymond Watts), amongst many others. "No Man is an Island" is a 1970 reggae song by Dennis Brown, a 1968 song by Joan Baez from her *Baptism* album, and a 1966 song by soul band The Van Dykes. "It Tolls for Thee" is the title of a 1962 episode of the TV western *The Virginian*, and also of a 2016 episode of the BBC's *Holby City* hospital drama. The passage has been widely cited in discussions of social responsibility to refugees, around the UK Brexit debate, and in online meditations against illness, including COVID (see Antley 2022). All of these different social and cultural resonances of the passage can be understood linguistically as examples of different instances of *mind-modelling*.

Very briefly, mind-modelling is the common human capacity for imagining the nature and characteristics of the speaker or writer of an utterance, based on the fundamental fact that every utterance presupposes another mind. This draws on the psychological notion of "Theory of Mind" (see Apperly 2011), extended particularly into processes of literary reading (see Zunshine 2006), though mind-modelling is a fundamental and universal human capability. The mind of the other person who is modelled is based on the embodied facts of your own existence, experience and condition, and varied on the basis of incoming linguistic and social information (see Stockwell 2020, 2022). All of the different readings and uses of "Meditation XVII" represent different mind-modellings of John Donne. Mind-modelling is both personal and social. The mind being modelled is prototypically face-to-face, but our cognitive capacities for mind-modelling extend to remote people, historical people, and fictional people, without exception.

Every different use of the Donne text represents a different example of mind-modelling by different readers. Though these are personal, they are not entirely idiosyncratic, because they are grounded in the cognition of the linguistics of the text. This makes mind-modelling explorable by stylisticians with a fully contextualised view of language. In the "No man is an island" text, there are three particular main stylistic aspects which would drive a reader's mind-modelling of Donne: addressivity, deictic positioning, and cognitive embodiment.

For example, as noted above, the text begins proverbially and generically, implying a universal addressivity. This is reinforced by all the indefinite articles in the text ("an island ... a piece ... a part ... a clod ... a promontory ... a manor"). It only moves towards a closer and more specific definite addressivity first with the second person possessive pronouns ("thy ... thine") and then with the definite direct non-generic first person pronouns ("me ... I"). Most of the text consists of declarative sentences, unmodalised, and verbs that are semantically static ("is ... is ... were ...were"). The only sole exception here would be "washed away", but even that is rendered less actional by the auxiliary ("be washed"). But the final two clauses start with an (emphatic) imperative ("And therefore never send to know"), signifying a direct power-asymmetric addressivity. Notice, too, how the clause buries you after two verbs ("send to know") — finally doing action and cognition — and renders you in a grammatical particle ("whom") as an indirect object of the clause ("the bell tolls for thee"). The syntactic imperative ("never send to know") actually disguises an embedded interrogative (meaning "do not send to ask for whom the bell tolls?"). So after this evasion and removal, the final clause is all the more direct and powerful: for whom? — for thee! The addressivity ramps up the authority and credibility of the "Donne" voice, while focusing in more and more particularly on "thee".

That final "thee" is thus what Herman (1994) calls *doubly deictic*, in the sense that it points both to the textual narratee as well as "outwards" to you, the reader. In traditional egocentric deixis terms, the first part of the text is not deictic at all: it is all generic until "thy" and "thine". It then shifts proximally to "me/I" and "whom/thee". The spatial deixis only cuts in with the sweep down from a European view to your own estate. And in temporal terms, only the final hint of futurity ("it tolls for thee", and the implicit future aspect of an imperative) moves the deictic centre away from a generic present. However, there is a great deal of positioning social deixis in the ideological aspects discussed above, which captures a sense of a particular world-view on the part of the "Donne" mind. And a consideration of the compositional deixis allows us to talk, from within a cognitive *linguistic* frame, about the differences in this text's experiential history from prose to poetry, and the registers it displays throughout, to model a complex relationship between our imagined contemporary "Donne" and a sense of the "Donne-ness" of the historical tradition with which the text has been read and re-used.

Finally, the concreteness of the metaphors across the text is generally embodied: theology, complex logic, life, time and death, community and perception are all abstractions rendered in highly material, bodily terms. The emotional content of these is as important as their simple meaning-mappings. For example, I am reminded by the unfamiliar and phonologically marked "Clod" in the text, achronologically, of William Blake's "clod" in his 1789 poem "The clod and the pebble". Of course, there is no influence of the later on the former use, but both perhaps are gesturing towards the biblical "clod of clay" out of which God formed Adam in the Book of Genesis (2:7). The Hebrew word in the original is עָפָר (*aphar*), generally translated variously as *dust / earth / soil / clay* (see Strong's 1890 *Concordance*). It is the same word used later in Genesis 3: 19 "Remember, man, that thou art dust, and unto dust thou shalt return". Farrugia (2006) notes that both the Judaic and Christian traditions have a longstanding expression that Adam was created from "a clod of earth" or "clay" (he cites writings by Augustine and Luther), and observes that the name "Adam" comes from *adamah* (clay), related to the word for "red", *adom* in Hebrew. "Clod", then, has a particular biblical and funereal resonance of which I imagine my mind-modelled Donne the theologian would have been aware. In the context of "Meditation XVII", this figures Europe as a garden of Eden, and the loss of a single life as a sinful refutation of divine purpose.

An approach from mind-modelling allows us to draw properly on our best current understanding of language to encompass matters of imagined creativity, intention, design, and craftedness, that would traditionally have been excluded from a purely linguistic account as inaccessible context. Similarly, our knowledge of historical positioning, ideological framings, our sense of other readers' treatments of the text, and our own emotional associations with words, phrases, and genres are all matters of contextualised language, and therefore the domain of linguistics. We cannot really speak of style without recognising that it is an inherently contextualised textual phenomenon.

Every reader models a "John Donne", and imagines him to be more or less historically authentic, depending on your sense of your own historical knowledge. It requires an interdisciplinarity of literary scholarship, stylistics, and readerly experience that Verdonk foresaw and once styled as "the new interdisciplinarity":

> the mind of readers is not a passive *tabula rasa* on which literary texts simply register. [...] readers themselves positively bring something to texts in order to activate them. On the one hand [...], this readerly processing is certainly influenced by the fact that language and language-users, literature and its readers, are all rooted in particular sociocultural contexts. Reading therefore involves a kind of self-definition on the part of readers, which can be associated with strong feelings of human solidarity. Yet [...] readers' "work" with texts also brings into play their most intimately personal perceptions, feelings and judgements. Small wonder that, in order to study a phenomenon so profoundly social and so intensely private, many scholars are at last breaking down traditional lines of disciplinary demarcation. (Sell and Verdonk 1994: 195–6).

Many years later, collecting together and reflecting on his life's work as a stylistician, Peter Verdonk reiterated his commitment to this integrated form of stylistics, and ended his valedictory lecture at the University of Amsterdam with the traditional formulaic but apposite closing words, "I have spoken". Echoing that same spirit, for this chapter, I am done.

References

Antley, M.A. 2022. *John Donne in the Time of COVID*. New York: Wipf and Stock.

Apperly, I. 2011. *Mindreaders: The Cognitive Basis of "Theory of Mind"*. New York: Psychology Press.

Arshagouni, M. 1991. The Latin "Stationes" in John Donne's *Devotions upon Emergent Occasions*. *Modern Philology* 89(2): 196–210.

Bex, T., Burke, M. & Stockwell, P. (eds). 2000. *Contextualised Stylistics: in Honour of Peter Verdonk*. Amsterdam: Rodopi.

Blake, W. 1789. The clod and the pebble. In *Songs of Innocence and Experience*, 53. Lambeth: Catherine Blake.

Culpeper, J., Short, M. & Verdonk, P. (eds). 1995. *Exploring the Language of Drama: From Text to Context*. London: Routledge.

Docherty, T. 1987. Donne's praise of folly. In *Post-Structuralist Readings of English Poetry*, R. Machin & C. Norris (eds), 85–104. Cambridge: Cambridge University Press.

Donne, J. 1610. *Pseudo-Martyr*. London: Walter Burre.

Donne, J. 1623. *Devotions upon Emergent Occasions, and Severall Steps in my Sicknes*. London: Thomas Jones.

Donne, J. 1633. *Poems, by J.D. With Elegies on the Authors Death*. London: J. Marriot.

Donne, J. 1635. *Poems, by J.D. With Elegies on the Authors Death* (rev. edn, editor unknown). London: J. Marriot.

Farrugia, M. 2006. Gn 1: 26–27 in Augustine and Luther: "Before you are my strength and my weakness". *Gregorianum* 87(3): 487–521.

doi Fetzer, M. 2013. *John Donne's Performances: Sermons, Poems, Letters and Devotions.* Manchester: Manchester University Press.

doi Gallagher, J. 2017. Poetics of obedience: John Donne's "A Litanie" and the oath of allegiance controversy (1606–1610). *Modern Philology* 115(2): 159–182.

doi Guibbory, A. (ed.). 2006. *The Cambridge Companion to John Donne.* Cambridge: Cambridge University Press.

Guibbory, A. 2015. *Returning to John Donne.* London: Ashgate.

Hemingway, E. 1940. *For Whom the Bell Tolls.* New York: Charles Scribner's Sons.

Herman, D. 1994. Textual "you" and double deixis in Edna O'Brien's *A Pagan Place. Style* 28(3): 378–411.

doi Horn, M. 2010. John Donne, godly inscription, and permanency of self in *Devotions upon Emergent Occasions. Renaissance Studies* 2(3): 365–380.

doi McCarthy, E. A. 2020. *Poems, by J.D.* (1633 and 1635), the O'Flahertie manuscript, and the many careers of John Donne. In *Doubtful Readers: Print, Poetry, and the Reading Public in Early Modern England,* 147–181. Oxford: Oxford Academic.

Merton, T. 1983. *No Man is an Island.* Cincinnati: Franciscan Media.

Morton, T. 2021. *It Tolls For Thee: A Guide to Celebrating and Reclaiming the End of Life.* London: Watkins.

Motion, A. 1999. Preface. In *John Donne's Devotions Upon Emergent Occasions and Death's Duel* (edited by A. Motion), xi–xxi. London: Vintage.

doi Sell, R. and Verdonk, P. (eds). 1994. *Literature and the New Interdisciplinarity: Poetics, Linguistics, History.* Amsterdam: Rodopi.

Stockwell, P. 2020. *Cognitive Poetics: An Introduction.* 2nd edn). London: Routledge.

doi Stockwell, P. 2022. Mind-modelling literary personas. *Journal of Literary Semantics* 51(2): 131–146.

Strong, J. 1890. *The Exhaustive Concordance of the Bible.* Cincinnati: Jennings and Graham.

Stubbs, J. 2008. *John Donne The Reformed Soul.* New York:. W.W. Norton and Co.

doi Sugg, R. 2007. *John Donne.* London: Palgrave.

Sullivan, E. W. 2016. "John Donne, Anne Donne, Vn-done" redone. *ANQ: A Quarterly Journal of Short Articles, Notes and Reviews* 2(3): 101–103.

doi Targoff, R. 2008. *John Donne, Body and Soul.* Chicago: University of Chicago Press.

doi Verdonk, P. (ed.). 1993. *Twentieth-Century Poetry: From Text to Context.* London: Routledge.

Verdonk, P. 2002. *Stylistics.* Oxford: Oxford University Press.

Verdonk, P. 2013. *The Stylistics of Poetry: Context, Cognition, Discourse, History.* London: Bloomsbury.

Verdonk, P. & Weber, J-J. (eds). 1995. *Twentieth-Century Fiction: From Text to Context.* London: Routledge.

Walton, I. 1658. *The Life of John Donne, Dr in Divinity, and Late Dean of Saint Pauls Church London.* London: R. Marriot.

Zunshine, L. 2006. *Why We Read Fiction: Theory of Mind and the Novel.* Columbus: Ohio State University Press.

CHAPTER 2

Reconstructing Kath

Memory, bereaved mind styles and plot
manipulation in Penelope Lively's
The Photograph

Catherine Emmott
University of Glasgow

Penelope Lively's *The Photograph* is a story which revolves around a dead
woman, Kath, and the memories of her by those closest to her. Readers of
the novel have to form a representation of her from information presented
in the thoughts of the bereaved characters, then reconstruct this
representation later in the story as more information accumulates. This
chapter examines the "mind styles" of these bereaved characters, including
stylistic features such as metalepsis, multiple-self metaphors and sentence
fragmentation. In addition, this study examines how these presentation
techniques create a sense of mystery about the dead woman and hide key
facts for plot manipulation purposes, so that the revelations at the end of
the story can then come as a surprise to readers.

Keywords: Penelope Lively, *The Photograph*, mind styles, bereavement,
metalepsis, multiple-self metaphors, sentence fragmentation, plot
manipulation, mystery

Introduction

Penelope Lively's novel *The Photograph* provides an interesting text for studying
the combination of impactful thematic writing — in this case the themes of
bereavement and memory — and the careful handling of foreground and background information needed for successful plot manipulation. The story revolves
around Kath, who has died some years before the story begins. In one respect, this
is an elegiac story about memories of those who knew her, since the recollections
and differing perspectives of her family and various acquaintances occur throughout the novel. The reader has to create a representation of her from these recollections, which is particularly challenging because these recollections are from

https://doi.org/10.1075/lal.44.02emm

self-oriented perspectives and have some major lacunae. Lively offers a revealing portrayal of the way in which the memory of her haunts the thoughts of the bereaved characters in the story, providing insights into how people come to terms with a sudden and unexpected death. In another respect, this is also a mystery story, with a puzzle to be solved. Indeed, there are elements of a detective story, with Kath's husband trying to collect evidence about her infidelity, but with a denouement which makes the characters and the reader radically reappraise her life and her death.

The key objectives of the book — to represent haunting bereavement memories and to create a compelling plot — might seem to be somewhat antithetical. Bereavement can lead to lingering memories, some of them, as Lively shows, remaining frozen in time and repetitive. Conversely, a compelling plot often requires the impetus for change in order to provide a surprising denouement for the reader. The combination of these different types of writing is nevertheless achieved in this novel since the eponymous photograph and other disclosures are catalysts for the bereaved characters to radically change their perceptions of the dead woman.

In this chapter, I focus on the stylistic techniques used to present the characters' mourning reflections. These include the use of repeated metalepsis to show how vivid experiences of Kath are triggered and keep recurring in her relatives and associates; the use of multiple-self metaphors to reflect the complex nature of her personal identity seen through the prisms of others' memories; and the use of sentence fragmentation to echo the characters' traumatised inability to engage fully with their memories of the day she died. In addition, I examine how the writing style supports the development of the plot, since the stylistic indicators of bereaved thought patterns also provide a means of creating a mystery about her and a medium for burying key details which are later brought together to support the surprising denouement when her secret personal history is revealed. Overall, this chapter will examine how Lively manages to combine a haunting portrayal of the thoughts of the bereaved with a compelling plot which prompts readers to reconstruct their representations of the dead woman.

Story summary

This story opens with the discovery of a photograph of Kath by her husband Glyn, providing evidence of her infidelity. She has died several years previously and Glyn is devastated suddenly to find that his extremely attractive late wife had an affair with her brother-in-law, Nick — the photograph shows them secretly holding hands together. Glyn then shares this knowledge with her sister, Elaine (Nick's wife), and embarks on a quest to find out whether or not this is a one-off affair or serial infidelity, searching through his memories of Kath for clues about her behaviour and also interviewing others who knew her. Glyn is a professional academic, so he believes he can use his research abilities to investigate his late wife's story, but unfortunately he is too personally involved and he does not have the listening skills to be able to act as a successful amateur detective in this case (see Lecomte 2022).

One of the notable features of the book is the multiple perspectives not only of Glyn and Elaine, but also of Nick, Oliver (Nick's ex-business partner) and Polly (Nick and Elaine's daughter). Most chapters are headed with either the individual names of characters (identifying the focaliser of the chapter, e.g. "Glyn") or the names of two characters as they meet together, e.g. "Elaine and Glyn" (generally focalised by one or both of the two mentioned characters). As we see these different perspectives, we see the current lives of the characters, but these lives are punctuated by their memories of Kath. In consequence, the reader is able to build up a mental representation of her, although this relies on intermittently-occurring, fragmented and incomplete information that is then reconstructed as we learn fresh details throughout the story.

As the story progresses, we find that Kath's infidelity was in fact a one-off affair, but there are hints from minor characters that there is something to discover about her state of mind in the time before her death. Underlying her apparently happy exterior, it seems that she was a troubled figure, and the secrets behind her hidden personality become the main mystery of the book. Towards the end of the novel, Glyn relives his memories of the day that his wife died, revealing to the reader that she committed suicide. At the denouement, her old friend Mary provides background information about Kath's life that might explain her state of mind leading to her death. She reveals to Glyn, Elaine and Oliver in separate conversations that Kath suffered distress due to two miscarriages, and that she was also particularly affected by her mother's early death. This leads to reappraisals of her by these main characters and a sense of general sadness. They return to their everyday lives, although with a fresh understanding of her.

Bereaved mind styles

Lively has written other stories about bereavement, most notably *Perfect Happiness* (1985) and *Passing On* (1990), which both examine the responses of characters to recent deaths. By contrast, *The Photograph* (2004 [2003]) examines the reactions of characters to new information about the deceased several years after the death. Rather than representing raw grief and the initial adjustment after a death,

The Photograph shows relatives and associates who have become relatively fixed in their thoughts about the dead woman, until they discover the new evidence of the photograph and gain additional information, which prompts their radical reconceptualisations of the past and also changes how they act in the present.

In order to interpret the novel it is useful to draw on Fowler's (1977, 1996) classic work on mind style, which provides a general way of viewing how a range of stylistic features in a text may be indicative of a way of thinking. This allows the reader to have a sense of experiencing a character's thoughts (e.g. by seeing how characters' thoughts can start to break down into fragments as they think about a death, as we will see later in this chapter). In Lively's *The Photograph*, the notion of mind style seems particularly relevant, although there might be some debate about whether we are seeing a cumulative bereavement mind style across several individually-presented characters (Palmer 2004) or, alternatively, separate individual mind styles, representing their professional and personal selves, interspersed with bereavement experiences that are similar in nature but stem from their different relations to Kath and their own circumstances.

Verdonk's work on style as "motivated choice" (Verdonk 2002:5, see also Verdonk 2006), is also particularly relevant here. Verdonk believed that the linguistic choices that a writer has made may be of key significance to the overall interpretation of a literary work when they are foregrounded, particularly when they are repeatedly selected, as is the case in *The Photograph*. Throughout his career, Verdonk applied this type of analysis to a number of texts about death and bereavement, looking particularly at the ironies of death and the haunting presence of the deceased (e.g. Verdonk 1988; 2013). Verdonk's focus has been mainly on poetry, so it is interesting to see in this study how the types of observations he made about poets can be related to Lively's novel, where the stylistic effects are sustained over the span of a full book. Although it is common for stylisticians to look at foregrounding, Verdonk's work is significant because he has also examined backgrounding. In his discussion of Auden's "Musée des Beaux Arts" (a poem about Bruegel's *Landscape with the Fall of Icarus*), for example, he explores the irony of how the countryside characters in the poem and the picture are so busy with their everyday lives that they miss the big event when Icarus falls, which happens as a background detail (Verdonk, 1988:39–64). As we will see later, this focus on foreground and background is significant for *The Photograph* because the central characters in the story have been so preoccupied with their own lives that they have failed to understand Kath's distress and hence they have not been able to engage with the reasons for her suicide.

This chapter will examine the thinking styles of the characters remembering Kath. The reader has to construct a mental representation of her since she only appears in the other characters' memories (see Emmott 1997 for a discussion of how characters are mentally represented in "character constructs"). As Judd (2003) suggests, there is some similarity between this novel and Daphne Du Maurier's *Rebecca*, where the eponymous character is dead before the story begins, but she has a significant haunting presence throughout the story. In Lively's *The Photograph*, the references to Kath are split across chapters, viewed from the perspectives of different characters. This makes it difficult to build up a representation of her, particularly since the memories generally suddenly appear from nowhere as characters are conducting their everyday lives. These memories are often incomplete and fragmentary because of the nature of memory. Also, the dead woman herself appears to have withheld key information about herself from those closest to her – hence, ironically, very minor characters sometimes know more about her previous state of mind than her family.

As the story progresses, the characters and readers have to reconstruct their memories of Kath as new information is revealed. Culpeper's (2001) work is particularly valuable for showing how the balance of impressions about a character can shift throughout a text – in this case, there is an initial relatively positive representation, mediated through the thoughts of those who supposedly knew her well, which changes to a very bleak overall picture by the end of the book. This significant shift in our perceptions can only be achieved by selectively presenting those aspects of her behaviour at the start of the novel which seem to show her as having been primarily a happy-go-lucky figure. Factors that may have suggested the converse are suppressed or minimised at that early stage. Eventually, the balance is shifted in a way that aims to make the final major reversal seem convincing. Later in this chapter, I will draw on Emmott and Alexander's (2014; 2020) work on foregrounding and backgrounding to show the strategies used to present very different versions of Kath at different stages in the novel.

Lively's portrayal of bereaved mind styles in *The Photograph* has a degree of stylistic experimentalism, as will become evident in the examples that follow (see Gavins 2013 for a useful discussion of the cline of experimentalism). Lively is not usually included on lists of experimental writers for her work in general, but it has sometimes been recognised that she has experimental aspects to some of her writing (e.g. Moran 1997), particularly in relation to her Booker prize-winning novel *Moon Tiger* (Lively 1988; see McGrath 2017).

Stylistic features of bereaved mind styles

In the first part of the stylistic discussion in this chapter, I will focus on the bereaved mind styles in the story. This is a very obvious aspect of *The Photograph* as we begin to read the novel. It is not until later in the story that it becomes apparent that these stylistic choices might have the secondary motivation of controlling the way in which information is presented for plot manipulation purposes — hence, I will leave discussion of those aspects until the final section. I will look first at the features that cross characters, and then examine how a sample individual mind style is created.

Memory triggers and apparent presence

Lively's technique for representing bereaved mind styles reflects the common reports of bereaved people who say that their deceased loved one may appear to be present in their physical space, often triggered by anything that reminds them of the deceased (Sabucedo et al. 2021). In *The Photograph*, these triggering experiences may be visual, auditory, or more generally experiential, and are described as "resonances" (p. 17). The triggers are various, and include objects (p. 1), a similar-looking person (p. 160), and particularly places (e.g. p. 28 and p. 156), but the memories can also be spontaneous so do not always have obvious triggers (p. 62).

Although these experiences are imaginary, there is a strong sense of presence. The techniques used can be explained using the narratological term "metalepsis" (Genette 1980, 1988, see also Fludernik 2003), which describes the crossing of different ontological narrative levels. In the following examples from *The Photograph*, the crossing is between the world of the imagination of the fictional characters and their everyday physical world. Although the characters know that Kath is dead, the writing style sometimes suggests, if read literally, that she is entering the scene. Of course, what they experience of her is only a product of their imagination, but nevertheless the metalepsis can portray an intense experience, particularly when it happens at regular intervals for specific characters and also for a number of characters.

The experience of triggering is achieved in a particular striking fashion at the very start of *The Photograph*, where she seems to physically enter the scene:

> Kath.
> Kath steps from the landing cupboard, where she should not be.
>
> (Glyn's thoughts, p. 1)

The repetition of her name here, particularly when formatted initially as a separate item in a sentence fragment in its own mini-paragraph highlights the triggering effect. The name is the very first word of the main text of the story, with only the chapter heading, "Glyn" above it. By "sentence fragment", I mean a word or words that are punctuated as a sentence, but do not form a syntactically complete sentence (Emmott et al. 2006a). Our empirical research has shown that these are particularly attention-grabbing with this additional paragraph formatting (Emmott et al. 2006b). The repetition of Kath's name also adds to this effect. At this stage, readers are not aware that she is dead, so the idea of her joining Glyn in the scene is strong. She does not just appear, but seems to actively step into the room towards Glyn, the focaliser, even though we soon learn that it is simply the case that her memory has been triggered by Glyn seeing a file which is marked with her writing fall from the cupboard. Then "She smiles at him" (p. 2). The effect is cumulative as Glyn continues to intermittently experience her presence throughout the story. Glyn sometimes finds this intrusive – the mention in the example above that she should not be in the cupboard is perhaps simply because her documents have been wrongly placed there, but elsewhere there is a hint of irritation, as we will see when we discuss other aspects of his mind style later.

There is no explicit signal in the above example, such as "he imagined". On occasions, though, there is a signal (for example, the expression "In the mind's eye" (p. 11)) which is used to preface Glyn recalling memories of Kath's habitual behaviour. Sometimes, an explicit memory trigger may preface her appearance, as with the name in this example, when someone has just referred to her:

> It is curious how her name instantly summons her. She is right there, for an instant, looking at him.   (Nick's thoughts, p. 94)

On many occasions, though, she just seems to appear, or her voice is suddenly heard as direct speech, for example when her sister Elaine is working and she hears the words "You're *so* judgemental", as if said to her by Kath directly (p. 29). There is no indication that Elaine is hallucinating voices, just that her sudden recollection is very intense.

Bühler (1990) identifies two primary types of imagination-orientated deixis (*deixis am phantasma*) in everyday life. People may imagine an object inserted into their context, as when someone tries to decide whether a new piece of furniture will look good in the room they are standing in, or they may imagine themselves entering another scene, as when they imagine themselves visiting a restaurant later. The idea was developed by Duchan et al. (1995) who use the term "deictic center" to describe the reader's current context at any point in a story. The term "inwards deictic transfer" (Emmott 2017) can be used to describe the examples from *The Photograph* above where Kath seems to be entering the focaliser's current context, but conversely, there are occasions when there is "outward deictic transfer" (Emmott 2017), where the focaliser is represented as moving into the imagination, which in the case below is a memory of a past encounter.

> he finds himself in Elaine's garden, with Kath, companionably gathering windfall apples   (Oliver's thoughts, p. 191)

Specific memories sometimes seem as if they (metaphorically) haunt particular characters and can be quite limited and fixed in form and often recurrent (signalled by the repeated adverbs at the end of the following example):

> she is this impervious presence in his head, re-enacting frozen moments. Saying
> the same things again and again.   (Nick's thoughts, p. 142)

In the reader's first encounter with Elaine's thoughts, at the very start of the second chapter, Elaine's memory is triggered by a place. Elaine is driving past the Town Hall Registry Office at the time and thinks of Kath's wedding day. This memory has become fixed and recurrent, again with the repetition of the name at the start highlighting the personal link and the repeated adverbs at the end of the example indicating recurrence:

> Kath.
> Kath always swims into view just here [...] Kath comes down the steps, again
> and again and again   (Elaine's thoughts, p. 28)[1]

These types of examples and other specific episodic memories recur repeatedly, so that the text becomes a series of glimpses of Kath and her past, with the information provided about her presenting a partial view of her from multiple perspectives.

Multiple selves

One very noticeable stylistic feature in Lively's work is that when Kath appears in the imagined context of the characters, she often appears in plural form. We can see this clearly in the two examples below:

> A whole troop of Kaths flit about him, stemming from different times and places
>   (Nick's thoughts, p. 94)

> several Kaths have arrived   (Elaine and Glyn's thoughts, p. 62)

One obvious reason for this plurality is that the characters have multiple memories of her that can be triggered or appear spontaneously at any point and sometimes these memories may occur in rapid succession or together. In the first example above, the text goes on to briefly list three separate memories in three

---

1. Throughout this chapter, ellipsis marks are enclosed in square brackets when I omit material in quotations simply to keep quotations as short as possible and focused. Ellipsis marks without square brackets are in Lively's original text. Ellipses are of stylistic significance in this novel, so this is an important distinction.

successive sentences. In the second example, Elaine and Glyn are having dinner together and both are simultaneously thinking of her as they talk. Glyn imagines a previous occasion when he was with his wife on a canal barge (described in more detail in a paragraph of several sentences) and at the same time Elaine is "experiencing several Kaths" (p. 62) (the details are not provided by Lively) and then Elaine recalls a more detailed (half page) memory of the day the photograph was taken.

Lively has expressed a belief in interviews (e.g. Crown 2009; McGrath 2017) and in her autobiographical work (e.g. Lively 2014) that memories are not linear — they can appear from any period in time. This achronology is seen repeatedly in *The Photograph*. These recurrent memories particularly affect Glyn, who is still living in the same house in which he and his wife lived together, so the house itself constantly triggers these memories.

> Kath is everywhere now, the landing is full of her, and the staircase, and the big brimming treacherous cupboard; there are dozens of her, from different times and at different places, all talking at once, it seems.   (Glyn's thoughts, p. 6)

Kath's plurality also reflects Lively's views on the nature of personal identity generally (i.e. in life as well as in death). Lively believes that if we know a person well, we often see the earlier versions of them as we look at them or remember them (the main characters are all represented as multiple selves at various points in *The Photograph*). The memories of Kath across time are particularly strong in her sister, Elaine, since she has known her throughout her lifespan:

> Elaine finds other Kaths crowding in. [...] Child-Kaths are mixed with grown-Kaths, so that the effect is of some composite being who is everything at once, no longer artificially confined to a specific moment in time — no longer ten years old, or twenty, or thirty, but all of those. This is a hydra-headed Kath
>   (Elaine's thoughts, p. 153)

Elaine thinks of her sister just after this quotation as a "multiple Kath" (p. 153), so Lively is presenting her as a multiple self who was there, continuous and changing, throughout their lives. Elsewhere, I have used Lakoff's (1996) term "split self" in other research about trauma (Emmott 2002) and that term might be appropriate in some cases in this book where we see distinct past and present versions of characters, particularly where they are sufficiently different in nature to have characteristics of two different entities. Nevertheless, the idea of the "multiple self" is perhaps more relevant to the parts of the text, as above, where many different versions of Kath seem to be fused onto each other rather than being held up for comparison.

One clear example of splitting of the self can be seen in the way that the adult versions of Kath become more difficult to handle after the discovery of the photograph, which provided evidence of her affair with Elaine's husband, Nick. This leads to the difficulty for Elaine of differentiating in her memories between whether her sister was, at any particular point, innocent or had at that point in time betrayed her, so determining Elaine's reaction to her and the extent to which she needs to reconstruct her view of her (p.149). Hence, there may sometimes be a moral dimension to the representation of Kath's different adult selves, which might be seen as a potential split in how she is perceived in the memories of characters (see Stockwell 2009: 160–7 for a discussion of these moral aspects).

It is not just that Kath is perceived as having multiple selves by specific characters, but also that she is fragmented across several minds, with different people holding different – and even contradictory – memories, leading to the existential question of how she can continue at all as an entity in the minds of these characters. In the novel *Perfect Happiness*, this is seen in relation to a deceased husband, where his widow asks how he can simply be "reduced to a matter of other people's thoughts" (p.26).

In some respects, there is reassurance in the fact that a joint representation is held by several characters since memories held only by a single person are vulnerable. In *The Photograph*, Elaine realises this when, after she has considered how, in her memory, Kath will "for ever and always" come down the Registry Office steps towards her (p.28), she qualifies this with the thought "Actually, just so long as I'm around" (p.28). Some memories appear to be communal, particularly for shared events such as Kath and Glyn's wedding, but even then characters may remember different fragments from different perspectives, and sometimes have contradictory memories.

These differing memories can be particularly difficult for those close to the deceased because they can challenge and undermine their own representations in a way that they feel is inappropriate. In *Perfect Happiness*, the result is "the capacity to dilute" the memory (p.34). In *The Photograph*, Elaine is exasperated when a minor character, Linda, starts to speak about Kath in clichés, believing that Linda has "no right to Kath" (p.161). Elaine wonders why Linda can't see that her comments are "a travesty" of her and that she is reducing her "to her own humdrum vision" (p.161). When Glyn hears the recollections of others who have additional knowledge of his late wife, he has feelings "of exclusion, of ignorance, of deprivation" (p.132).

The nature of memories: Fragmentation and memory loss

Another key stylistic feature in *The Photograph* is the use of sentence fragmentation at moments when characters contemplate Kath's death. These moments are only occasional, but are heavily foregrounded as the thoughts of characters seem to suddenly break down syntactically.

In texts generally, sentence fragmentation can be foregrounded to different degrees. In stories, fragmentation is used for multiple purposes (Emmott et al. 2006a), such as evaluations, topic introductions, reiterating descriptive information from an earlier sentence, and reflecting the slowness of thinking processes during moments of discovery. Lively uses fragments in some of these standard ways, but her use of fragmentation becomes more radical when it is combined with ellipsis and underspecification in thoughts and speech. References to Kath by her name or pronouns are left without verbs, and events are left unspecified after time indicators. "That day.", in the example below, is left unexplained, although immediately afterwards there is a chapter with that heading which explains what happened on the day of her death.

Back then. When She. When.	(Glyn's thoughts, p. 2)
Back then. When. After.	(Glyn's thoughts, p. 17)
"Must have been there since she — Since then."	(Glyn's speech, p. 58)
That day. When Kath.	(Nick's thoughts, p. 204)

This reluctance to think about her death appears to reflect trauma. In speech, too, characters either refrain from mentioning death or delay in mentioning it, without discussing the details further:

"I was told she —"	(Clara's speech, p. 123)
"devastated when — When she — So sad."	(Linda's speech, p. 162)
"Kath ... died"	(Oliver's speech, p. 72, Lively's ellipsis)

Burke (2010:130) provides a useful discussion of aposiopesis (breaking off in speech) in relation to the use of dashes and ellipses to convey emotion. These stylistic features are clearly evident in the above examples. This general reluctance to think and talk about death reflects a societal norm in British culture (where the story is set), but also provides an opportunity to withhold information from the reader for plot reasons, as discussed later.

In the above examples of thought and speech, characters have the relevant knowledge about Kath, but they do not want to engage with it mentally or are reticent in speech. In addition to this, details about her are withheld because characters have gaps in their memories, for various reasons — for example, memory is generally fallible, but also sometimes her relatives and friends have been inattentive to her or simply not present at a key point in her life.

So although bereavement memories can be intrusive (as discussed earlier), memories of loved ones can also be frustratingly incomplete for the participants. In *The Photograph*, we are given the impression that there are limits to what is normally recalled by the characters and that some of the characters are usually unwilling to probe further. Kath's husband, Glyn, only starts to interrogate his memories about her after his discovery of the photograph. Hence, memories are described by metaphors that show their inadequacy. Some memories seem to have deteriorated or have become compressed, so that "tracts of it have gone down the sluice" (p.63) and are now "compacted into a handful of vibrant moments" (p.139). Elsewhere, parts of the memories are simply missing, so, for example, Kath becomes just a face and a voice "like the Cheshire cat" (p.29) and "everywhere there are perforations. There are holes through which [she] slips away." (p.25) or lacking in detail since there is just an "impressionistic blur of things said, things done" (p.25).

As the story progresses, though, some of these lacunae are filled, with new details "bubbling up from the vaults of memory" (p.125). Liquid metaphors are used here and elsewhere to show the reconstruction of memories, so we learn that "A stone has been cast into the reliable, immutable pond of the past, and as the ripples subside everything appears different" (p.59). Earthquake metaphors are used to show a more significant shift in memory (a "seismic jolt", p.154). These reconstructions of memory can be distressing for the main characters when new information challenges their core views about people they thought they had known well but who appear in a very different light.

Filtering Kath's representation through communal and individual mind styles

The ways of representing bereavement discussed so far are largely shared by the main characters. Although different characters are generally thinking about Kath separately, they have similar experiences of her suddenly entering their thoughts and there is some similar content. In this respect, it could be argued that the reader sees what Palmer (2004) terms "intermental" thought since there is a sense in which this community of relatives and friends experience the same bereavement and share a representation of the dead woman.

Nevertheless, we also see individual mind styles represented and the actual memories of Kath may have significant differences. Oliver, who is perhaps the most objective of her main observers, muses that:

> She has become like some mythical figure, trawled up at will to fit other people's
> narratives. Everyone has their way with her, everyone decides what she was, how
> things were.   (Oliver's thoughts, p. 173)

The Photograph's strength as a novel is that it convincingly shows how those who
knew her try to integrate bereavement memories into their own lives, and the
book shows these experiences of remembering as they occur in the characters'
individual mind styles. Since it is so central to the story, I will discuss Glyn's
individual mind style in detail and then briefly mention the way the individual
thoughts of the other key characters are handled.

Glyn's mind style is skilfully drawn, to show a portrait of an academic who
has learnt to live with recurring memories of his late wife, although he views these
with both fondness and a sense of intrusion into his working day. It is important
to recognise Glyn's overall professional and personal mind style for a number of
reasons:

i.   It forms the backdrop to his intermittent bereavement memories of Kath, so
      recognising it provides a more balanced view of his thinking style than just
      focusing on examples from the bereavement memories.
ii.   It shows how he tries (and largely fails) to solve the mystery of her life, as a
      result of his intense jealousy after he discovers the photograph.
iii. It explains his inattentiveness to her when she was alive.
iv.   It provides a contrast to her own personality since she seems to be unable
      to sustain a career herself.
v.   Glyn's mind style also controls some of the flow of information relevant to
      the plot, which will be discussed in the next section.

Glyn is portrayed as an academic who is, by his own judgement, "a facts man, par
excellence" (p. 23). "Dispassionate appraisal" (p. 17) is his method of working. The
discovery of the photograph acts as a catalyst, jolting him into action and he is
driven largely by jealousy to play the role of an amateur detective searching for
"evidence" (p. 15) and "motive" (p. 118), as well as interviewing "witnesses" (p. 116)
and following up every "clue" (p. 101). Glyn assumes that he can transfer his professional research skills into his investigations. His way of thinking as an academic permeates his mind style. Kath becomes Glyn's "area of study" (p. 101) and he
looks at the problem as he "would at any other major piece of research" (p. 101).
He believes that he will be successful in this since this is his *"métier"* (p. 117) and
"a five-star capacity for obsession is what makes him a painstaking researcher"
(p. 118). Even a false trail in his investigations is compared to an unrewarding trip
to an archive (p. 116). Ironically, although he is a successful academic, he is over-
confident in his abilities to solve this personal mystery. He is so overcome with

jealousy that he is unduly suspicious about some of those that he interviews and he cannot fully engage with what these characters are telling him about his late wife. Also, he fails to factor in the emotional elements in her life which may have driven her to suicide.

During her life, Glyn had prioritised his work, and his reaction to the new distraction posed by the photograph is that:

> Kath is getting in the way of his work, which was not allowed, as she well under-
> stood.   (Glyn's thoughts, p. 3)

The photograph pushes her into the forefront of Glyn's mind, so his mind style in the book is comprised not only of the intermittent bereavement memories that are triggered or come from nowhere, but she also takes over his main thoughts, where he attempts to rationalise what has happened, actively trying to discover further information about the past, form hypotheses, and re-consider both her habitual behaviour and the details of specific previously forgotten episodes in the past. Intermittently, though, he is subject to memories that give away the extent to which he seems to have somewhat neglected her, since the gaps in his memory are partly due to the times he was often away or not listening to her, as well as the natural decay of memory.

The Photograph is primarily a book of multiple mind styles. In their own ways, the other main characters are generally too preoccupied with their own lives to engage fully with Kath, apart from in the moments when she suddenly appears to them. Elaine is a successful garden designer, who prides herself on her organisational powers. The text portrays her mind style with gardening details, she views life using gardening metaphors, and many of her intermittent memories of her sister are triggered by memories of her in garden settings. Her memories reveal her uneasy past relationship with Kath, where she was dismissive of her, even though she attempts to justify her behaviour. Nick is obsessed with his own projects. He remembers Kath when other characters prompt him to do so, but he views the affair as being in the past and he is more concerned about his failing marriage with Elaine. Polly is a busy young professional now and she was only a child when she knew Kath, so her memories are of fun times with her (Polly's thoughts are conveyed in an extended monologue to her boyfriend and other speech). Oliver, who took the photograph, was more peripheral in Kath's circle and has a new professional and personal life.

Sadly, none of these characters were available to support Kath, either during her life or on the day of her death, due to their circumstances. Only her friend Mary, who appears at the denouement, listened to her fully. The other characters primarily focused on her attractive appearance, not her underlying state of mind.

Ironically, Glyn and Elaine were inattentive to what she said in life and now she haunts their thoughts in death.

Plot: Mystery and resolution

The Photograph is not just a representation of bereavement. It also has a carefully-constructed plot — it is a mystery story with a detective element. The standard schema of mystery and detective fiction is that key information is hidden until the subsequent resolution stage (Emmott and Alexander 2014, 2020; Tobin 2018). In this story, there is a garden path effect, so Glyn is in fact trying to solve the wrong mystery for much of the book. The main mystery as perceived largely through his eyes and through his investigations, is that of his wife's infidelity. However, as the novel progresses, it becomes evident that this is no longer the main issue since there is no evidence that Kath was repeatedly unfaithful. The real mystery for Glyn and the other key characters becomes why she was sufficiently distressed to kill herself and it is this mystery that is explained at the denouement.

A number of strategies are used by Lively to control the information flow in the story in order to create the mystery and provide the revelations at the end of the book, as will be shown in the following discussion.

Suppressing information: Omission and burying

Within mystery stories, the late placement of key information can be used to control the questions that the reader asks. The key information that is omitted is the fact that Kath has committed suicide — the story of her death is finally told in the chapter before the denouement. The characters know that she killed herself, so this is only a revelation for the reader. This very late disclosure (p. 208–9) may prevent the reader from asking questions about the nature of her death, since the focus has been on her infidelity, not how she died.

How is it the case that such a key fact is not mentioned earlier? The main reasons for this seem to be:

i. The main characters know she committed suicide, so this fact can be regarded as given information for them and does not need to be shown in their thought processes.
ii. Some of the stylistic features used to represent bereavement cover up this fact. The fragmentation, for example, can be interpreted as representing trauma, but the incomplete and under-specified language prevents discussion of her death.

iii.   The characters do not want to think about the details of her death, so "That day.", the day she died, is not recalled until towards the end of the book.

iv.   There are social taboos about talking about death and some characters do not want to discuss the details of their past lives.

It is only the reader who has been in the dark about the fact that Kath has committed suicide. By contrast, the explanation of *why* she did this is unknown to the reader *and* the key characters until the end of the story. When the characters are unaware of facts, this may make it easier to suppress the information because the characters do not need to hide anything, but this leads to a strategic issue. There has to be some prior mention of the relevant information in the story since otherwise the ending will come as such a surprise that the reader may be dissatisfied. A primary technique used is to mention information in the earlier and middle parts of the story, but to make it seem inconsequential to the eventual revelation.

In this story, there are two topics that need to be mentioned as a basis for the later denouement, but which need to be presented as not significant at the earlier stages in the story. These pieces of information are both reasons why Kath may have been so distressed that she killed herself: (i) she seems to have been particularly badly affected by the death of her mother and (ii) she had two miscarriages and appears to have had an unfulfilled desire for children.

Kath's reaction to her mother's death is handled partly by delimiting it to a particular point in her biography. We are told that she was very close to her mother and distressed by her death, to the extent that it affected her mood significantly for a year afterwards, altering her appearance (p. 46). However, this mood shift is not presented as an ongoing problem, and there is considerable emphasis on her attractive and apparently happy persona. In addition, the other characters sometimes minimise the mother's role. Elaine was not as close to their mother as Kath was, so she is relatively dismissive of her (p. 45). When Glyn finds the mother's letters in his late wife's possessions after her death, he sees no reason to be interested in them (p. 4). The text, therefore, does not dwell on the mother's influence and the lack of full appreciation of the mother's role by Elaine and Glyn may prompt the reader not to pay too much attention to this information until the denouement.

The topic of children is repeatedly mentioned throughout the book. Many of the memories of the characters include children, and, more specifically, there are a lot of mentions of Kath and Polly, Elaine's daughter, enjoying themselves together. Some hints are given that Kath may have wanted children herself, but we are not made aware of her distress at being childless until the end of the story when the two miscarriages are revealed.

The manipulation in this case is to present Kath's appearances with children in general and particularly Polly as being simply part of her everyday life and not as relevant to a theme of unachieved motherhood. Glyn firmly dismisses the idea in his thoughts in the first chapter of the book.

> Kath had an affinity with children. They drifted her way, and she to them. Perhaps if…
>
> God, no. Kath as a mother? She with the attention span of a butterfly. And, anyway, I never wanted children.   (Glyn's thoughts, p. 13, Lively's ellipsis)

Glyn's perspective here pushes us towards his evaluation, but also this example is part of a broader context, following on from a discussion of how his late wife was startlingly attractive and how she mesmerised men, women, and even children. The topic controls the way we perceive the information and the emphasis at this point is more on her attractiveness than on any feelings she might have had about motherhood.

Other mentions of Kath's relations with children and, in particular, Polly as a child are frequently handled by embedding them within episodic memories that again occur without any evaluative context — it is only in retrospect that we might realise that cumulatively we have frequently seen many glimpses of her spending time with children, and that she seemed to derive pleasure, sometimes intense pleasure, from this. In the example below, this view of Kath is embedded in Elaine's memories of Polly.

> This Polly has shrunk by a few years. She is four, or thereabouts. She is dancing. She is dancing with Kath […] Polly and Kath face each other, holding hands — small Polly, grown-up Kath — and they whirl about the room. […] Their faces are rapt, smiling, intent. Polly gazes up at Kath and they whirl on and on. For ever, apparently.   (Elaine's thoughts, p. 49–50.)

Polly is the main topic in this example and this memory follows directly on from another memory about Polly in Elaine's thought. Hence, Polly is the primary focus and this memory seems unlikely to prompt any questions about Kath's childlessness, particularly since there is little at this stage in the novel to cause any suspicion that she is unhappy about her childless state. Other characters also have many memories of the two together including Kath plaiting Polly's hair (p. 82, p. 177) and Polly helping her to gather windfall apples (p. 191). As we will see later, these memories of Kath's relations with Polly are re-worked later in the novel, but in the earlier parts of the book they do not appear to have any significance as a possible factor leading to her death.

Re-balancing and hinting

Culpeper (2001) has studied how attributes of a character can be changed, so that a radical shift in our mental representation of a character can be achieved by the end of a story. In mystery and detective stories, it may serve the interests of the plot to change the reader's perception of a character. If this is a significant change, then it needs to be done gradually throughout the book if it is to be convincing so we may start to see changes in the middle part of a book. Unless there is some reason for a change in personality mid-way through a story, the differences need to be accounted for in some other way, such as presenting new information or hinting that all is not as it seems.

In the case of Kath, there is a major shift between the beginning and end of the book. At the start of the book, there are references to her smiling, laughing, and apparently being happy (e.g. p.79), she had plenty of friends (p.24), she was "not fettered by obligation" (p.11), and she had her own life when Glyn was away for work reasons (p.24). By the end of the book, there is a substantial reversal and she is presented as someone who was sufficiently distressed to have committed suicide.

This is a considerable change in perception for the main characters, but in the middle part of the book, there are suggestions by minor characters that something was not right in her life (see Woloch 2004 for a detailed study of the role of minor characters in stories). This creates a sense of mystery about her, but also prefaces the radical turn-around in the main characters' mental representations by the end of the story.

Two of these minor characters appear during Glyn's investigations. When interviewing Peter Claverdon, a man who employed Kath at a music festival, he meets Claverdon's partner — the emphasis is on a small plot twist since Glyn has been wondering if Claverdon had been having an affair with his late wife, but realises when his male partner arrives that Claverdon is gay. The partner only appears for a page of the text, but has the opportunity to say about her time at the festival:

"What a shame it all went wrong. She was so upset"   (p.123)

Glyn is oblivious to this at the time, but we are told that "he will hear it later, much later" (p.123). The comment is under-specified — we do not know what went wrong — but it is also foregrounded by the mention of Glyn's subsequent attention to it.

Later, Glyn goes to visit another minor character, Ben Hapgood, an artist who has painted Kath. After a discussion about her with this artist, Hapgood's wife describes in passing how Kath was very good with the Hapgood children and what fun they had with her, and she says:

> "What a shame it was she never ... not that she ever said anything, but one always sensed —"   (p. 129–30, Lively's ellipsis)

Glyn again ignores this small comment at the time. Later, though, he thinks again of the people in these two completely separate encounters and we see some of these words directly repeated in his head as a "continuous repetitive refrain" (p. 133), This has the effect of foregrounding these elements of these conversations that he had previously dismissed.

A pattern has therefore been established for the reader and continues. Elaine has an encounter with another minor character, her cousin Linda. Again, the emphasis is on other matters, but Linda slips in these observations about Kath:

> "I gathered she'd just had that nasty little upset, poor dear, so she was rather under par. [...] Such a shame —"   (p. 161)

Elaine does not follow up on this at the time, but, like Glyn, she keeps thinking of this afterwards:

> Later, she hears Linda again. That nasty little upset. Under par.   (p. 162)

This partially fragmented text is in a paragraph of its own, which foregrounds it. A further repetition, placed in a prominent position at the end of this scene, also uses a sentence fragment for foregrounding purposes:

> Cousin Linda hangs around all evening, saying that again. And again.   (p. 162)

These minor characters — Claverdon's partner, Hapgood's wife and Cousin Linda — occur in separate scenes and speak to different main characters, Glyn and Elaine. Nevertheless, the reader can bring together these observations to start forming a communal view (Palmer 2004). The characters are too minor to have any internal representation of their thoughts about these matters, but their observations have an effect on the mind styles of the two main characters, producing a reverberating effect that can prompt doubts in these main characters.

As the book progresses, the occasional doubts of the main characters become more frequent when judged together, so that their interpretations of Kath's attributes start to switch. We see her preoccupation sometimes when she is in the presence of children (p. 62), and some of the main characters wonder about the fact that she didn't have children (p. 106). There is an evaluative shift from seeing her as a happy-go-lucky person to viewing her as someone who had no real purpose in life (p. 82). Characters start to recall occasions when perhaps she may have been sad (p.112) or might have been crying (p.185), even though these had not been mentioned before. By the time we learn of her suicide, her persona is represented in an increasingly bleak way (p.196) and the denouement reinforces this, adding background to suggest that there were times when "beneath the surface gaiety something darkly thrashed" (p.220).

Denouement: Explanation and reconstruction

In *The Photograph*, the denouement resembles in some ways the classic final exposition in many detective stories where all the characters meet together to hear the conclusions of the detective. However, here the explanation is given by Mary, an old friend, not the amateur detective. It is conveyed in meetings with three of the main characters, Glyn, Elaine and Oliver, on separate occasions in the story world, but the reader sees these occasions consecutively, giving the sense of a communal communication.

Mary provides new information about Kath's two miscarriages. As her best friend, she was the only person Kath confided in, so she can also offer insights into her state of mind. It is ironic that Glyn, as her husband and the would-be detective, is not the one to have discovered this information, but it reflects his lack of engagement with his late wife, as seen in his mind style, since he was too dazzled by her beauty and too preoccupied with his work to be fully aware of her state of mind. The need for an explanation has become increasingly evident throughout the book, due partly to the re-balancing and hinting about Kath discussed earlier, but also as a result of the revelation to the reader that she has committed suicide, just before the exposition chapter.

A key strategy in detective stories is for the detective to tell us that the solution was obvious all along. Even where it was not really obvious, a statement of this type can make the solution seem more credible so it acts as a persuasive strategy. In *The Photograph*, there is a statement of this type between the revelation of Kath's suicide and the explanation. This comes from Oliver, who plays a more objective and thoughtful role in the story than the other main characters. He says that when he heard of her suicide, he thought "yes, this was always on the cards" (p.216) and that:

> in some disturbing way what had happened was heralded, that there had always been something troubled about Kath, something that set her apart. Behind and beyond her looks, her manner, there had been some dark malaise. But nobody saw it, back then, he thought. All you saw was her face. (Oliver's thoughts, p.216)

In presenting Mary's explanation, the strategy is not only to disclose new information about Kath — her two miscarriages and her distress at her mother's death —

but to rework episodes that we have seen in the rest of the novel. Oliver prepares us for this by saying:

> He found himself searching for times with Kath, and each sequence that arrived was subtly changed by what had happened; [the day of her death] had kicked away old assumptions — what had seemed unexceptional was now quite other.
>
> (Oliver's thoughts, p. 216)

We see Mary explaining about the miscarriages to Glyn, then we also see these key revelations mediated through Elaine's thoughts as she leaves Mary's house. This technique allows the key disclosures and Elaine's reaction and memories to be brought together in a compact way, which might not have been possible if the whole meeting had been portrayed directly. Elaine thinks about "Kath's non-children" (p. 227) and, in her head, it appears as if she is directly addressing her, although it is clear that this is an imaginary Kath. As Elaine is a mother herself, she can presumably empathise with Kath's childlessness more than Glyn, who has said he did not want children — hence, it seems appropriate that we see the reaction to this revelation through her eyes.

> The non-babies are now loud and clear, who did not exist a couple of hours ago. Kath's non-children. [Elaine now thinks differently about Kath in consequence.]
> Why didn't you *tell* me? says Elaine.
> She sees Kath with Polly, dancing with her — small Polly, grown-up Kath — she sees her plaiting Polly's hair, she sees her coming into the kitchen with Polly and a brimming basket of windfall apples.
> I always thought you didn't particularly *want* children, says Elaine. [...]
> The non-children eclipse much else. She hears the non-children louder than anything that has been said. It is the non-children above all who have skewed things. They keep coming back — faceless, formless, significant.
>
> (Elaine's thoughts, p. 227)

The technique here is to bring in portions of some of the many previous mentions of Kath and Polly, now condensed together but the reader is aware of their frequency throughout the novel. No direct comment is made about the relationship with Polly, but it is clear from the surrounding simulated direct speech and the fact that this is sandwiched between the discussion of the "non-children" that the implication is that Kath's intense engagement with Polly indicates her love of children and gives some indication of the fact that she might have been devastated by her childlessness. The mentions of the non-babies are foregrounded, not only by repetition, and the use of a sentence fragment, but there are also what Stockwell (2009; 25) terms "attractors", here loudness, eclipsing and skewing things, and the words "above all" and "significant".

Conclusion

The Photograph is a carefully crafted novel which manages to embed a well-constructed plot within a moving portrayal of bereavement mind styles. Jordison (2018; host's announcement, paragraph 3) has commented on Lively's writing generally as follows:

> Lively has an unusual ability to bend the rules of structure, voice and chronology — but never at the expense of compelling storytelling. She writes with such smooth skill that, as a reader, you are barely aware that you are reading something that could easily be termed "experimental".

Up to a point, the representation of bereavement and the mystery-detective plot may seem like very different genres, but they fit together well in this story. The writing style for bereavement memories is sometimes under-specified and fragmented and the episodic memories may be decontextualised. These features can be used to withhold or detract from plot relevant information until the mystery is explained, as far as it can be explained in a story about suicide. Both the reader and the characters create representations of Kath after her death, and then subsequently reconstruct these representations as new information surfaces about her distressed mental state.

References

Bühler, K. 1990. *Theory of Language: The Representational Function of Language.* Amsterdam: John Benjamins.

Burke, M. 2010. *Literary Reading, Cognition and Emotion: An Exploration of the Oceanic Mind.* New York and London: Routledge.

Crown, S. 2009. A life in books: Penelope Lively. *The Guardian.* 25 July 2009. <https://www.theguardian.com/books/2009/jul/25/life-books-penelope-lively-interview> [Accessed 29 August 2023].

Culpeper, J. 2001. *Language and Characterisation: People in Plays and Other Texts.* Harlow: Longman.

Duchan, J. F., Bruder, G.A, & Hewitt, L. E. (eds). 1995. *Deixis in Narrative: A Cognitive Science Perspective.* Hillsdale NJ: Lawrence Erlbaum Associates.

Emmott, C. 1997. *Narrative Comprehension: A Discourse Perspective.* Oxford: Oxford University Press.

Emmott, C. 2002. "Split selves" in fiction and medical "life stories". In *Cognitive Stylistics: Language and Cognition in Text Analysis*, E. Semino & J. Culpeper (eds), 153–181. Amsterdam: John Benjamins.

doi Emmott, C. 2017. Immersed in imagined landscapes. *The Stylistics of Landscapes and the Landscapes of Stylistics*, J. Douthwaite, D. F. Virdis, & E. Zurru (eds), 45–60. Amsterdam: John Benjamins.

doi Emmott, C. & Alexander, M. 2014. Foregrounding, burying and plot construction. In *The Cambridge Handbook of Stylistics*, P. Stockwell and S. Whiteley (eds), 329–343. Cambridge: Cambridge University Press.

doi Emmott, C. & Alexander, M. 2020. Manipulation in Agatha Christie's detective stories: rhetorical control and cognitive misdirection in creating and solving crime puzzles. In *Stylistic Manipulation of the Reader in Contemporary Fiction*, S. Sorlin (ed), 195–214. Bloomsbury: London.

doi Emmott, C., Sanford, A. J. & Morrow, L. I. 2006a. Sentence fragmentation: Stylistic Aspects. In *Encyclopedia of Language and Linguistics*, K. Brown (ed), volume 4, 241–251. Oxford: Elsevier.

doi Emmott, C., Sanford, A. J. & Morrow, L. I. 2006b. Capturing the attention of readers? Stylistic and psychological perspectives on the use and effect of text fragmentation in narratives. *Journal of Literary Semantics*, 35(1): 1–30.

Fludernik, M. 2003. Scene shift, metalepsis, and the metaleptic mode. *Style*, 3: 382–400.

Fowler, R. 1977. *Linguistics and the Novel*. London: Methuen.

doi Fowler, R. 1996. *Linguistic Criticism*. 2nd edn. Oxford: Oxford University Press.

doi Gavins, J. 2013. *Reading the Absurd*. Edinburgh: Edinburgh University Press.

Genette, G. 1980. *Narrative Discourse*. Ithaca NY: Cornell University Press.

Genette, G. 1988. *Narrative Discourse Revisited*. Ithaca NY: Cornell University Press.

Jordison, S. 2018. Penelope Lively webchat: on Egypt, Englishness and her first memory. 1 August 2018, host's announcement posted 27 July 2018, <https://www.theguardian.com /books/live/2018/jul/27/penelope-lively-webchat-post-your-questions-now> [Accessed 11 February 2024].

Judd, E. 2003. Just the facts. *The Atlantic monthly*, July/August 2002, 144.

Lakoff, G. 1996. Sorry, I'm not myself today: The metaphor system for conceptualising self. In *Spaces, Worlds and Grammar*, G. Fauconnier & E. Sweetser (eds), 91–123. Chicago IL: Chicago University Press.

doi Lecomte, H. 2022. Sherlocking one's way into empathetic and generic (rebirth): Inquests of mourning in Penelope Lively's *The Photograph*. *Études Britanniques Contemporaines*, 62, <https://journals.openedition.org/ebc/11958> [Accessed 29 August 2023].

Lively, P. 1985. *Perfect Happiness*. London: Penguin.

Lively, P. 1988. *Moon Tiger*. London: Penguin.

Lively, P. 1990. *Passing On*. London: Penguin.

Lively, P. 2004 [2003]. *The Photograph*. London: Penguin.

Lively, P. 2014. *Ammonites and Leaping Fish: A Life in Time*. London: Penguin.

McGrath, C. 2017. "A writer writes": Penelope Lively's fiction defies the test of time. *New York Times*, 4 May 2017, <https://www.nytimes.com/2017/05/04/books/review/penelope-lively -profile-purple-swamp-hen.html>, [Accessed 29th August 2023].

doi Moran, M. H. 1997. The novels of Penelope Lively: A case for the continuity of the experimental impulse in postwar British fiction. *South Atlantic Review*, Winter, 1997: 101–120.

Palmer, A. 2004. *Fictional Minds*. Lincoln NE: University of Nebraska Press.

doi Sabucedo, P. , Hayes, J & Evans, C. 2021. Narratives of experience of presence in bereavement: sources of comfort, ambivalence and distress. *British Journal of Guidance and Counselling*, 49(6): 814–831.

doi Stockwell, P. 2009. *Texture: A Cognitive Aesthetics of Reading*. Edinburgh: Edinburgh University Press.

doi Tobin, V. 2018. *Elements of Surprise: Our Mental Limits and the Satisfactions of Plot*. Cambridge, MA: Harvard University Press.

Verdonk, P. 1988. *How Can We Know the Dancer from the Dance: Some Literary Stylistic Studies of English Poetry*. Ph.D. thesis, Amsterdam University.

Verdonk, P. 2002. *Stylistics*. Oxford: Oxford University Press.

doi Verdonk, P. 2006. Style. In *Encyclopedia of Language and Linguistics*, in Brown, K. (ed), Volume 12, 196–210. Oxford: Elsevier.

doi Verdonk, P. 2013. *The Stylistics of Poetry: Context, Cognition, Discourse, History*. London: Bloomsbury.

doi Woloch, A. 2004. *The One vs. the Many: Minor Characters and the Space of the Protagonist in the Novel*. Princeton: Princeton University Press.

CHAPTER 3

Motivation and textual meaning in the stylistics of poetry
"Dulce et Decorum Est"

Lesley Jeffries
Lancaster University

This chapter assesses Verdonk's work on poetry through the lens of my own work on textual meaning in poetry. Using Wilfred Owen's war poem "Dulce et Decorum Est" as an illustration, it re-examines the attempt in Jeffries (2022) to establish whether a framework originally applied to ideology could be developed into a more general model of textual meaning. The broader project concluded that the framework of Textual Conceptual Functions (TCFs) as originally developed cover much of what might be seen as consensus about the stylistic choices in poems, though there is additional contextually based meaning arising from individual readings of poems. The approach provides a systematic way to identify and assess aspects of a poem's meaning that would not necessarily be found by investigating formal linguistic features alone or by a literary historical or social approach.

Keywords: contemporary poems, textual meaning, Wilfred Owen, "Dulce et Decorum Est"

Introduction

Peter Verdonk's interest in the language of poetry is well-known and his influence on those of us who work in this area is significant and lasting. Whilst there is no doubt that poetry, of all the genres, allows the reader the latitude to draw different ideas, emotions and interpretations from the page, nevertheless, there is a level at which we can demonstrate consensus from the choices made by the poet, which then feed into these different directions of travel by individual readers. Short et al (2011) suggest that differences of interpretation between readers tend to be minor and cannot vary infinitely, adding that we should rather consider them different

https://doi.org/10.1075/lal.44.03jef

readings of a higher order interpretation. I believe that Peter Verdonk would have agreed.

This chapter will reflect on the contribution of Verdonk's work on poetry through the lens of my own work on textual meaning in poetry. A recent research project (Jeffries 2022) attempted to establish whether a framework originally applied to ideology in political language and news reporting (Jeffries 2010b) could be developed into a more general model of textual meaning which would provide a systematic approach to ideation in texts, and specifically in contemporary poems. The theoretical implications of proposing such a model are to place stylistics more centrally as one of the pillars of linguistics, rather than seeing any kind of text analysis as dependent on, and subservient to, general linguistics. One of the stated aims was to provide a rigorous and transparent account of the textual meaning of a number of poems which could be used as the basis of comparison, both with other poems and with other accounts of the same poems.

Here, I will use Wilfred Owen's anti-war poem, "Dulce et Decorum Est" as the test case by which to consider the potential contribution of my theory of textual meaning to the question of motivated meaning.

Peter Verdonk's legacy

Verdonk's explorations in the stylistics of poetry are conveniently found collected in Verdonk (2013), where we can see the development of his thinking about poetry through the years. Like me (Jeffries 1993), he started out by using the basic building blocks of a largely structuralist linguistics to provide a systematic analysis of poems at all the levels from phonetics to semantics, often using these tools to explicate the ways in which foregrounding can be linguistically triggered. This approach reflected both the linguistic mainstream of the time and the prevailing view that stylistics was an application of linguistic insights to the question of literary criticism. I don't have space here to go into the history of the development of stylistics (though see Jeffries and McIntyre 2025 for more on this), but it is worth noting that this field has become increasingly independent and confident in its own status as a sub-discipline of linguistics, and, I would argue, one that should be seen as being central to linguistics itself.

One difference between my starting point and Verdonk's is that his explicit purpose was to contribute a linguistic explanatory underpinning to literary criticism whereas I have always been more interested in using texts, including poems, to discover how language works. Verdonk's articles, then, often start with a literary hunch and he then uses linguistic analysis to provide support for this specific interpretation of the evidence. In Chapter 3 of Verdonk (2013: 26), for example, he begins a discussion of Auden's poem "Museé des Beaux Arts" by describing the pictures of the artist Brueghel upon which Auden's poem is thought to be based. He then continues (Verdonk 2013: 26):

> Wishing to relate these contextual factors to the meanings of the poem's linguistic structures or text, I propose to perform a literary stylistic analysis for which I will exploit, though rather informally, the techniques of discourse analysis.

Verdonk's concern, therefore, was primarily with the poem and he starts here with the contextual features. My work, by contrast, starts with the text and stops short of the contextual for reasons given below. Both are, of course, valid ways to approach the language of poems and Verdonk and I agree that we are aiming for a relatively objective way to use linguistics in literary criticism, based on its transparency and replicability which mark out stylistics as belonging more in (scientific) linguistics than literary criticism.

Though Verdonk never takes the argument that far, he nevertheless argues that although literary criticism necessarily involves some subjectivity on the part of the analyst, having some evidence to back up your interpretation is a good way to proceed. I agree that being able to say why you interpret a text in a particular way is fundamental to being able to build up a case and have a sensible discussion with analysts who may disagree with you or may wish to nuance the interpretation in a slightly different way. The key thing is to have a shared and agreed vocabulary to use for these discussions. Literary criticism might be criticized itself for not having such a shared language in which to operate, though Verdonk (2013: 12) is keen to make clear that he sees literary criticism and stylistics as inextricably linked:

> The question which often arises about this relational aspect of literary stylistics is "Which of the two interests comes first when examining a literary text, the linguistic or the literary?" The answer is that means and ends, language and literary function, must receive our equal attention and it must be shown that they are interdependent. In other words, a given prominent feature in the text that appeals to first impression may be either literary or linguistic. If this observation is literary, stylisticians will seek linguistic evidence, and if it is linguistic, they will attempt to suggest its potential literary effect.

There are significant assumptions here, which I would perhaps want to question. First of all, there is the undeclared assumption that literature somehow works differently from other texts. Whilst literature is clearly one of the more inventive genres of human language use, I would argue that we should be considering literature as working in fundamentally the same way as other texts, albeit with different aims and often using style in more extreme ways than other more mundane genres. The second assumption is that our concern with literature as stylisticians is primarily with foregrounding (*prominent feature*). Whilst this is undeniably a major focus of literary stylistics, there is another, more backgrounded, level of style, which can also be discovered through the kinds of analysis proposed in this chapter.

What Verdonk's (2013) collected articles do is to trace the development in his thinking over the years in line with that of stylistics, moving from linguistic levels to discourse analysis and functional grammar to pragmatics. Each of these developments in his work demonstrated the value of the new approach, though at times one of the earlier approaches (usually the most basic one) is needed in addition to the "new" one. In other words, even when talking about functional, discourse-based, or cognitive aspects of a poem's style, one always needs recourse to terms coming from syntax and other fundamental linguistic fields. Towards the end of the collection he moves to cognitive poetics and readers' meaning, reflecting the changing focus of stylistics itself, and he makes clear that he embraces this move towards a more reader-centred type of stylistics.

What Verdonk does not appear to do, however, is to integrate all these different insights into a higher-level framework. His work reflects the development of stylistics, as a broad field of many different theories and models, not explicitly in conflict with each other, but nevertheless lacking any overarching model of how they fit together in the pursuit of understanding textual meaning. Ultimately, though, what Verdonk was trying to achieve was a linguistically informed literary criticism which complements more traditional approaches to verbal arts. He wanted to reconcile linguistic and literary approaches to literature and those who knew him would see this as typical of this man of peace.

Textual meaning

Much of what Verdonk achieved in his writing about poetry demonstrates the value of a rigorous stylistic approach to how poems make meaning, though as mentioned above, he was less concerned to try and merge all the insights of linguistics into a single model of textual (and specifically poetic) meaning. This wider linguistic ambition is one that I have been grappling with for a number of years, first of all in relation to political language and news reporting (Jeffries 2015) and latterly in a return to the language of poetry (Jeffries 2022). In this section I will try to summarise the argument for a specific concept of textual meaning which overlaps in various ways with the basic structures of language (lexico-grammar) and with the usage models of pragmatics, but which can be identified as operating on a separate level from these.

What I intend by textual meaning is the way in which language choices in all texts produce an idea of the events, context, actions, artefacts and so on within the world of the text. Note here that I am not explicitly using Text World Theory (see Werth 1999; Gavins 2007), though I am borrowing the fundamental metaphor of the text-world as a useful analytical concept. Whilst we can explore the superficial linguistic meaning of a text using core concepts from descriptive linguistics (from phonetics to semantics, via phonological, morphological and syntactic layers), I see textual meaning as being additional to, though concurrent with, this basic semantico-syntactic meaning, whilst being produced by the same linguistic choices.

If we consider just one example from a poem analysed in some detail in Jeffries (2022), it may serve as justification for the wider concept of textual meaning as explored below. U.A. Fanthorpe's poem "Men on Allotments" (Fanthorpe 2005) conjures up a scenario of gardeners on their allotments on a Sunday and amongst other comparisons, the background sounds of a suburban setting are described as follows:

> Pop music from the council estate
> Counterpoints with the Sunday-morning bells

This is a straightforward description of two contrasting sounds that can be heard simultaneously by the gardeners on the allotment site, though the verb (*counterpoints*) is an explicit trigger of oppositional meaning and sets the two sounds into a binary relationship which is superficially unique to this poem. Thus, if asked what the opposite of *pop music* is, an English speaker would almost certainly not reply *Sunday-morning bells*, though they might respond with *classical music* or something similar. What this demonstrates is the capacity for binary relationships between words or phrases (or sometimes higher level structures) to be created in the text itself and just for that particular co-textual moment. The result is that this poem sets up a temporary opposition which can be seen as a specific version of a more conventional opposition between secular and religious living, with the people on the council estate listening to secular music when the churchgoers are being called to worship by the bells. What is not made explicit at this point, but becomes clearer as the poem progresses, is that the men on their allotments fit into neither of these categories. On the one hand, their god-like nature is hinted at as they *grope to life* the potatoes and see *the casual holiness* of the beans, but the poem celebrates less the men's imperfect creative power and more the overwhelming power of the plants themselves, which quickly outstrip the gardeners' attempts to control them.

Returning to the question of textual meaning, I would argue that this example demonstrates the simultaneous creation of linguistic (i.e. semantic-syntactic, propositional) and textual meaning. In this case, the lexico-grammar of the lines tells us simply that there are two competing musical sounds audible from the allotment site, whereas the textual meaning implies that these sounds are symbolic of a social opposition between the secular and the religious. This superficial contrast between secular and religious lives is the background against which the men on their allotments are seen not to fit into the conventional binary, since they are god-like in their growing and yet flawed in the face of the power of nature itself. This interpretation of one of the larger themes of the poem is found in a layer based on the propositional meaning but adds ideational content to this basic level.

What this example demonstrates is that, in addition to the basic surface meaning of a text, based on the propositional meaning created by its lexico-grammar, there is a layer of meaning (the co-textual) that defines aspects of the world of the text through a set of textual features, one of which is the creation of opposition. We will explore the other textual features below. Meanwhile, the following section will explore the "other" interface between (co-)textual and contextual meaning.

Poetry as text

As Verdonk repeatedly stated and stylisticians often feel the need to acknowledge, readers take different messages from their reading of literature (and, it is implied, particularly from "great" literature). Such comments are sometimes taken as an argument against the usefulness of stylistics. However, it is logical to argue that texts (not just literary ones) are made up of choices from the range of potential linguistic options and that these choices together create at least some consensus as to their meaning. To argue, as some do, that there can be no such consensus, seems to me to lead to a complete breakdown in the potential for human communication. Whilst it is clear that communication between human beings is flawed and sometimes dysfunctional, there is nevertheless plenty of evidence that on the whole human beings do manage to connect with each other through language. The integrationist theories of language (Harris 1981) by which all meaning is construed as entirely contextual and constructed by participants in communication does not, it seems to me, explain how language itself works, though it rightly suggests that much communication is made up of more than linguistic content. As with many conflicts in the field, the answer is probably that both integrationist and what integrationists call "segregationist" approaches to describing human communication throw some light on a very complex phenomenon.

Poems, as a general rule, are dislocated in time and space compared with other genres and text-types. This is not to say that poems fail to reference contemporary (or other) issues or that poetry doesn't reflect the language and times in which it is written. Neither does it deny that some poetry (e.g. love poetry) is written and used very specifically in an interpersonal or interactional way. However, most poems are written to be read (or read aloud) at a time and place remote from their creation. The result is that the communicative situation that poems occupy is very different from everyday language and, for example, conversational implicature works differently in poetic texts. Poetry is not, in any normal sense, necessary for communicating, and so there is little value in asking to what extent the text flouts Gricean maxims of quantity (it's all excess) or quality (much of it is invented) or relevance (poems tend to go off at a tangent) or manner (clarity is not the aim or the achievement of much poetry). Eco (1984) provides some basis for the use of the Gricean maxims in text analysis when he argues that an excessive attention to some textual detail, which appears to be insufficiently motivated by the surrounding co-text and the stylistic norms of the text, can produce symbolic interpretation on the grounds that it is otherwise unjustifiable. In addition, some poems will include narrative structures where interpersonal communication between characters is available for analysis by such frameworks as Grice's Cooperative Principle and politeness theories etc. But it remains generally the case that poetry occupies a relatively de-contextual position in relation to interaction.

Paradoxically, and despite this characteristic, of poetry being largely decontextual, there is a sense in which poetry is the most allusive and thus vague of genres. My work on poems has shown a range of ways in which indirect allusion beyond the mundane surface meaning is an essential part of their textual meaning and dependent on the standard features of textual meaning in the framework. Thus, for example, the syntactic ambiguity operating between lists and appositional structures allows poems to provide open meaning where the items listed can be seen as separate, or identical or both. Most of the features of the framework introduced below can thus contribute to poetry's indirect and allusive meaning.

A framework for poetic analysis

The approach to textual meaning in poetry described in this chapter developed from the framework called Critical Stylistics (Jeffries 2010b; 2014) which was intended as a systematic way to approach ideation in non-literary texts, specifically texts relating to politics and political reporting. I use the term ideation, borrowed from Halliday and Matthiessen (2004), but in a slightly differently way to refer to the construction of a particular view of the world through textual choices. In relation to political language, I was interested in demonstrating how ideation may also exhibit ideological meaning, but although this can also be present in poems, the work described here aimed to discover whether my view of ideation through textual choice can be the basis of a more generalised theory of textual meaning which encompasses literary and aesthetic effects as well as ideological ones. The label "Critical Stylistics", therefore, no longer applies to the wider application of the framework, and the term "textual meaning" has largely taken over from it.

There are some caveats about this approach to poetic meaning, since I am not attempting to build into the framework those aspects of poetry which are more to do with music than meaning (see Jeffries 1993). There is a place for linguistic discussion of these aspects of the poetic genre which largely distinguish it from other genres and text-types. However, except where the sound patterning or manipulation of formal structures creates one of the kinds of textual meaning I am concerned with (e.g. evoking through sound), the music of poetry is not currently included in the model (though see Fabb and Halle 2008; Tsur 2017 and Tsur and Gafni 2022 for work in this area).

Another boundary I would wish to draw comes between the textual and the pragmatic, or contextual, aspects of meaning. Whilst the boundaries between most linguistic categories are not set in stone, it is nevertheless useful to make a theoretical distinction between meanings that are triggered by some aspect of textual choice and those which are entirely a product of the context, including the background and experience of the reader.

The "Critical Stylistic" framework originated in my work on the textual construction of opposition (Jeffries 2010a) which persuaded me that some meanings are created, as it were, dynamically, within a text, as a result of the interplay between the choices made by producers of texts and the content of that text. The framework asks, "What is the text doing?" and that question is broken down into more specific questions, such as "What is the text naming?" and "What is the text contrasting?". Each of these questions refers to the "Textual-Conceptual Functions" or TCFs for short. The reason for this rather unwieldy label is to make explicit their role as a bridge between the lexico-grammatical choices (thus textual) and the ideation-building (hence conceptual). The TCFs, then, are form-meaning dyads in a general sense, but as there is often a range of forms delivering the TCFs, sometimes with a prototypical form at the centre and fuzzy boundaries, there is no one-to-one relationship between form and meaning.

Table 1. Textual-conceptual functions in textual stylistics

Chapter and TCF label		Meaning	Form(s)
1.	Naming and describing	Labels the people and things (concrete and abstract) in the world of the text.	Noun phrases, including adjectival modification. Adjectival phrases.

Table 1. *(continued)*

Chapter and TCF label	Meaning	Form(s)
2. Representing processes	Presents the events, actions and states in the world of the text and how they relate to the people and things named and described.	Choice of main (lexical) verb transitivity types.
3. Prioritising	Provides information on the more or less significant participants (or artefacts) in a scene.	Placement in syntactic structure (e.g. subordination or fronting)
4. Representing time, space and society	Creating a scenario in time, space and with social structures in which there is a specific point-of-view which the reader/hearer is invited to take up.	Deixis.
5. Equating and contrasting	Presents aspects of the world of the text as similar (equating) or in an oppositional relationship (contrasting)	Intensive relational structures and apposition (equating). Syntactic and semantic triggers including, for example, *Not X but Y* frame.
6. Listing (formerly Enumerating and exemplifying)	Lists all the items in a category (enumerating) or some of the items that illustrate a category (exemplifying)	Lists of words, phrases or clauses which perform the same function in the higher level structure.
7. Alluding (formerly Implying and assuming)	Making non-propositional meaning available to reader/hearer.	Definite noun phrases and triggers of logical presuppositions (assuming). Triggers (e.g. *and*) of conventional implicatures.
8. Negating	Denying, refusing or otherwise negating some aspect of the text.	Core negators (no, not), pronouns (none), morphemes (de-), lexical items (deny).
9. Hypothesising	Presenting potential scenarios.	Modality from modal verbs through modal adverbs (probably) and adjectives (probable) to lexical verbs of opinion (e.g. suspect).
10. Representing others' speech and thought	Presenting the prior (or imagined) speech or thought of other speakers.	Direct, indirect and free direct reporting mechanisms.

Table 1. *(continued)*

Chapter and TCF label	Meaning	Form(s)
11. Evoking (new to the framework)	Producing a response in the reader directly linked to the linguistic choices and relevant to the poem's content.	Onomatopoeia (sound) Layout (image) Line-breaks and stanzas (form) Long, delayed or extended clause elements (structure) Minor sentences (structure)

The final general point to make about the TCFs in this framework is that they are typical of many stylistic features in being able to make meaning locally in a text as a one-off effect or make meaning through their patterning across a text or part of a text. Thus, the effects of these TCFs are sometimes momentary and yet may also often be cumulative.

Methodology

It may be worth noting here that providing a framework for analysis is not the same as setting out a methodology and it is therefore incumbent upon researchers to find ways to apply a framework to data in a rigorous and transparent way which will address the research questions of the project. My aim in Jeffries (2022) was to find out whether the framework was appropriate for poems, and I treated each poem in the same way, by annotating templates for each TCF for each poem before considering the effects of individual features and patterns of features evident in the textual choices.

The research was carried out in three stages. First I worked on familiar poems which would allow me to ascertain whether the analytical process produced a recognizable stylistic description reflecting the literary merits and effects of these texts which I knew well. Next, I chose a second set of unfamiliar poems and went through the same process, but this time in order to explore poems with which I was unfamiliar and establish whether the method would work as a way to engage with the style of new texts. Finally, I asked the editor of a poetry magazine (Peter Sansom, editor of *The North*) to choose another set of poems for me to work on as a way of avoiding researcher bias in the selection of the poems.

The final stage of the process in relation to each poem individually was to write a commentary bringing together the features observed through the TCF analysis in such a way that the textual meaning of the poem is interpreted. Writing a commentary of this kind is entirely separate from the process of identifying the textual features themselves, which often result in multiple lists and tables rather than a coherent account of the textual meaning itself. Such commentaries may work best line-by-line or thematically, though as the commentary on the poem below demonstrates, it is often best to use an amalgamation of both approaches.

"Dulce et Decorum Est"

In order to reflect and celebrate Verdonk's habit of first debating theoretical concerns and then putting those concerns into practice on a single poem, I will now demonstrate the result of the methodology explained and introduced theoretically above. The poem is one that many know well, Wilfred Owen's "Dulce et Decorum Est":

Dulce et Decorum Est

Bent double, like old beggars under sacks,
Knock-kneed, coughing like hags, we cursed through sludge,
Till on the haunting flares we turned our backs,
And towards our distant rest began to trudge.
Men marched asleep. Many had lost their boots,
But limped on, blood-shod. All went lame; all blind;
Drunk with fatigue; deaf even to the hoots
Of tired, outstripped Five-Nines that dropped behind.

Gas! GAS! Quick, boys! — An ecstasy of fumbling
Fitting the clumsy helmets just in time,
But someone still was yelling out and stumbling
And flound'ring like a man in fire or lime. —
Dim through the misty panes and thick green light,
As under a green sea, I saw him drowning.

In all my dreams before my helpless sight,
He plunges at me, guttering, choking, drowning.

If in some smothering dreams, you too could pace
Behind the wagon that we flung him in,
And watch the white eyes writhing in his face,
His hanging face, like a devil's sick of sin;
If you could hear, at every jolt, the blood
Come gargling from the froth-corrupted lungs,
Obscene as cancer, bitter as the cud
Of vile, incurable sores on innocent tongues, —
My friend, you would not tell with such high zest
To children ardent for some desperate glory,
The old Lie: *Dulce et decorum est*
Pro patria mori.

Whilst it is not always possible for copyright reasons, I try where possible to introduce whole poems so that readers can refresh their memories or read them for the first time as a complete text. This does not mean that I am against pulling the poem apart to expose its workings, and this is what I did with this much-loved and familiar poem. I first of all examined the core textual conceptual functions (TCFs), Naming (and Describing), Representing processes (transitivity), Prioritising (structure) and Representing time, space and society (Deixis). I then went through the poem again for each of the remaining TCFs and made notes on relevant observations, whether or not the same phrases or words had already been commented upon in other parts of the analysis. Having been through this repetitive process, I considered whether this was a poem which lends itself to line-by-line commentary (some are better treated thematically) and concluded that a mixture of the two would be best for presenting the results. The result is in the following paragraphs.

We can see one pattern of naming in this poem by first considering only the noun phrases (and pronouns) referring to people across the text. The first stanza introduces the plurality of the soldiers, including the narrator, in the first-person plural pronouns (*we, our*) and the third person noun (*men*) often summarized by the determiner alone (*many, all, all*). The sense of large numbers of anonymous soldiers being used as cannon fodder is strong, though the inclusion of the narratorial voice (*we*) provides the reader with reassurance that this is an account by someone who was there. Note that personal deixis is working alongside naming here, using the first person plural pronoun (*we*) to establish an early point-of-view (that of the narrator-plus-comrades). The second and third stanzas bring the focus (and the point-of-view) much more narrowly to a single soldier who is dying from mustard gas (*someone, a man, him*) and the narrator (*I, my, my, me*) who is witnessing this horror. In the final stanza, the deictic centre remains on the narrator's point-of-view, but there is now also a focus on an addressee, with the second person pronoun (*you*) repeated three times. Although readers may be implicated in the reference of this pronoun, and may choose to position themselves as the addressee, it is also possible to read this stanza as having a specific addressee through the vocative phrase *My friend* which introduces the final, devastating condemnation of war in the reproach to those who use the Latin motto (*Dulce et decorum est pro patria mori*). Whilst the narrator is still present by implication through these direct address forms, he is reabsorbed into the collective (*we*) as the cog in the machine that he undoubtedly is. I am making an assumption here, but presumably at this point in 1917 all active soldiers are men, despite the creation of the Women's Army Auxiliary Corps in that same year. The now dead soldier remains in the scene, but now as a grotesque image of a body thrown onto the cart and jolted by the uneven road (*we flung him in*; *his face*; *his hanging face* etc.)

What is quite striking when you separate out the naming of these people from other naming in the poem is that the people are often referred to minimally by a single word, often a pronoun. The main exceptions to this are the already mentioned vocative (*My friend*) and the intended addressees of the final Latin motto: *children ardent for some desperate glory*. This final naming of those who are presented as vulnerable to manipulation (presumably young recruits) stands out against all the other naming of people who are barely described at all. The result is a foregrounded focus on these young lives blighted by unreal expectations of war.

By contrast with the single-word naming of people in most of the poem, other aspects of the scene are described in more detail using a range of adjectival and participial (i.e. deverbal) descriptors: *bent-double; knock-kneed; coughing; haunting*; asleep; blood-shod; *lame; blind; drunk; deaf; tired; outstripped; clumsy; misty; thick green; green; helpless; smothering; white; hanging; froth-corrupted; vile; incurable; innocent; high; old*. Taking these descriptors out of context empha-sizes their collective focus on the incapacity of the soldiers and the visual effect of the mustard gas. Some of the resulting noun phrases are not unusual at first glance. Thus *the white eyes* is foregrounded semantically because we normally describe eyes from the colour of their irises, which are never white. The reader is therefore alerted to the rolling eyes of the dead soldier by this simple phrase. Note also that once the soldier is dead, the parts of his body that are mentioned become impersonal, with the definite article (*the*) being used both for the eyes and in relation to *the blood* and the *froth-corrupted lungs*. They also begin to take over his lost agency as the Actors (*the white eyes writhing*). This underlines the public nature of death in warfare and the lack of personal control over one's body after death. Simpson (1993: 111–112) notes a similar effect in William Golding's descrip-tion of a man (the eponymous Pincher Martin) drowning in the sea, where what he calls "body-part" Actors seem to have agency of their own (e.g. "The lips came together and parted").

By contrast with the lack of agency of the soldiers, both alive and dead, some of the artefacts of war become animated in other naming processes. Thus, the shells (*Five Nines*) which the soldiers are retreating from show signs of animacy being characterised as *tired* and *outstripped*, both words more normally used of animate beings and *the clumsy helmets* have the soldiers' fumbling panic trans-ferred to themselves as though it were a fault in the helmets and not the fin-gers of the soldiers. This personification by adjectives is not an unusual feature in poetry and would be commented upon by an alert close reader, but a systematic account of the naming in the poem allows us to contrast the animacy of weapons and equipment with the impersonal presentation of the dead soldier's body parts, showing a topsy-turvy world in which things are not as expected.

If we consider the representation of processes, events and states (i.e. transitivity) in the poem, together with any relevant peripheral TCFs that occur, what we find is that Supervention (i.e. unintentional material actions) dominate:

> *coughing, lost, went, stumbling, floundering, drowning, guttering, choking, drowning, gargling*

Notice that the verbs in the early part of the poem are also predominantly continuous (*-ing*) participles, which provide some of the deictic effects of continuity whereby both the apparently endless march back to base and the repetitive scene of the dying soldier are symbolized.

Working with any version of transitivity categories can throw up problems with them or suggest ways in which they work differently. Here, for example, the verb GO (*went*) is only identifiable through its complements (*lame, blind, drunk, deaf*), demonstrating that verbs may appear to belong in different categories according to their co-text. Alternatively, one could see this as a function of the specific verb sense — there being one Supervention meaning of this common verb, where others may be Material Action Intention (he went to school) or even Verbalisation (he went "Hello"). This illustrates a general point about linguistic description, which is that categorisations, from word classes to speech acts, are often only provisional, being labels for phenomena which are often only points on a (two-dimensional) cline or identify areas of multi-dimensional spaces analogous to vowels on the vowel chart in phonetics. Despite this problem of description, these proto-categories may be seen as "real" to the extent that they label differences which are identifiable and thus provide a vocabulary with which to talk about linguistic form and meaning.

If we consider some of the other verbs, we also find that what are normally straightforward intentional material actions (MAI), such as *march*, can be partially interpreted as Supervention if we look at their context (*men marched asleep*). Thus we get the clear sense that although the men are marching, they are not fully in control of their actions, being so tired they are comatose. In other cases, the MAI verbs demonstrate that the actions, though intentional, are nevertheless flawed or ineffective: *fumbling, cursed through sludge, trudge, limped*. These verbs are somewhere between the MAI and the Supervention categories because they are actions taken intentionally, though the flawed nature of their execution is clearly not intentional. This shows that transitivity analysis on its own does not capture the full effect of verb choices in this poem and it confirms what the project reported in Jeffries (2022) found, which was that there may be a need to identify cross-cutting dimensions within the description of processes, events and states, to recognize that some MAI verbs represent actions that are very much less than the fully intentional actions that this categorization implies.

Against this background of involuntary or problematic action/movement, there are two stand-out (foregrounded) actions of verbalization (in addition to the Free Direct Speech, "*Gas! GAS! Quick boys!*"). Note that the first (*yelling out*) is an example of Narrator's Presentation of Voice in Speech presentation terms, since we don't know what is said, whereas the second (*tell*) is a full case of direct speech (DS), with addressees made explicit (*children*) and, though there are no quotation marks, the Latin motto as the direct speech itself. The dying man is incoherent as we are not told what he yells, nor whether he is even yelling words, but we know that his verbalization expressed his pain and fear. By contrast, the speaker at the end (*My friend*) is given a full hearing, with the context explaining both how he speaks (*with such high zest*); to whom (*children ardent for some desperate glory*) and what he says. His language is represented faithfully. Thus, in addition to the propositional meaning of this last long sentence, we also have the textually constructed contrast between the lack of voice of the dying soldier and the clear message given by those far from the field of battle who want to recruit more soldiers to the cause.

The other minor pattern of verb choice relates to the question of witness. The beginning of the scene is captured by the list of continuous participles (*yelling out, stumbling, floundering*) following the shared auxiliary verb, *was*, and the apparent endlessness of this horrific scene is experienced as a series of continuing actions whose characteristics are captured by the completeness symbolism of the three-part list. This seems like an inescapable trauma. However, the next sentence provides a sense of closure when, after some initial adverbials (*Dim through the misty panes and thick green light, / As under a green sea*), a clause including the simple past tense *saw* (*I saw him drowning*) breaks the spell and implies that at least that part of the horror is complete as witnessed by the narrator. This moment of explicit witness (*I saw*) is foregrounded both deictically (simple past tense amongst the continuous verb forms) and in transitivity terms (Verbalisation amongst a sea of Supervention/MAI). Having provided this respite, the next short stanza shows that even after the soldier is dead, the horror continues in the dreams of the narrator/witness where the three-part list (*guttering, choking, drowning*) again suggests the complete nature of the horror repeatedly witnessed.

The other example of Verbalisation in the poem is in the last stanza, where there is a change of point-of-view, with the conditional clauses placing the addressee (*My friend*) as the perceiver in a series of Mental perception verbs: (*watch; hear*). The hypothesizing nature of these conditional clauses means that the reader (and addressee) is asked to imagine the scenario where the addressee is witnessing the same events as the narrator (*you too*), though the narrator's and fellow soldiers' point-of-view is also present implicitly in the detail of the actions and the description of the dead soldier's face.

Having considered the representation of first naming and then processes, events and states, albeit with some input from other TCFs such as speech presentation, listing and deixis, I will now turn to the question of how the syntax of the poem produces effects through the Prioritising and Evoking TCFs, with mention of other TCFs where relevant. The structure of the sentences in this poem is varied, but works with the other TCFs to produce a number of effects:

> Bent double, like old beggars under sacks,
> Knock-kneed, coughing like hags, we cursed through sludge,
> Till on the haunting flares we turned our backs,
> And towards our distant rest began to trudge.

Before the reader reaches the main clause (underlined) in this sentence, they have to negotiate a three-part list of adverbials which together emphasise the complete physical breakdown of the soldiers and this delay in finding out what's happening directly evokes the drawn out process of getting back to safety. However, the main clause itself is no comfort (*we cursed through sludge*) and is followed by a pair of subordinate adverbial coordinated clauses which show that the main clause is not the relief it might seem to evoke, but simply a stage in a longer process of getting back to the distant camp.

By contrast with this opening sentence, the final sentence of stanza one gets straight to the point (*all went lame*) and then presses the point home by reducing the following clauses, eliding first the verb, and then the reduced subject (predeterminer only):

> S   P   C
> All went lame;
> ~~all went~~ blind;
> ~~all went~~ Drunk with fatigue
> ~~all went~~ deaf even to the hoots...

The diminishing of the clauses in this way evokes the erasing of the men's faculties and the men themselves. Note here that the parallel structures in this case form a four-part list which unlike the symbolic completeness of a three-part list implies excess and the final part contains a long noun phrase (*the hoots / Of tired, outstripped Five-Nines that dropped behind*). This is foregrounded against the previous clauses where there are no or only one-word (*fatigue*) adjective complements and it evokes the long trail of nameless soldiers traipsing back to their base to rest and recuperate.

The next stanza brings the scene to life, using Free Direct Speech presentation, by quoting the men in the scene (*Gas! GAS! Quick, boys!*) This is noticeably a series of minor sentences with no verb even implied, directly evoking the voices of the men being attacked (who wouldn't be speaking in complete sentences) and increasing the immediacy by missing out a reporting clause. The following sentence again begins with a minor structure (no verb) which appears to be a two-part list of a NP (*an ecstasy of fumbling*) and a non-finite nominal clause (*fitting the clumsy helmets just in time*). The contrast of these timeless (because verbless) clauses with the following clause, where tense and aspect are reintroduced, is evocative of the scene playing out in front of the narrator's eyes:

> But someone still was yelling out and stumbling
> And flound'ring like a man in fire or lime. —

The evocation of action in time, because of the use of a finite verb (*was*) is foregrounded against the ongoing (timeless) background of the men trying to get their helmets fitted. It brings the dying man into focus and evokes the momentary hope that he will be able to get to safety before the following sentence dashes that hope, using a long introductory sequence of adverbials (underlined) to evoke the slow-motion horror of watching him die:

> <u>Dim through the misty panes and thick green light,</u>
> <u>As under a green sea</u>, I saw him drowning.

This is followed by a similar structure, also adverbial-heavy at the beginning, which evokes the repeated dreams of the narrator, with a three-part (i.e. complete) list of the process of dying which the narrator is doomed to watch forever:

> In all my dreams before my helpless sight,
> He plunges at me, guttering, choking, drowning.

The final stanza is an extreme example of what I used to call syntactic iconicity (Jeffries 2010c), but which I am now incorporating into the framework as structurally evoking direct responses from readers. In this case, the sequence of two long conditional clauses before we get to the main clause evokes both the length of the original experience (the horror) and the repeated memory of it — at the same time delaying the hypothetical reaction of the addressee to the scene they have little chance of witnessing (*you would not tell*).

> If in some smothering dreams, you too could pace
> Behind the wagon that we flung him in,
> And watch the white eyes writhing in his face,
> His hanging face, like a devil's sick of sin;

> If you could hear, at every jolt, the blood
> Come gargling from the froth-corrupted lungs,
> Obscene as cancer, bitter as the cud
> Of vile, incurable sores on innocent tongues, —
> My friend, you would not tell with such high zest
> To children ardent for some desperate glory,
> The old Lie: *Dulce et decorum est*
> *Pro patria mori.*

Although the process of analysis involves looking at each TCF individually, there are times (this is one) when addressing them together better reflects the reality of the poem's effect. Some TCFs happen in the same place but have independent ideational effects — others work together on a single effect.

At the broadest level, then, this final stanza has the TCFs of prioritizing (structure), hypothesizing (modality), negating and evoking all working together to produce a parallel imagined scenario in which the addressee gets to experience the war in the same way as the narrator and reacts to it by deciding not to use the Latin motto to drum up new recruits. Note that the effect of the negating TCF is that it produces two scenarios — positive and negative. In this case, paired with the modal (*would*), the *not* produces an image of what could happen if the addressee had witnessed these scenes contrasted with what will actually happen, because the addressee is not in fact witness to the scene described.

Through lack of space, I have said little about Alluding here, though there is a very strong thread of existential presuppositions running through the poem up until the last stanza. So, there is no doubting that the world of the poem contains all that the definite noun phrases refer to (e.g. *the haunting flares, their boots*) and this is a relatively unremarkable aspect of the text. However, the setting up of the whole last stanza is foregrounded against this background of things and people that are presupposed. It is created as a logical presupposition by the conditional, modal and negated structure I have just discussed. This logical presupposition is that the hypothetical scenario is not the one that can be assumed, but rather the reverse.

At the same time, the individual lines and phrases in this final stanza contain examples of equating which are separate from the overlapping TCFs discussed above:

> like a devil's sick of sin;

> Obscene as cancer, bitter as the cud
> Of vile, incurable sores on innocent tongues, —

These similes are the culmination of a series of earlier similes which set the scene:

like old beggars under sacks
coughing like hags
like a man in fire or lime
As under a green sea

Unusually, there appear to be no constructed opposites in this poem, which we might find surprising, given the theme. Neither does Owen favour metaphor on the whole over simile, though a cognitive metaphor approach would one see some of the more unusual personifying collocations (*haunting flares*; *eyes writhing*) as metaphorical. Whilst I have often been asked whether metaphor ought to be included as a TCF in the framework, I don't see it as operating at the same level as it is a purely conceptual notion which can be delivered in so many different textual ways. Like personification and other literary devices, metaphor is a step further away from the textual choices of the writer than most of what I am describing. This means that such labels might be helpful at the interpretative end of the process, but they do not strike me as a helpful part of the analysis itself. Evoking, however, is clearly one of the main ways in which texts, particularly poems, make meaning, and one that Verdonk (2013: 83) sees as vital to literary work:

> Further, I am in full agreement with Leech, who has argued that the contribution to meaning made by the literary text as a formal object lies primarily in the principle of iconicity, that is, "its very physical substance imitates or enacts the meaning that it represents".
>
> (Leech 1987: 86)

Conclusions

I have no space here to comment in detail about evoking through sound (*sludge*, *trudge*) or evoking through form (e.g. the effect of enjambement) and there are other purely textual insights that I have not managed to fit in here too, such as an assessment of the adjective *blood-shod*. This is not intended to be the last word on the style of this complex poem, though it has attempted to show how an underlying analysis of each of the textual-conceptual functions can be built into a coherent attempt to interpret the poem through its language. I am deliberately leaving the additional echoes of meaning that come from context, such as writing this analysis during a phase of spreading warfare in the world, for a separate kind of commentary, though one that might usefully draw on the linguistic analysis proposed here. Similarly, there can be other contextual observations relating to the history of the specific war Owen is writing about or relating to literary traditions and intertextuality. None of these is excluded by the proposals in this chapter, though they may be enhanced by the textual insights it provides.

Using "Dulce et Decorum Est" as an illustration, this chapter reflects on the attempt reported in Jeffries (2022) to establish whether a framework originally applied to ideology could be developed into a more general model of textual meaning which would provide a systematic approach to ideation in contemporary poems and bring forward evidence for aesthetic judgements and observations. My conclusions from the broader project were that the TCFs as originally developed cover much of what might be seen as consensus about the stylistic choices in poems, though there is, as already mentioned, additional contextually-based meaning that will arise from our own personal, societal or historical readings of poems. The value of the approach demonstrated here is to provide a systematic way to identify and assess those aspects of the poem's meaning that would not necessarily be flagged up either in a commentary based on formal linguistic features alone, as in the early type of stylistics, or by a literary scholar with historical (albeit anachronistic) or social context as their frame of reference. Thus, I see the approach as providing what used to be called a "discovery procedure" and confidence that, were another scholar to repeat the process, much the same account of the poem's textual meaning would be produced. The caveat to this claim is that some of the TCFs (e.g. prioritising) are so all-encompassing that two scholars may each only find themselves commenting on a subset of the potential observations. However, there should be no problem in each recognising and acknowledging the observations of the other if they are grounded in the model in the same way.

The two changes made to the framework as a result of applying it to poetry were already anticipated but became more urgent in working on poems. For methodological reasons, separating out the core TCFs from the peripheral ones is a way to organise the analysis and helps with writing a commentary where TCFs are overlapping or concurrent. Analysing poems also underlined the need to add Evoking (iconicity), a phenomenon I had long been working on in relation to poetry (Jeffries 2010c), but which had never arisen in my work on non-literary texts. This project confirmed to my satisfaction that it was indeed a new TCF that could be added to the list, rather than working at a different level or angle, as metaphor does. This extending of the list of TCFs is not done lightly. Some fields of linguistics (e.g. transitivity, speech act theory) suffer from an ever-extending list of labels for ever more detailed features of language whose consequence can be to dilute the usefulness of the relevant framework. However, I am relatively confident that Evoking works in much the same ways, and at the same level, as the established TCFs of the earlier model, being linked to certain forms, but not limited by them and producing a limited range of effects that are interpretable in relation to the specific co-text in the poem.

In summary, here are my main theoretical conclusions after applying the framework to poems:

- Textual meaning exists in poetry as well as other genres, though there may be some differences of emphasis and execution more typical of poetry than other genres and text-types;
- A tripartite structure of language with textual meaning sitting between the structural and the contextual is theoretically helpful and demonstrates the centrality of stylistics to linguistics (i.e. it is not just a kind of applied linguistics);
- There is no theoretical objection to — and much to be gained from — teasing out strands of linguistic structure and meaning (as happened in the early days of modern linguistics), despite the fact that they work concurrently in the text itself. This is not, I would contend, a kind of "segregationalism" (see Harris 1981) but a productive and insightful way to make progress in describing different parts of human communication.

The project also demonstrated the following general points in about textual meaning in relation to poetry:

- Poetry uses the same range of textual features (TCFs) as other texts, albeit with different effects;
- The textual-conceptual approach to poetic meaning seems to provide a way to get under the skin of poems without being overly formalistic nor too vaguely literary about it.

There is, as always, more work to do. Whilst future research could usefully be focussed on finding evidence of the psychological reality of the textual layer of meaning, I would propose that we also need an agreed meta-theory of language to make progress in understanding how each of the lower levels of language work together, whichever theoretical approach is adopted at these levels.

On the detail of the framework, there is more to be done on working out how the TCFs fit together and what different models of each feature (possibly informed by different theoretical standpoints) can offer. I do not see this kind of eclecticism as a problem as long as it is explicit and rigorous in its approach. The application of the framework to other genres will help to produce an ever more robust model of textual meaning which can be applied to texts across the board.

On poetry itself, my work so far has only been able to apply this approach to a very small number of poems and all they are also all lyric poems in English, most of them from British poets. A real test of the approach which I would be fascinated to see is how it would work with dub poetry, slam poetry and poetry and poems from other languages and traditions.

One of the things I shared with Peter Verdonk was a love of the language of poetry. Despite superficial differences in our approaches to the style of poems,

I think what comes across from his writing is an attitude I also have, which is that stylistics has something to offer those who want to understand how poems make meaning by providing evidence from linguistic choices for the interpretations being put forward. This is what I understand by the concept of style as "motivated choice". Let us leave the last word to Peter:

> I wish to make the obvious point that the way in which stylistics and literary criticism each approach a literary text exemplifies a particular perspective, namely, a perspective on the study of literature. Thus, very generally speaking, literary criticism directs attention to the larger-scale significance of what is represented by a product of verbal art. On the other hand, stylistics tends to focus on how this significance can be related to specific features of language, that it, to the linguistic texture of a literary work. Following this argument, I think the literary critical and stylistic perspectives are complementary, or perhaps the poles of a dialectical process.
> (Verdonk 2013: 172)

References

Eco, U. 1984. *Semiotics and The Philosophy of Language.* Bloomington, IN: Indiana University Press.

Fabb, N. and Halle, M. 2008. *Meter in Poetry: A New Theory.* Cambridge: Cambridge University Press.

Fanthorpe, U.A. 2005. *Collected Poems.* Calstock, Cornwall: Peterloo Poets.

Gavins, J. 2007. *Text World Theory: an introduction.* Edinburgh University Press.

Halliday, M.A.K. & Matthiessen, M.I.M. 2004. *An Introduction to Functional Grammar.* London: Edward Arnold.

Harris, R. 1981. *The Language Myth.* London: Duckworth.

Jeffries, L. 1993. *The Language of Twentieth Century Poetry.* Basingstoke: Macmillan.

Jeffries, L. 2010a. *Opposition in Discourse.* London: Continuum Books.

Jeffries, L. 2010b. *Critical Stylistics.* London: Palgrave.

Jeffries, L. 2010c. "The Unprofessionals": Syntactic iconicity and reader interpretation in contemporary poems. In *Language and Style*, D. McIntyre & B. Busse (eds), 95–115. London: Palgrave.

Jeffries, L. 2014. Interpretation. In *The Cambridge Handbook of Stylistics*, P. Stockwell & S. Whiteley (eds), 469–486. Cambridge: Cambridge University Press.

Jeffries, L. 2015. Language and ideology. In *Introducing Language and Linguistics*. N. Braber, L. Cummings & L. Morrish (eds), 379–405. Cambridge: Cambridge University Press.

Jeffries, L. 2022. *The Language of Contemporary Poetry.* London: Palgrave.

Jeffries, L. & McIntyre, D. 2025. *Stylistics* (Second Edition). Cambridge: Cambridge University Press.

Leech, G. 1987. 'Stylistics and functionalism', in Fabb, N., Attridge, D., Durant, A. and MaccCabe, C. (eds) *The Linguistics of Writing: Arguments between Language and Literature*. Manchester: Manchester University Press. 76-88.

Short, M., McIntyre, D., Jeffries, L. & Bousfield, D. 2011. Processes of interpretation: using meta-analysis to inform pedagogic practice. In *Teaching Stylistics. Teaching the New English*. Jeffries, L. & McIntyre, D. (eds), 69–94. London: Palgrave.

doi Simpson, P. 1993. *Language, Ideology and Point of View*. London: Routledge.

doi Tsur, R. 2017. Metre, rhythm and emotion in poetry: a cognitive approach. *Studia Metrica et Poetica* 4(1): 7–40.

doi Tsur, R. & Gafni, C. 2022. *Sound – Emotion Interaction in Poetry. Rhythm, Phonemes, Voice Quality*. Amsterdam: John Benjamins.

Verdonk, P. 2013. *The Stylistics of Poetry: Context, Cognition, Discourse, History*. London: Bloomsbury Academic.

Werth, P. 1999. *Text Worlds: Representing Conceptual Space in Discourse*. Harlow, Essex: Pearson Education Limited.

CHAPTER 4

Stylistics and motivated choice in Seamus Heaney's "Orange Drums"

Mick Short

In this chapter I will perform a stylistic analysis of "Orange Drums, Tyrone, 1966" by Seamus Heaney, one of Peter Verdonk's favourite poets (cf. his discussions of poems by Heaney in Verdonk 1993: 57–65 and Verdonk 2002). I will mainly indulge in what has sometimes been called "steam stylistics" (Carter 2007, Gavins & Stockwell 2012), which concentrates on motivated choices at all linguistic levels in relation to meaning, effect and style. Steam stylistics has, of course, been supplemented in recent years by a number of useful analytical approaches, such as corpus stylistics (e.g. McIntyre & Walker 2019, Semino & Short 2004), narrative analysis (e.g. Alber & Fludernik 2010, Herman 2013), cognitive stylistics (e.g. Gavins and Steen 2003, Stockwell 2002), and Text World Theory (e.g. Gavins 2007, Werth 1999). My main motivation in this chapter is to analyse the language of the poem in as much detail and as dispassionately as I am able, to characterise the text and my understanding and appreciation of it. This approach, allied to being as open, honest and truthful as we can be, lies, in my view, at the heart of the stylistics enterprise. Given that I have now been retired for more than ten years, I am not as up to date on the various new approaches to analysis as I might once have been, but hopefully, others can add to, and correct, my mainly steam-driven attempt. I have supplemented my analysis with some corpus-based work, however, along with the occasional remark in relation to the other approaches referred to above. Peter Verdonk similarly used steam stylistics accompanied by insights from more recent approaches to the field when he analysed texts. "Orange Drums", which is usefully short enough to analyse in stylistic detail in a short paper, shows Heaney developing his distinctive poetic voice and, although not one of his finest poems, certainly has its own poetic merits. Peter Verdonk himself used it as part of an unpublished talk he gave to an early PALA conference.

Keywords: corpus stylistics, cognitive stylistics, linguistic stylistics, narrative analysis, Seamus Heaney, steam stylistics, Text World Theory

https://doi.org/10.1075/lal.44.04sho

The poem

"Orange Drums, Tyrone, 1966" was first published in 1975, in Heaney's *North* collection (Heaney 2001 [1975]: 63). Because detailed stylistic analysis is easier to follow when the text is presented along with it, I had hoped to quote the poem here. Unfortunately, it has proved impossible to do this, owing to differing assumptions among the various publishers involved. So for those who do not have *North* to hand, I provide here two alternatives of what appear to be stable online versions of the text:

1. https://irelandtour.sunygeneseoenglish.org/resources/poems/heaneys-orange-drums-tyrone-1966/ provides an exactly accurate rendering of the original text.
2. https://posc284.posc.sites.carleton.edu/uncategorized/poetry-of-place-and-conflict/ quotes the poem accurately except for the fact that it does not provide the original four-line stanzaic divisions. The poem is also presented some way down this web page but it can be accessed easily by searching the page for "Artifact 6", the heading under which the poem is presented.

Initial observations and my overall understanding of "Orange Drums, Tyrone, 1966"

The title of the poem positions the reader in a particular time and place which, in turn, helps us to build the text-world of the poem as we read it. Like Peter Verdonk, I assume that part of my duty as an academic reader of poetry is to make sure that I am as aware as possible of the linguistic, historical and cultural knowledge that the writer of the poem and his contemporary readers would have had when responding to the poem. In text-world terms, this then becomes my discourse-world knowledge, which I have in mind when approaching the text critically. There is an important theoretical issue here, of course. I assume that it is part of my duty as an academic reader-critic to align myself through research, initially at least, with the relevant linguistic and contextual assumptions which Heaney and his contemporaries would have had at that time and in the same culture. Hence the discourse-world I assume when responding critically will be different from my first reading of the poem. Many postmodern critics assume that it is critically valid to take up such more naïve, "readerly", positions. But that would be another paper. I now outline the contextual information which will be helpful to others as they read the poem and my commentary on it.

Tyrone is in Northern Ireland, and in 1966 on the 12th of July (the date of the annual Orange/Protestant marches through areas where Catholics live), Heaney would have been a young man, with a "Green", Catholic background, not an "Orange", Protestant one. He was the son of a Catholic cattle farmer, 27 years old, married with a young son and about to begin lecturing in Modern English Literature at Queen's University, Belfast. His first volume of poetry, *Death of a Naturalist*, was published in 1966, the year he wrote "Orange Drums". The Orange march described in the poem effectively takes place in the run-up to the violent sectarian "Troubles" in Northern Ireland, which are conventionally said to have begun in 1969, when British troops were first deployed, and to have ended with the Good Friday agreement of 1998, though opposed sectarian feelings on the part of many were in evidence long before then and indeed continue to this day. Although Catholic by birth and education, Heaney tried throughout his life not to take sides in the sectarian debate, seeing his poet's role as portraying carefully the complexities of life in the round and not accepting its reduction to simplistic statements, including partisan assumptions of political or religious certainty. And this is what we can see emerging in this early poem. He evokes a march for the reader which, given his Catholic background, he would feel threatened by, but which he does not criticise. In other words, this early poem can be seen as part of the development of his distinctive, involved yet not overtly sectarian, poetic voice.

The commentary in "Orange Drums" is focused almost exclusively on describing one drummer as he marches in an Orange parade. Indeed, the poem's title focuses us on the drum itself, rather than the drummer. Heaney restricts himself throughout the poem to referring to people and things other than himself in the parade. Although we feel his edginess as a spectator, he does not criticise the drummer, this particular march, or Orange marches in general. Rather, his attitude seems more descriptive, if not entirely dispassionate. Although not one of his very finest poems, "Orange Drums" has much to recommend it and is worthy of careful critical consideration.

It is helpful when exploring the development of Heaney's distinctive poetic voice, to compare the version of "Orange Drums" in the first (1975) edition of *North*, in which the poem first appeared, with the most recent edition. The two versions of the poem are identical except for the penultimate line. Originally that line was "The pigskin's scourged until his knuckles bleed" but Heaney changed it in the final version to "The goatskin's sometimes plastered with his blood". The changes Heaney made indicate (a) his desire for more accurate description and (b) a wish to play down unnecessarily emotive sectarian responses. Although pigskin was used more often for drums in earlier times (it was probably more easily available), goatskin is quasi-universal for lambegs these days and "pigskin" has more negative associations than "goatskin" as pigs are often assumed to be dirty, with goats being less so. In addition, "plastered with his blood", though also negative in associative terms, is less so than "scourged until his knuckles bleed". "Scourged" also has strongly emotive biblical associations. Christ was scourged while on the Cross, an allusion which is effectively removed from the final version of "Orange Drums".

Below I use collocational analysis in addition to steam stylistics to show, where relevant, the discourse/semantic "prosodies" of words in the poem. By 'relevant' I mean where a discourse prosody is discernible in the corpus data and where it is relevant to the interpretative remarks I am making (i.e. supports or goes against my interpretative view). The corpus used for the collocational work was BNCWeb, with a span of four words either side of the node. A Mutual Information (MI) value of >3 was assumed as the cut off for statistical significance.

Overall structure

The poem is relatively simple and straightforward grammatically. The title consists of a two-word noun phrase plus a one-word location and a date, suggesting a diary entry or radio commentary and positions readers as if we are observers in the text-world context described above. The text-world depicts a Northern Irish setting and there is a close correspondence between the text-world and the real-world context in which Heaney wrote the poem. The main body of the text, excluding the title, is 89 words long and consists of three stanzas, each four lines long, and is pretty straightforward linguistically. It has seven sentences (two each in stanzas 1 and 2, and three in stanza 3), averaging 19.5 words per sentence, close to the norm for written English prose. The rhyme scheme is in the familiar ABAB form, consisting of four half rhymes and two full rhymes, and the basic metre is iambic pentameter. The poem is also simple in Text World Theory terms. There are no embedded, alternative or modal worlds apart from the one described. Heaney thus makes us focus exclusively on the one world evoked by his commentary. Below, I analyse the poem a stanza at a time.

Stanza one

"Orange Drums" opens *in medias res,* with definite reference in the opening two lines: "The lambeg", "him" and "his". The narrator (Heaney, we assume, as there is no indication of another narratorial voice) apparently presupposes that we already know what a lambeg is (I confess that I didn't!) and that we have experienced other Orange marches (which have been taking place annually since 1796) and know the significant role that lambegs have played in them. So we are positioned by the opening commentary as if we, like Heaney, are witnessing the march ourselves. The pattern of definite reference continues and the deictic "there" in line 3 (the only straightforward deictic term in the poem) also helps to position us with Heaney, watching the procession from a somewhat distanced viewing position. Effectively, then, the deixis, especially for those with real-world knowledge of Heaney's life and the Troubles in Northern Ireland, helps the reader take on the discourse-world assumptions necessary to envisage the text world of the poem. Moreover, because there are no references in the text to the observer, the narration is effectively indeterminate between 1st-person and 3rd-person.

"There" indicates a physically distal perspective and alerts the reader to the possibility of an attitudinally distanced one too, something which is borne out by the initial description of the drummer and his drum. The reference to the drummer's belly suggests that he is overweight: a search for the collocates of "belly" using BNCWeb reveals five relevant terms. In terms of Mutual Information (MI) value they are: "whale" (MI value = 7.5665), "swollen" (MI value = 7.3293), "pot" (MI value = 6.4641), "huge" (MI value = 4.6872) and "fat" (MI value = 4.3329). The concordance list for "belly" also includes three body-related terms which themselves are often associated with plumpness: "thighs" (MI value = 8.5794), "buttocks" (MI value = 8.5327) and "breasts" (MI value = 7.4245). The gross physicality of the description of the drummer is also underlined by the reference to "his haunches".

The lambeg, as much as the drummer, is the main focus of attention throughout the poem. The drum is the subject and topic of all three main verbs in sentence 1: the intransitive verb "balloons", the transitive verb "weighs" and the transitive participial verb "lodging", all of which invite the reader to infer pragmatic implicatures. The drum, not the drummer, is portrayed as active in all three verbs and so it appears to be almost quasi-sentient and in control. The lambeg "balloons at his belly", a semantically deviant (and so metaphorical) foregrounding which is underlined by the /b/ alliteration across the three lexically full words, emphasising the size of the lambeg and belly together. There is also alliterative foregrounding linking "lambeg" as Subject to the verb "lodging", which has the semantically deviant auditory noun "thunder" as its Object.

A corpus search for "lodging" and the other grammatical variants of the LODGE lemma brings up various metaphorical uses of the term in relation to renting a room or to sending written documents in support of formal objections, complaints or appeals. But the sense here is clearly more basic, relating to placing something in an intended location. The Object of "lodging", "thunder" is not a physical object, of course, and so a metaphorical meaning has to be inferred. The noise of the drumbeat is thus portrayed as very loud indeed, like thunder, and the agentive source of the loud noise is the drummer's drum/belly. Paul Simpson, my Northern Ireland "informant", points out that this rather ironised depiction is underlined by a pun in relation to "lodging". The Orange Order is often referred to as the Orange Lodge because the Grand Lodge of Ireland, which supports the Orange Marches to this day, was formed in 1725 to uphold the Protestant Reformation and the "Glorious Revolution" of 1688.

But perhaps the most foregrounded word in the first sentence, "grossly", which modifies "lodging thunder", is line initial, and is also foregrounded through semantic deviation ("thunder" can't normally be placed anywhere) and grammatically by its placement before the deictic 'there'. "Grossly" is also very negative in collocational terms: all 13 items in its list of collocates are semantically or pragmatically negative and at least six of them are grammatically negative too. The fifth-strongest item in terms of MI value is "overweight", which coheres with the collocational effects associated with "belly" which I have discussed above.

Table 1.

Word	Mutual information value (>3)
under-represented	11.384
underestimated	10.1499
inflated	9.8418
negligent	9.578
overweight	9.4921
exaggerated	9.252
unfair	9.1238
indecent	8.962
inaccurate	8.7443
inadequate	8.494
inefficient	8.393
offensive	8.0765
misleading	7.2327

The final line and sentence of stanza 1 is a passive construction with "he" as the acted-upon Subject/Topic and, inferentially, the drum (the referent of the noun clause "what he buckles under") is in the Agent slot. There is an obvious semantic opposition in "He is raised *up* by what he buckles *under*" (my italics), which is underlined by the word-initial /ʌ/ assonance between the slant-opposites "up" and "under". The drummer cannot literally be raised up by a heavy object which he is carrying; and the most likely inference seems to be that the awkward size, positioning and weight of the lambeg, which has to be held on its side so that it can be beaten on both sides, forces him into a more upright posture, head back, so that the drummer can bear its considerable size and weight while drumming. The use of the verb "buckle" is also of interest. Its only BNCWeb collocates with an MI value above 3 are "knees" (8.698), which occurs in the previous line of the poem, "under" (5.3336) and "down" (4.4092). The two adverbs can also be seen in cognitive metaphor terms as part of the GOOD IS UP / BAD IS DOWN schema. Readers familiar with Gerard Manley Hopkins may also recall his famous use of "buckle" in "The Windhover" and want to see an allusion/intertextual connection here; but as far as I can see, such an interpretative move would be unhelpful, except in the sense that both uses involve a sudden change in body shape. But I can see no obvious interpretative connection between a bird of prey suddenly diving towards its prey and a drummer being borne down by the weight of his huge drum.

Stanza two

As in stanza one, the drummer's active role is played down in favour of his drum. In spite of the fact that "He", referring anaphorically to the drummer, is the Subject of the main clause in the first sentence of stanza two, the focus of the sentence as a whole is really the lambeg and how it dominates the man. He parades in a secondary, acted-upon position, behind the drum which weighs him down; and, in the fronted adverbial clause, it is the seasoned rod which the drummer uses to beat the drum that is the Agent of the clause, not the drummer. The stanza's second sentence also has a fronted clause, a concessive adverbial "though the drummers / Are granted passage through the crowd", which, although it implicates that the drummer is marching, portrays him merely as one of a group, with the crowd apparently in control of whether the drummers can march through them or not. The crowd is also described as "nodding", which I first assumed, on the grounds of textual relevance, must be in response to the rhythmic beating of the drum. But it also indicates the approval/support of the crowd, which the collocates for "nodding" make clear. In a list of 16 collocates, the one with the highest MI value is "thoughtfully" (8.1957), the next highest is "smiling" (7.8397), "approval" is fifth highest (5.6406) and "agreement" is seventh highest (5.454).

The final line and sentence of stanza two effectively summarises the dominant role of the lambegs: "It is the drums preside, like giant tumours." The '"It is" + Complement (= NP + non-defining relative clause) + Adverbial' structure gives three-way emphasis to "drums", "preside" and the end-weighted Adverbial simile, all in one short sentence. As elsewhere, the drums are Subject to a dynamic verb, and "preside", has obvious associations of power and control. Pragmatically, the "'it is" + Complement' structure appears to cancel an assumption that something other than the drums would normally be Subject to "preside" and, indeed, "drums preside" is foregrounded because the expression is semantically deviant. "Preside" normally expects a human Subject (and indeed a person with enough social power to chair a formal meeting or gathering of some kind), not an inanimate object. The collocational search for 'preside' gives just two collocates, "over" (MI: 6.3498) and "meeting" (MI: 5.3751). The sentence- and stanza-final Adverbial, already foregrounded by virtue of its end-weighted position and its textually separating comma, also contains an innovative simile/metaphor DRUM IS TUMOUR, where the lambeg is portrayed negatively as being cancer-like. Large cancerous tumours are more threatening than small ones, of course, and this one is "giant", adding to the oppressive characterisation of the drum.

Stanza three

In stanza one, the noise of the drums was compared to thunder, connoting a possible oncoming storm/threat. Then, in stanza two, the tumour comparison suggested a possibly cancerous health threat which would be much more worrying in personal terms, terminal even. Finally, stanza three, which has a nexus of foregounding devices, increases yet again the sense of imminent threat as we and Heaney watch the march together.

The first sentence of stanza three foregrounds syntactically the semantically deviant Adverbial "To every cocked ear, expert in its greed" by fronting it. The "cocked ear" schematically assumes that an unidentified noise, possibly threatening, has been heard nearby. Most humans can't move their ears independently; normally only animals like cats, dogs and deer do this, when noises possibly signalling an imminent threat are heard. Although at first glance there are no apparent significant prosodies in collocational terms for "cocked" (its only BNCWeb collocates with an MI greater than 3 are "hat", "position" and "into"), in the context of the developing Northern Ireland Troubles the fact that guns need to be cocked before firing clearly evokes associations of guns and possible injury or death as a consequence of them being fired. A Google search on "cocked position" brings up a welter of links to web pages about guns or muscle contraction (immediately before flight, perhaps?). Moreover, although a Google search on "cocked hat" brings up many contemporary hits for fashionable hats, the original cocked hat was a tricorne, worn by many military officers and there are many hits for this semantic area too. Even today, to be knocked into a cocked hat is an idiomatic expression indicating that the person referred to has been thoroughly defeated.

All this appears at first sight, then, to encapsulate the worry of a Catholic observer. Moreover, it is also important to note that "every cocked ear", besides itself being foregrounded semantically, as we have seen, is modified by the semantically deviant phrase "expert in its greed". This metaphorical expression clearly cannot cohere straightforwardly with the viewpoint of a threatened Catholic observer. Indeed, it can best be understood in relation to the Protestant majority in the crowd of onlookers, celebrating the march. "Expert in its greed" suggests that most of the crowd are listening expectantly for the march, which they will often have watched in previous years. Heaney is thus portraying the opposing attitudes of the two major religious and social communities in Northern Ireland. What feels positive for Protestant onlookers is threatening for Catholic observers. The crowd of Protestant supporters are clearly waiting in triumphal anticipation for the marchers, though Heaney and other Catholics, living nearby in the houses along the streets where the march is taking place, would feel threatened by it. In point of view terms, then, Heaney (a) observes things from his own viewpoint and (b) takes into consideration the viewpoint of others with opposing opinions. But then, in the semantically deviant "expert in its greed" he also implicates (c) his own antipathetic response to (b). Hence the point of view position expressed is both complex and sophisticated.

"His battered signature subscribes 'No Pope'" in line 2 of the final stanza is clearly semantically deviant, and so metaphorical, in a number of ways. As it is physical objects which are normally beaten, "Battered" modifying "signature" is semantically deviant and so metaphorical. The most likely inference appears to be that "signature" refers metaphorically to the rhythm of the battered drumbeat. There are 21 collocates for "battered" with an MI above 3. Below I present the top 10 collocates, all of which refer to physical objects of some kind.

Table 2.

No.	Word	Mutual information value (> 3)
1	trilby	11.6646
2	refuges	11.1564
3	wives	8.6707
4	suitcase	8.3915
5	refuge	7.8105
6	truck	7.0427
7	hat	6.7926
8	leather	6.4136
9	tin	6.222
10	boots	5.9478

The highest collocate is "trilby" (11.6646) and its superordinate, "hat" (6.7926), is seventh in the list. The trilby hat is commonly worn in Protestant marches in Northern Ireland. The list also contains four other physical objects used by people, along with other terms related to the maltreatment of other human beings, particularly in terms of power relations in close social, including domestic, relationships. "Wives" (8.6707) is third in the list, "refuges" (11.6646) is second and its singular, "refuge" (7.8105), is fifth. In our discourse-world we know that maltreated people, including wives and partners in domestic circumstances, sometimes have to leave their homes and live in refuges. So the significant collocations for "battered" seem to be alerting us to human-to-human violence, which connects, in turn, to the broader sectarian disagreements in the Northern Ireland Troubles.

There is a very strong nexus of foregrounding in the second line of the final stanza. A drum, not its "signature" is normally beaten, and so "battered signature", referring to the beaten drum's rhythm, is clearly metaphorical, referring to the regularity of the drumming beat. In turn, "his battered signature" is the Subject of "subscribes", which has "'No Pope'" as its Object. Both the SV and the VO relations here are semantically deviant and needing interpretation. I wondered at first whether the watching crowd might be chanting "No Pope" to the insistent rhythm of the lambeg's beat but my Northern Irish informant tells me that is not common.

So, eventually I inferred that Protestant onlookers might be imagining the words in their heads as they listened to the beat of the lambeg. This inference seems somewhat unsatisfying, though, which I find rather disappointing. If others can come up with a better interpretation, theirs would be preferable to mine and, indeed, would also help to improve the overall standing of what is already a pretty good poem. I do also have some other hesitancies about the last lines of the poem, as I will try to explain below.

The third line of the last stanza is the simple sentence "The goatskin's sometimes plastered with his blood". Plastering literally has to do with putting a plaster skim on walls or other surfaces when a house is being built. Here the metaphorical analogue appears to be that the drummer's blood is covering (part of) the drum's goatskin, presumably because, in text-world terms, he accidentally bangs his hands on the rim of the lambeg as he beats the drum hard with his rods. To my mind, the analogue is a little unsatisfactory as, although his blood will be spread onto the goatskin, it is unlikely to cover it entirely, like plaster spread on a wall, as the lambeg is so large. There is also an ambiguity in the past participle "plastered" in terms of whether what is being described relates just to the present moment or is a more general result of drumming at previous marches; but the poem as a whole seems to be describing one particular march, not marches in general.

I also have some difficulty with the last line of the poem, "The air is pounding like a stethoscope". Final lines of poems, particularly short ones, automatically attract end-weighting foregrounding because of their position in the poem; and this final line is also one of only two full rhymes in the poem, foregrounding it internally and, through its phonetic parallelism with "'No Pope'", suggests an important pragmatic interpretative connection between the two lines.

Overall, then, the heavy foregrounding at the end of the poem suggests that we will find important interpretative significance to go with it. But from what I can see (again, perhaps others can improve on what I say) the lines do not quite seem to be able to bear the foregrounded weight they have been given and, indeed, seem to lack precision. The simile "like a stethoscope" does not quite seem to work in meaning terms. Firstly, "stethoscope" has positive as well negative associations schematically (it can be an important part of a process to alleviate or cure medical problems), which are difficult to ignore, and in spite of the phonetic parallelism it is not obvious how to connect the medical tool to "'No Pope'" and the socio-political assumptions underlying such a real or imagined "chant". Secondly, the relationship between the metaphor in "the air is pounding" and "stethoscope" does not quite fit semantically, even though sound vibrations are involved in both cases. Unlike the drumbeat, which emanates from the drummer deliberately beating the drum, the heartbeat referred to in the medical domain is not *intended* by the medical patient. The stethoscope is merely the instrument that amplifies the sound of the *autonomic* beating of the patient's heart, or noises in other parts of a patient's body, so that a doctor can hear them clearly.

Concluding comments

In the above discussion of stanza three of Heaney's "Orange Drums" I have been trying to flesh out the interpretative difficulties I have experienced in trying to respond in detail to it. This is why, despite the impressive writing in its first two stanzas, which I have tried to map out in the earlier parts of this chapter, I think that "Orange Drums" is not quite as fine as some of Seamus Heaney's other poems. I have tried, in a way I think is important for stylistic analysis and distinguishes it from most mainstream literary approaches, to make my thoughts about the poem as clear as I can, with detailed analytical support for my views, so that others can criticise them, improve on my account and, at the same time, improve the standing of what is already a very interesting poem. I hope that such consideration might, in turn, contribute to our understanding of the general relationship between literary appreciation and textual analysis and interpretation.

Acknowledgements

I am grateful to Joanna Gavins and Paul Simpson for comments on earlier drafts (and in Paul's case, for reading the poem to me in an appropriate accent) and to Dan McIntyre, who supplied me with the collocational data referred to in this chapter.

References

Alber, J. & Fludernik, M. (eds) 2010. *Postclassical Narratology. Approaches and Analyses.* Columbus, OH: Ohio State University Press.

Carter, R. 2007. Response to special issue of *Applied Linguistics* devoted to Language Creativity in Everyday Contexts. *Applied Linguistics* 28 (4): 597–608.

Gavins, J. 2007. *Text World Theory. An Introduction.* Edinburgh: Edinburgh University Press.

Gavins, J. & Steen, G. (eds). 2003. *Cognitive Poetics in Practice.* London: Routledge.

Gavins, J. & Stockwell, P. 2012. About the heart, where it hurt exactly, and how often. *Language and Literature* 21 (1): 31–50.

Heaney, S. 2001 [1975]. *North.* London: Faber & Faber.

Herman, D. 2013. *Storytelling and the Sciences of Mind.* Cambridge, MA: MIT Press.

McIntyre, D. & Walker, B. 2019. *Corpus Stylistics. Theory and Practice.* Edinburgh: Edinburgh University Press.

Semino, E. & Short, M. 2004. *Corpus Stylistics. Speech, Writing and Thought Presentation in a Corpus of English Writing.* London: Routledge.

Stockwell, P. 2002. *Cognitive Poetics.* London: Routledge.

Verdonk, P, 1993. Poetry and public life. A contextualized reading of Seamus Heaney's "Punishment". In *Twentieth Century Poetry. From Text to Context*, P. Verdonk (ed), 112–33. London: Routledge.

Verdonk, P. 2002. *Stylistics.* Oxford: OUP.

Werth, P. 1999. *Text Worlds: Representing Conceptual Space in Discourse.* Harlow: Longman.

CHAPTER 5

"Truth is ugly"
Style, structure and tone in "Swansong"

Dan McIntyre
Uppsala University

In this chapter I analyse the lyrics to "Swansong", a relatively obscure song by the comedy duo Kit Hesketh-Harvey (1957–2023) and Richard Sissons, known professionally as Kit and the Widow. "Swansong" is a sombre reflection on the impact of humans on the natural world, and ends with a challenge to the reader/listener to consider their own culpability for the environmental damage described in the text. It is, then, a text driven by a clear purpose, albeit one that was produced as entertainment. In this respect, the text does not simply prioritise the poetic function of language (as is often the case in poetry), wherein the focus is on the message for its own sake. "Swansong" also exploits the conative function of language, which is aimed at directing behavior and action (it is aimed both at entertaining the reader/listener and at spurring them into some kind of action). I argue that the text does this by creating tonal discrepancies between the structure and propositional content of the lyrics, and between the propositional content and the music (Part XIII of Camille Saint-Saëns's orchestral suite *Le Carnaval des Animaux*). The stylistic analysis that I present aims to describe the means by which this is achieved. Ultimately, I argue that a greater understanding of the means by which the text functions offers insights into the nature of Roman Jakobson's six functions of language, thereby demonstrating the utility of linguistic stylistics.

Keywords: foregrounding, grammar, grammetrics, lyrics, metre, music, poetic function, tone

Introduction

Peter Verdonk's masterful analysis of W. H. Auden's poem "Musée des Beaux Arts" (Verdonk 1987)[1] takes as its title Friedrich Nietzsche's dictum "We have art in

---

1. Verdonk's 1987 article is reprinted in the collection of his work entitled *The Stylistics of Poetry* (Verdonk 2013: 23–36). Subsequent references are to the version of the article in that book, since it is easier to access than the original publication.

https://doi.org/10.1075/lal.44.05mci
© 2025 John Benjamins Publishing Company

order that we may not perish from truth".[2] The sentence that precedes this one in Nietzsche's work is rather more prosaic: "Truth is ugly", says Nietzsche (1913: 264). In this chapter I want to suggest that this second sentiment is at the heart of a markedly different object of study to the one that Verdonk (1987) analyses, but that the ultimate idea behind this text is not dissimilar to that expressed in "Musée des Beaux Arts". My focus is on a relatively obscure text. It is not high art of the kind exemplified by Auden's poem (for reasons that I will explain), though neither can it be classified easily as popular writing. My analysis is of the lyrics to "Swansong" by Kit Hesketh-Harvey (1957–2023) and Richard Sissons.

From 1982 until 2012, Hesketh-Harvey and Sissons performed as a duo known professionally as Kit and the Widow. The pair produced primarily musical comedy, though in a vein that stood in marked contrast to the alternative comedy that was dominant in Britain at the outset of their careers and that eventually became the new mainstream. What Kit and the Widow offered was in the tradition of cabaret-style entertainment that traces its lineage through the music hall-inspired comedy of acts like Flanders and Swann.[3] While Hesketh-Harvey and Sissons enjoyed a degree of mainstream success on radio, and in the West End and on Broadway, their type of comedy was never really in vogue and it is fair to say that their appeal was niche rather than broad.[4] That is, Kit and the Widow's work occupies a middle-ground between the literary and the popular. "Swansong" is to some degree unrepresentative of their output, eschewing, as it does, humour for pathos. It is a sombre reflection on the impact of humans on the natural world, and ends with a challenge to the reader/listener to consider their own culpability for the environmental damage described in the text. It is, then, a persuasive

---

2. The quotation is from section 822, Book III of Friedrich Nietzsche's *The Will to Power*, a collection of Nietzsche's writings published shortly after his death in 1900. *The Will to Power* was edited by Heinrich Köselitz, Ernst Horneffer, and August Horneffer. It was originally published as *Der Wille zur Macht* in 1901 and then in an expanded edition in 1906. The first English translation was by Anthony M. Ludovici who translates the line in question as "Art is with us in order that we may not perish through truth" (Nietzsche 1913: 264).

3. Flanders and Swann were a musical duo who performed comic songs between the late 1940s and the late 1960s, of which the most well-known today is perhaps "The Hippopotamus". The stereotype of wry, witty wordplay over jaunty, light piano music (of the kind offered by Flanders and Swann and the like) was satirised by the comedy double-act Alexander Armstrong and Ben Miller in *The Armstrong and Miller Show* (BBC One, 2007–10); though as a marker of how unfashionable Flanders and Swann's brand of comedy had then become (and, by extension, that purveyed by Kit and the Widow), it is unlikely that many of the show's audience would have been able to identify the objects of Armstrong and Miller's affectionate satire.

4. It is interesting, however, to note the mainstream success of the Australian comedian Tim Minchin, whose musical comedy also centres on clever wordplay — though Minchin's music and comedy has an altogether harder edge to it.

text driven by a clear narrative purpose. At the same time, it is also a text that was produced as entertainment, and that was performed in a musical theatre revue (Kit and the Widow 1991) sandwiched between more obviously comic songs. In this respect, the text does not simply prioritise what Jakobson (1960) terms the poetic function of language (as is often the case in poetry), wherein the focus is on the message for its own sake. "Swansong" also exploits the conative function of language, which is aimed at directing behavior and action (it is aimed both at entertaining the reader/listener and at spurring them into some kind of action). It is, then, a different kind of text to Auden's "Musée des Beaux Arts". While Auden's poem is an observation of "the horror of the human condition" (Verdonk 2013: 36), "Swansong" focuses on a particular societal issue with the aim of drawing the reader/listener's attention to their own role in perpetuating environmental damage. While it too follows the dictum that "We have art in order that we may not perish from truth", it achieves its objectives by demonstrating Nietzsche's second dictum that "Truth is ugly".

There is a final reason for my choosing to analyse "Swansong" and this is that, like Auden's poem, it is also inspired at least in part by an existing artwork; in this case, Part XIII of Camille Saint-Saëns's orchestral suite *Le Carnaval des Animaux* (*The Carnival of the Animals*). Where "Swansong" differs from Auden's poem is in laying bare the ugly truth that, paradoxically, its artistry attempts to make more palatable.

The Carnival of the Animals and "Swansong"

Camille Saint-Saëns composed *The Carnival of the Animals* in February 1886, primarily for his own amusement. Fearing that it would detract from his image as a serious composer, he refused to allow the work to be published in his lifetime (Stegemann 1991: 42), though he did later consent to publication of Part XIII of the suite, entitled "Le Cygne" ("The Swan"). This particular movement, for cello and two pianos, is perhaps the most well-known of the whole piece and inspired the solo dance "The Dying Swan", choreographed in 1905 by Mikhail Fokine for the Russian Prima Ballerina Anna Pavlova. As with the other movements, the music is intended to be imitative of the animal for which it is named. In the case of "The Swan", Rees (1999: 262) notes that the lines of the melody, played adagio on the cello, "suggest the graceful contours of the swan's neck [...] while the two pianos magically suggest the ripples and water-drops of river foliage through which the majestic creature glides". The movement as a whole is used as the music to "Swansong", though the lyrics are sung to an original melody over the top of this. Whether or not we accept Rees's (1999) argument concerning what the music represents, it is slow, serene and calming and this contrasts sharply with the propositional content of the lyrics. This propositional content is undoubtedly inspired by the title of the 13th movement, as becomes clear when the swan is referenced directly in line 29 (see the lyrics, below). Hesketh-Harvey and Sissons may well also have been influenced by Fokine's notion of the dying swan, given the lyrical focus of lines 37 and 38 and, indeed, the title, about which I say more below.

"Swansong" appears on the album *Les Enfants du Parody (Lite)* (Kit and the Widow 2008). Since no published version of the lyrics exists, what follows below is my own transcription, based on a performance of the song that formed part of the theatre show *Lavishly Mounted* (Kit and the Widow 1991), a recording of which is available on YouTube.[5] For ease of reading, I have punctuated the lines and divided them into stanzas based on syllable count and musical divisions in the performance. While my analysis does incorporate commentary on syllabic and metrical elements, I refrain from discussing punctuation and other aspects of graphology since these are my own impositions on the text. The lyrics incorporate a number of culturally-specific references which may be difficult to interpret for some readers outside the UK. The likely candidates include "Fairy liquid" (a brand of soap for washing dishes), "brollies" (an abbreviation of *umbrellas*), "Doc Martens" (a brand of distinctive heavy-duty boots, often associated with societal sub-cultures such as punk and goth), "Rocket Thunder" (likely an invented product but reminiscent of brand names for cheap strong cider), "Golden Wonder" (a brand of potato crisps), "plastic fobs" (objects attached to key rings, sometimes taking the form of a device for operating electronic appliances — e.g. locks – remotely), "Henley" (a well-to-do town on the banks of the River Thames, famed for its annual royal regatta), "Bacofoil" (the brand name for a type of aluminum foil used in cooking), and "Sellafield" (a nuclear facilities site in Cumbria, England).

Swansong
Fairy liquid, squeegees and dismembered brollies   [1]
Coca cola cans and rusting shopping trollies
Several discarded single black Doc Martens
Hordes and hordes and hordes of old McDonalds cartons
Half a Fiat 126 to claim the insurance   [5]
Prophylactics way beyond mankind's endurance
Tesco bags and bits of orange nylon rope and — look, there are

---

5. See https://www.youtube.com/watch?v=PPOLdT4ewNA

Bottles labelled Cherryade and Rocket Thunder
Empty packs of cigarettes and Golden Wonder
Toys that you get given free at service stations   [10]
Plastics fobs from Henley members' reservations
Orange peel and Castrol superlube containers
Bacofoil and Adidas athletic trainers
Double blade disposable blue razors and — look, there are

Parts disintegrating, bits of perch and tench and,   [15]
Floating, recent life that won't bear close attention
Shiny pools of manganese and benzochloride
Sulphrous waves of petrofluoride
Sewage treated and untreated in profusion
Drainings from an engine sump in part solution   [20]
Old car batteries sitting on the glorious placid shoreline leaking acid

And washed down from lovely shimmering Derwent Water
One whole sheep marked "Radioactive do not slaughter"
Cannisters with skull and crossbones part revealed
Cannisters unmarked just saying "Sellafield"   [25]
Banks of vegetation standing rotting sweetly
Banks where vegetation's given out completely
There I sat down and I

Saw a swan of purest whiteness gently lying
Saw a swan of purest whiteness slowly dying   [30]
Saw a swan enmeshed in bits of anglers' twine
Poisoned by the lead weights on a fishing line

And many people rushing forward who cried to see it
Many people rushing forward who tried to free it
Saw the swan who lifted up her failing head   [35]
Saw them gasp to hear her as she quietly said

"You'll no doubt have heard how swans refrain from crying
"Up until the moment that we find we're dying
"Charming but as you can see by then it's not much use
"Quite apart from which swans aren't responsible, you know,   [40]
"So, what's your excuse?"

"Swansong" is a prescient comment on the impact of humans on the environment, a theme that is even more relevant today than when the lyrics were written.
The overall tone may be characterised as contemplative, and of sadness rather
than anger, though the song is no less powerful for that. In the analysis that follows, I begin by describing and commenting on the structural elements of the

text before going on to consider wider contextual issues that impact on its interpretation.

Structure, music and context

Verdonk (2013:25) notes that the style adopted by W. H. Auden at the end of the 1930s is impactful in part because of its juxtaposition of casualness of tone and seriousness of subject. He notes, for example, a "seemingly rambling syntactic structure" (Verdonk 2013:30) to Auden's "Musée des Beaux Arts", marked partly by the prevalence of run-on lines. This, Verdonk argues, is a contributory factor to the casualness that critics have attributed to the text. "Swansong" clearly differs in this respect, in that its text style is highly structured and its propositional content serious. Nonetheless, the irony that Verdonk perceives in Auden's mixing of the casual verbal medium and the serious subject matter is present to some degree in "Swansong" in the contrast between the music (in which the swan is represented as magisterial amidst the beauty of nature) and the lyrics (where the swan appears only in its moment of dying). There are, then, a number of elements to be considered analytically. These are the poetic and grammatical structure of the lyrics, the music to which they are set, and the context in which the text is interpreted. I will begin by considering poetic structure.

Poetic structure

As mentioned above, my division of the lyrics into stanzas is suggested both by syllable structure and repeated musical sequences. The first four stanzas of the lyrics are highly structured, with only slight variations from a trochaic hexameter structure. Each line of the first two stanzas (barring the directional "look — there are" in lines 7 and 14, about which I say more below) comprises 12 syllables of six stressed/unstressed feet. (In performance, the definite article in line 5 is unstressed and appended to the word *insurance* to ensure the pattern of 12 stressed/unstressed syllables). Stanzas three and four begin to break this pattern with final lines that extend beyond the 12-syllable limit imposed by the trochaic hexameter structure. In stanza three this is line 21 ("Old car batteries sitting on the glorious placid shoreline leaking acid"), where the extended syllabic structure may be seen as imitative of the "leaking acid" (i.e. the line is uncontained by the poetic form in the same way that the acid is uncontained by the batteries from which it leaks). And in stanza four, line 28 ("There I sat down and I") is only six syllables, which has the effect of foregrounding the line and thereby increasing the anticipation for what comes next, i.e. the description of the dying swan which is the crux of the narrative. Stanzas five and six depart from the established structure, with the final couplet in each consisting of 11 rather than 12 syllables. In stanza seven, the metrical foregrounding is increased further, with 13 syllables in lines 39 and 40. This serves to throw the final five-syllable line ("'So, what's your excuse?'") into relief, by virtue of its comparative shortness, foregrounding the question that is aimed as much at the reader as at the swan's addressees within the text-world.

Grammatical structure and grammetrics

Each stanza of the lyrics is progressively more complex grammatically than the one that precedes it. The increasing complexity of the text — in terms of poetic structure, grammatical structure and grammetrics — is imitative of the increasingly messy landscape of the swan. In this respect, the text functions as an iconic representation of the landscape of the text-world.

Line one of stanza one begins with three simple noun phrases consisting of either a head noun ("squeegees") or a head noun pre-modified by a noun or adjective ("Fairy liquid", "dismembered brollies"). The noun phrases in lines two and three pile up the premodifiers while in line four there is post-modification for the first time, in the form of the prepositional phrase "of old McDonald's cartons". Post-modified noun phrases also make up lines five, six and seven. This series of noun phrases has a somewhat disorienting effect as a result of (i) there being no syntactic connections between them and (ii) it providing none of the requisite linguistic information to anchor the reader in a specific text-world. Instead, what the reader is likely to experience is the effect of a series of snapshots, coherent only as a result of the head nouns in each case belonging to the same semantic field of litter and rubbish. The stanza ends with an imperative ("Look — there are") which serves to establish an implied addressee (the reader/listener) and to indicate that more such images are imminent.

Stanza two continues in this vein, but with added complexity in some of the noun phrases. The post-modification in lines eight and ten, for instance, is via a relative clause, compared to the phrasal post-modification of lines seven and nine. Line 14 repeats the directive to pay attention to more impending images.

The pattern of increasing grammatical complexity continues in stanza three. The adverbial ("floating") in line 16, for example, is the first instance of a grammatical structure that is not a noun phrase. But it is not just the sentence structure that is more complex in this stanza. There is also a shift to more complex grammetrics. As Verdonk (2013:174) explains:

> Grammetrics refers to the relationship between grammatical structure and metrical organization. For example, the grammatical units of a poem may synchronize with metrical units, which may result in a tightly structured encasement of a particular line of thought. For example, the two opening lines of Pope's *An Essay on Man*: "Know then thyself, presume not God to scan;/The proper study of Mankind is Man". Or, conversely, run-on lines or enjambments may interrupt the grammatical structure in the middle of a constituent.   (Verdonk 2013: 174)

In stanzas one and two, the grammatical and metrical units of each line are in accord. But in lines 15 and 16, the syntactic unit extends beyond the metrical unit, giving rise to the complex rhyme of "and tench and" with "attention". The consequent foregrounding effect draws attention to the fact that this is the first indication that the items conveyed in the noun phrases so far are all found in close proximity to water (indicated by the references to fish: "perch and tench"). This, of course, is significant given the later appearance of the swan. Each line of this stanza also contains lexical items from the semantic field of liquids ("floating", "pools", "waves", "sewage", "drainings", "shoreline"), further foreshadowing the connection between the items inventoried and their impact on the natural environment of the swan. The semantic quality of the polluting items listed in stanza three is also of a markedly more hazardous nature than those listed earlier, representing an increased level of threat, e.g. "benzochloride", "petrofluoride", "acid". This semantic pattern continues in stanza four.

Stanza five makes use of syntactic parallelism to imply that (i) the swan referred to in lines 29–31 is in each case the same swan, and (ii) the reason for the swan's death is its entanglement in fishing line, one more example of the litter and rubbish referred to so far. The parallelism is clausal (predicator, object, adverbial in lines 29 and 30: "Saw a swan of purest whiteness gently lying / Saw a swan of purest whiteness slowly dying"; predicator, object in line 31: "Saw a swan enmeshed in bits of anglers' twine"), phrasal (noun phrase consisting of a head noun post-modified by a prepositional phrase: "a swan of purest whiteness"; adverb phrase consisting of an adverb pre-modified by an adverb: "gently lying", "slowly dying") and lexical ("Saw a swan of purest whiteness"). It works to emphasise the cause-and-effect connections between lines 29 and 31. That is to say, the swan has become enmeshed in the anglers' twine, which prevents it from moving, which prevents it from feeding and defending itself, which in turn will be the direct cause of its death (human pollution being the obvious indirect cause). Line 32 ("Poisoned by the lead weights on a fishing line"), a further post-modification of the noun phrase in line 31, describes an additional consequence of (or reason for) the swan's entanglement, adding a further layer of distressing detail to the scene.

In stanza six, lines 33 and 34 are parallel syntactically. Both consist of a complex noun phrase with "people" as its head, post-modified by two relative clauses "[who were] rushing forward who cried to see it / [who were] rushing forward who tried to free it"). The only difference between the two lines is at the lexical level in the second relative clause, and here the variant elements are phonologically parallel: *cried, see it* and *tried, free it*. The parallelism suggests that those people upset by the swan's state and those trying to free it are one and the same. The repetition of the verb phrase is also suggestive of a burst of action. It is notable that *rushing* is the first verb of conscious movement in the lyrics.

Lines 35 and 36 ("Saw the swan who lifted up her failing head / Saw them gasp to hear her as she quietly said") repeat the verb phrase "saw", though the parallel structure in line 36 is elided in order to fit the trochaic hexameter. That is to say, the "saw" that begins line 36 is part of the relative clause post-modifying "swan". Lines 35 and 36 may thus be paraphrased as "[Many people] saw the swan who lifted up her failing head / [Saw the swan who] Saw them gasp to hear her as she quietly said". This shift in perspective from the people to the swan breaks the established pattern of external description, thereby foregrounding the words and thoughts of the swan which are revealed in lines 37 to 41.

Foregrounding in the final five lines

A number of instances of foregrounding can be observed in the final five lines of the lyrics. First of all, this is the first and only instance of direct speech in the song. Second, this direct speech is reflective of the swan's perspective (albeit reported by the narrator/performer), which departs from the narrator/performer's perspective which has been predominant so far. Third, there is semantic deviation in the magic realism that gives the swan the ability to talk. Finally, there is a slight metrical deviation in lines 39 and 40 (13 syllables as opposed to 12), whose length serves to highlight the extreme shortness of the final line (just five syllables). This congruence of foregrounding (Leech 2008: 64–5) gives emphasis to the final five lines, thereby directing special attention to them and — by extension — their propositional content, especially that of the final line. The swan's speech alludes to the mythic belief that swans sing only at the moment of their death. This belief is the origin of the term *swansong*, described in the *Oxford English Dictionary* as "A song like that traditionally believed to be sung by a swan that is about to die", "any final performance, action, or effort". The song's title encompasses both of these meanings, the final action of the dying swan being to ask humans to reflect on their behaviour. The swan's quiet acceptance of its fate is affecting. Despite its suffering, it addresses its audience calmly and with dignity, making the question in the last line of the song all the more poignant.

Music, performance and tone

The linguistic and metrical analyses in the sections above offer some thoughts on how the language of the lyrics contributes to the overall impact of "Swansong" on readers/listeners. But a full account of this necessitates some consideration of both music and performance and the wider context of the song.

It is, of course, not necessary to know that the music to "Swansong" is from Saint-Saëns's *The Carnival of the Animals*. Being unaware of this does not detract from the impact of the stylistic effects generated in the lyrics. But for those listeners aware of the music and the circumstances of its composition, a further effect is produced. *The Carnival of the Animals* was composed by Camille Saint-Saëns as a lighthearted piece of music (Stegemann 1991: 42) and "The Swan" was intended to reflect the magisterial nature of the bird. These sentiments are in clear opposition to the propositional content of the lyrics to "Swansong", which describe a rubbish-strewn landscape and its impact on the swan of the title, whose majesty and freedom has been curtailed as a result of it. The incongruity of the music and the lyrics gives rise to irony, challenging the reader to consider the relationship between human activity and the natural world.

I claimed at the outset of this chapter that the tone of "Swansong" is contemplative and of sadness rather than anger. Tone is a difficult concept to define, as Verdonk (2013: 25) notes, though his definition of it as a subsidiary element of style is helpful. He explains that style refers to a writer's mode of expression while tone encompasses the particular attitude or perspective conveyed by that (Verdonk 2013: 25). In essence, it is the stylistic choices in the lyrics to "Swansong" that convey the tone. For example, the prevalence of concrete noun phrases as opposed to, say, declarative sentences in which a clear opinion is proffered, has the effect of simply directing the reader's/listener's attention to particular images. That is to say, no explicit evaluation of these is offered; no outright condemnation is given. The narrator/poetic persona's opinion, then, is only available via pragmatic implicature, which indicates something less forceful than outright anger. The resulting contemplative tone of sadness and resignation is, I would argue, accentuated in the performance of the song (I refer here to the performance referenced in note 5). This is understated and restrained. Hesketh-Harvey sits on a stool, relaxed, with his hands lightly clasped, and sings quietly, almost *parlando*. This is at odds with the formality of the music and with his attire (he is dressed in white tie and tails). And at 3m 14s into the song, having sung the word "So" (line 41), he shrugs in apparent resignation.

One further point is worth making which I believe impacts on the tone. This is the fact that, despite Kit and the Widow primarily performing comic songs, there is little humour in the propositional content of "Swansong". Some of the rhymes and the general metrical/rhyming structure may be seen as indicative of a humorous genre. There is also the incongruity of prosaic brand names and highly structured poetic form, though whatever humour might emerge from this is not capitalized on. And line six ("Prophylactics way beyond mankind's endurance") implicates, via the Gricean maxim of manner (Grice 1975), not only an overuse of plastic as used in the production of condoms but also the exhausting amount of sex that humans must be having to warrant their manufacture. But on the whole, this is not a funny song. For readers/listeners lacking contextual knowledge of the artists, the general lack of humour does not detract from the power of the song or its performance. But for those aware of Hesketh-Harvey and Sissons's usual act, the poignancy of the song is increased. This can be explained as follows. First, as Attardo (2009) notes, experiencing humour depends on being primed to expect it. Specifically, he explains that "the situation must be framed or keyed as humour (in the Goffmanian sense)" (Attardo 2009:166). Fans of Kit and the Widow are almost certainly primed in this way. This priming is increased for listeners experiencing the song within the context of a musical theatre revue (as in Kit and the Widow 1991) or an album of otherwise humorous songs (Kit and the Widow 2008). But in these contexts, the expectations of the listener are not met. That is, the priming for humour is frustrated and the release which is expected following the prolonged seriousness of the text (see Morreall 2023) never occurs. This is in line with Yoon's (2018) experimental findings concerning the nature of surprise and its key role in the creation of humour. Yoon demonstrates that it is possible to create increased levels of surprise by lowering an audience's baseline level of arousal prior to exposure to humorous material. Nonetheless, what is always necessary for the creation of humour is a successful resolution to an incongruity (Yoon 2018 offers the example of a punchline to a joke). In the case of "Swansong", an audience primed for humour is likely to be nonplussed by the fact that the song does not appear to be very funny. In effect, the presence of a non-humorous song in a light-hearted revue creates an incongruity. The effect of this change of tone is to induce calm in the audience. Were the song to end with some kind of punchline, this would then be perceived as all the more surprising (and consequently more humorous) than if this reduction of the audience's baseline level of arousal had not been effected. But "Swansong", of course, does not end with a punchline — or, indeed, with any other kind of resolution to the incongruity of performing a serious song in a situation that is primed for humour. This lowering of baseline arousal followed by a lack of resolution is what accounts for the likely increased sense of poignancy and reflection in an audience that was expecting humour.

By the same token, it is also the case that there is no resolution to the narrative advanced in the lyrics, it ending in a state of what Bremond (1973) terms disequilibrium. This fact, combined with the lack of humour, compels the reader/listener to focus on the significance of the song's propositional content and, in particular, the question in its final line.

Conclusion

What I hope to have demonstrated in my analysis of "Swansong" is that while it reflects the same underlying belief that Verdonk (2013) finds in Auden's "Musée des Beaux Arts" (namely "We have art in order that we may not perish from truth"), it does so using a different set of stylistic techniques (i.e. internal deviation from formal structures, and tonal discrepancies) that follow from the notion that "Truth is ugly". This is done in order to further an environmentalist agenda without resorting to polemic. Where "Swansong" is similar to Auden's poem is in drawing on an existing work of art (in this case, *The Carnival of the Animals*), not only for inspiration but to strengthen its core idea. In analysing the text, including its lyrics, music and the context of its performance, I have been inspired by the techniques developed and deployed by Peter Verdonk across his long career.

In effect, Peter Verdonk's careful and precise approach to the description, analysis and evaluation of the language of poems, exemplified in his classic collection *The Stylistics of Poetry* (Verdonk 2013), constitutes a method for reading, understanding and enjoying this most complex of verbal art forms. What sets it apart from much stylistic work is the care that Verdonk takes to integrate both linguistic and literary analysis. This is demonstrated, for example, in his detailed explanation of the linguistic locus of the literary concept of tone (Verdonk 2013: 25). This combination of the literary and the linguistic increases the utility of such literary concepts, and the techniques that Verdonk (2013) advances are able to explain nuances of meaning in poetic language — such as the text discussed in this chapter — that would otherwise be subject only to intuitive response. This is why his work will endure.

References

Attardo, S. 2009. Salience of incongruities in humorous texts and their resolution. In *In Search of (Non)Sense*, E. Chrzanowska-Kluczewska & G. Szpila (eds), 164–79. Newcastle-upon-Tyne: Cambridge Scholars Publishing.

Bremond, C. 1973. *Logique du récit*. Paris: Seuil.

Grice, H. P. 1975. Logic and conversation. In *Syntax and Semantics*, Vol. 3: Speech Acts, P. Cole and J. L. Morgan (eds), 41-58. New York, NY: Academic Press.

Jakobson, R. 1960. Closing statement: Linguistics and poetics. In *Style in Language*, T.A. Sebeok (ed.), 350–77. Cambridge, MA: MIT Press.

Kit and the Widow. 1991. *Lavishly Mounted*. Theatre performance. Vaudeville Theatre, London. 25 March — 13 April.

Kit and the Widow. 2008. *Les Enfants du Parody (Lite)*. The Classical Recording Company Limited.

Leech, G. 2008. *Language in Literature: Style in Foregrounding*. Harlow: Pearson.

Morreall, J. 2023. Philosophy of humor. In *The Stanford Encyclopedia of Philosophy* (Summer 2023 Edition), N. Zalta and U. Nodelman (eds), <https://plato.stanford.edu/archives/sum 2023/entries/humor/>.

Nietzsche, F. 1913. *The Will to Power: An Attempted Transvaluation of All Values*. Volume II (*Book III and IV*). A.M. Ludovici (trans.). Edinburgh and London: T. N. Foulis.

Oxford English Dictionary, "swansong, n.", September 2023. <>

Rees, B. 1999. *Camille Saint-Saëns: A Life*. London: Chatto & Windus.

Stegemann, M. 1991. *Camille Saint-Saëns and the French Solo Concerto, from 1850 to 1920*. Aldershot: Scolar Press.

Verdonk, P. 1987. "We have art in order that we may not perish from truth": the universe of discourse in Auden's "Musée des Beaux Arts". *DQR: Dutch Quarterly Review of Anglo-American Letters* 17(2): 78–96.

Verdonk, P. 2013. *The Stylistics of Poetry: Context, Cognition, Discourse, History*. London: Bloomsbury.

Yoon, H.J. 2018. Creating the mood for humor: Arousal level priming in humor advertising. *Journal of Consumer Marketing* 35(5): 491–501.

CHAPTER 6

Where owls nest in beards
Making sense of Edward Lear's *Books of Nonsense*

Katie Wales
University of Nottingham

In this chapter I analyse the 200 limericks which comprise Edward Lear's *Book of Nonsense* (1846, 3rd revised edition 1861) and *More Nonsense* (1872), which, word and illustration together provide a rich database for the study of the textual landscapes and readers' mental representations. Degrees of incongruity between real world expectations of "normal" behaviour and that of Lear's world(s) invoke corresponding gradations of humour, even surrealism and subversion. In order to show the extent of Lear's creativity in language I make a working distinction between "nonsense" at the discourse level involving sound and word play; and "absurdity" at the text-world level. I give due consideration throughout to possible differences of world-views and responses between nineteenth-century and present-day readers; and between adults and children.

Keywords: absurd(ity), grammetrics, limerick, nonsense, surreal(ism), text-world

You may call it nonsense if you like,... but *I've* heard nonsense, compared with which that would be as sensible as a dictionary.

(*Through the Looking Glass,* Lewis Carroll [1871])

Introduction: Lear, sense, nonsense and humour

Always a passionate promoter of the "inseparability of form and meaning" in poetry (1988:15), Peter Verdonk later wrote: "The text encodes a verbal inter-action... between writer and reader, in which the former, directly or indirectly, invites... the latter to make sense of the formal structure and to create conceivable contexts for it" (1993:3). This statement anticipates the critical position of Text World Theory (Werth 1999, Gavins 2007) that poems and novels create "worlds"

https://doi.org/10.1075/lal.44.06wal

in people's minds, whilst at the same time it re-affirms the importance of form for its contribution to interpretation and effects.

In this chapter, I analyse a particular genre of poetry and the work of one particular writer for its rich potential for a study of form, textual landscapes and mental representations: the 200 illustrated "limericks" which comprise Edward Lear's *Book of Nonsense* (1846, 3rd revised edition 1861) and *More Nonsense* (1872) for children.[1] As we shall see below, neither Lear himself nor his contemporaries used the term *limerick* (first recorded by the *OED* in 1898 for this type of verse), so I shall follow him and call his collections "poems". The genre has always been associated with comic potential and in Lear's poems in particular degrees of discrepancy or incongruity between our real world expectations of "normal" behaviour and those of Lear's text-world(s) create corresponding gradations of humour, absurdity and subversion. Simpson (1998: 48) is right to argue that "no necessary and sufficient condition can be isolated which will guarantee that a text will have a humorous outcome" and that the reception of a work as comic discourse "depends largely on the predisposition of the reader". I would add that this reader must be historically and culturally situated. I return to potential differences of predisposition and reception between nineteenth-century and present-day readers, adults and children, in due course.

Lear consistently called his poems "Nonsense", but they are not "gibberish" and they are hardly "meaningless" in the way that Lewis Carroll's poem *Jabberwocky* is in *Through the Looking Glass* (1871), with its consistent use of neologisms or "pseudo-language" (Samarin 1969: 70). (However, I return to Lear's occasional use of "meaninglessness" below.) In everyday usage "nonsense" and "absurd(ity)" are often used interchangeably, as the negatives to "good" or "common sense", where "sense" is a matter of social, cultural and conceptual agreement rather than linguistic (see also Strachey 1888: 335, Stewart 1979: vii; and further discussion below). So it can be argued that Lear's image of owls nesting in beards, from what we ordinarily know about ordinary owls and beards, is "nonsense" or "absurd", illogical or irrational, even fantastic or surreal. Following Deleuze (2003: 71), however, I would argue that Lear's poems illustrate not a negative lack of sense (French *sens*), but a positive excess: a bundle of potentialities of meaning, without a fixed direction (also French *sens*), seemingly "pointless": unlike common sense which imposes the "right" direction. In order to appreciate fully the humour and poetic effects, and also the emotive undertones of the poems,

---

[1] All quotations are taken from *The Book of Nonsense and More Nonsense* (?1895), published "from the original authentic edition" by Frederick Warne & Co. Ltd [unpaginated]. There are actually 109 verses in *BN* and 103 in *MN*. The title of my chapter acknowledges not only a popular bird in Lear's verses but also the favourite bird of Peter Verdonk.

I make here my own distinction where possible between *nonsense* at the formal level, involving sound-play and word-play; and *absurdity* at the text-world level, involving incongruities or illogicalities of schemata and propositional meaning: both working to "unsettle fixed positions for the reader" (Shires 1988: 282); but also amply and richly illustrating, at both levels, what Attardo (2001: 100) calls "hyperdetermined humor [sic]".

In the three sections that follow I analyse in detail first the recurring patterns of grammar and verse form, and then the characteristically idiosyncratic text-world topography, actors, actions and dialogue. I would stress here that I am using Text World Theory as a "heuristic device", rather than subscribing to any single specific "analytical method" (Gavins & Lahey 2016: 5). It is not always easy to make a distinction in discussion between the effects or significance of formal features and those of world-building. Nonetheless, we should be able to see that Lear's verses have a fairly consistent set of "rules" and features which bring a coherence to the whole and create their own "sense".

Later in this chapter, I also consider pertinent relations between the poems and the visual illustrations provided for each verse by the author-artist himself. Verdonk (2005: 235) writes generally of the potentially productive or creative interaction between word and image, which, I would add, remains underexplored in stylistic and text-world theories. For a rich appreciation of Lear's books of *Nonsense,* the illustrations help readers to immerse themselves in a fantasy world by the double stimuli of viewing and reading; and they also heighten the comic and emotive effects. As a result, readers create a strong mental impression of what is to be expected from his work and can begin to appreciate Lear's unique contribution to a new ludic genre of poetry.

Grammetrics and language play

In his own Introduction to *More Nonsense* (1872), Lear describes how he was inspired by the suggestion of a friend to use a particular verse form for creating his own "Rhymes and Pictures", with lines beginning "There was an Old Man of Tobago". In fact, despite Lear's own strong preference for "Old Man" as we shall see below, the original title was "There was a sick man of Tobago", and this is the title on one of the earliest of Lear's surviving drawings of the verse (1831–7):

(1)   There was a sick man of Tobago
       Liv'd long on rice gruel and sago;
       But at last to his bliss,
       The physician said this -
       "To a roast leg of mutton you may go."   (Noakes 1985: 167)

This had come from Richard Scrafton Sharpe's *Anecdotes and Adventures of Fifteen Gentlemen* (1822) (*AA15G*), itself undoubtedly influenced by *The Adventures of Fifteen Young Ladies* (n.d.) (*AA15YL*), possibly also his own composition; and *A History of Sixteen Wonderful Old Women* (1820) (*H16WOW*) of uncertain authorship (see examples in Tuer [ed] [1898, 1986: 393–398; 425–428). All these poems were printed in five lines. On the cover of Lear's first (anonymous) edition of 1846 appears a poem in two lines, perhaps for reasons of space:

(2)   There was an Old Derry down Derry, who loved to see little folks merry;
So he made them a Book, and with laughter they shook, at the fun of that
Derry down Derry!   (Uglow 2017:151)

I return to the significance of "Derry" in my concluding section. Some editions print the verses in three or four lines, hence with internal rhyme as in (2) (see also the lay-out in Byrom 1977 and Uglow 2017, following Jackson's edition 1947). Here I follow the lay-out in editions even within Lear's own lifetime which print the verses in five lines as with his predecessors.

As the collections cited above suggest, the verse form was already well established by the time that Lear came to write his own versions, but there is no doubt that Lear's rhythms are more polished generally than his predecessors'. As Tigges (1987:118) rightly states, like the sonnet the limerick is a "formal strait-jacket" with a fixed rhyme scheme and restricted metrical possibilities: he aptly calls the verse form "the sonnet of nonsense" (Tigges 1987:117). As "There was a sick man of Tobago" shows above, two lines of three strong stresses are followed by two lines of two strong stresses and a final line of three again. The first two lines normally consist of an iambic foot (x /) followed by two anapaests (x x /), with the possibility of a final unstressed syllable, as in the place name "Tobago" and its rhyme "sago". Over three-quarters of Lear's verses favour a relative clause with *who* or *whose* in the second line, a strong iambic pattern. The third and fourth lines can have an iambic foot (x /) and an anapaest (x x /) or two anapaestic feet, depending on the syntactic construction, and with or without a final unstressed syllable. Lear shows a strong preference for *so-* and *but-* clauses in the third line, which normally introduce anapaests. The final line can have either an anapaestic foot or iambic followed by two more anapaests. In Lear's verses then there is no place for dactyllic feet (/ x x) or trochaic (/ x). Moreover, there is no possibility of varying the two anapaestic feet of the first line and this determines the selection of his protagonists and their habitat. The choice of "Old Man" or "Old Person" is not arbitrary: "There was an Old Man of Kent" (x / xx / x /) is not possible, although "There was an Old Man of Dundee" is (x/ xx/ xx /); and "There was an Old Person of Kent" (x/ xx/ xx/) and "There was an Old Person of Kentwell" (x/ xx/ xx/ x).

The pairing of lines one and two, and three and four, with the return to the metre of line one in line five is normally matched by the rhymes: two pairs of couplets and then a return to the rhyme of line one. "The sick man of Tobago" in (1), however, has a new rhyme in the fifth line. Lear only occasionally adopts this scheme (four examples in *BN*, none in *MN*). He is slightly more likely to repeat the rhyme of the second line (seven examples in *BN*, three in *MN*). At the very least the rhyming word of the first line is repeated in the last, as in the opening verse in *BN*:

(3)   There was an Old Man with a beard,
       Who said, "It is just as I feared! -
       Two Owls and a Hen
       Four Larks and a Wren,
       Have all built their nests in my beard!"

Overwhelmingly, however, he favours the whole repetition of the protagonists and their place of origin, a practice that occurs sporadically in *H16WOW*: three quarters of *the verses of BN* and four fifths *of MN* follow this formula, as in

(4)   There was an Old Man of Kilkenny,
       Who never had more than one penny;
       He spent all that money
       In onions and honey,
       That wayward Old Man of Kilkenny.

The "action" is therefore completed in the fourth line. Unlike a joke, there is no "punch-line": the effect is rather to suggest a satisfactory sense of closure, even the occasional sense of a lyrical refrain (Byrom 1977: 50).

Most significantly, however, it introduces the reader to a "narrator", who comments on the activities in the text-world through the use of the summative, and often evaluative, adjective: "That *wayward* Old Man of Kilkenny". His presence is reinforced by the distancing, even non-empathetic alienating effect of the deictic *That*: to be contrasted with *This* which features in some of the first lines of *H16WOW* ("*This* thrifty Old Woman of Norwich"). Critically evaluative adjectives out-weigh neutral or non-critical adjectives in both *BN* and *MN*: e.g. *repulsive, horrible, unpleasing, capricious, (BN); morbid, deluded, imprudent, nasty (MN)* versus *elegant, affable, placid (BN); amusing, funny, remarkable (MN)*, with *ecstatic, amiable* and *lively* in both. Do the critical evaluations suggest the voice of "common sense"? I return to the significant similarity between the narrator's attitudes and those of the text-world enactors "They" later in this chapter. But Lear is always playing with us, as he plays with words. There is a "slippage" of certainty, nothing is necessarily what it might seem. Why is the Old Man of Peru judged to be *intrinsic*? Or the Old Man at a casement *incipient*? Or the Old Man of Toulouse *turbid*? These are not usual collocations with human beings. Sometimes there is an apparent incongruity between the activity described and the narrator's judgment: the adjectives are not what might be expected. Why is the Old Man of Grigor *eclectic* for standing on his head? Or the Old Man of Vienna *nasty* for drinking camomile tea and tincture of senna? (A transferred epithet here, perhaps). The narrator's reliability can be questioned. The frequent polysyllabic adjectives in this line help the rhythm, but clearly Lear makes no concession to his younger readers. They must puzzle out what they mean, and also how they are pronounced, if they read the verses themselves. *Mendacious, judicious, abstemious* and *umbrageous* would trip up childish tongues, yet at the same time give delight from their mere sound. Subtle word play abounds: *ombliferous* is the Young Person of Crete, but the word does not exist; nor does *scoobious* for the Old Man of Cashmere and the Old Person of Grange. Readers are free to find their own interpretations.

Further, the word-play in these last lines is at one with the word-play in the main part of the verses, Lear delighting in the careful choice of words which give relish in reading: the Latinate pun for the Old Person of Cromer who falls over the cliff and is thus *concluded*; the Old Person of Rye being chased by a *virulent* bull. An Old Man of nowhere in particular falls *casually* into a kettle; a Young Lady of Norway *casually* sits in a doorway; an Old Person of Ems falls *casually* into the Thames. Early twentieth-century readers might here be reminded of the graceful action of Charlie Chaplin or Buster Keaton; late twentieth-century readers reminded of Del Boy falling into the bar in a 1989 TV episode of *Only Fools and Horses*. (However, only the Young Lady of Norway escapes unfortunate consequences).

Just as the last line has come to be a marker of his work, so the first line also evokes the prototypical Lear verse: the invariable "There was + {Old/ Young} {Man/ Person} of [place]". It might be expected that, in Nash's terms (1985:34) *there was* is a "pre-location" or "signal", a "preparation for the discharge" of the comic verse; or, in Simpson's terms (2000:244) the "set up". This is certainly plausible, for it does call the verse into existence at the moment of utterance. Yet it is not the existential opening of a joke beginning, for example, "There was this old man...". For despite the nominal end-focus, Lear's *There was* means "There existed", confirmed by its strong stress. Its significance as a deictic trigger for the text-world's chronotope (in the Bakhtinian sense) I return to in the next section.

Again, the places specified are important markers of the topography, to which I shall return also in the next section; but as rhyming words yoked with words in the second line the place-names provide another vivid illustration of Lear's word play. The need to rhyme the first and second lines, and the normal difficulty in making place-names rhyme because of their characteristically non-typical or even "exotic" phonemic structures forces the readers' attention onto the rhyming process itself. *Melrose* must have its stress on the last syllable and so must *Spit-head*. As the verses accumulate so our expectation is heightened of creative and witty collocations, like *Rhodes* and *toads, Leeds* and *beads*. Sound is foregrounded, the names are de-properised almost. Place-names like *Loo, Dargle* and *Minety* sound funny anyway. It is like a children's game, to make a rhyme out of a place-name: the stranger the name, the more difficult the rhyme, and the funnier the outcome: as in *Smyrna/ burn her; Corsica/saucy-cur; th'Abruzzi/ foot see; Portugal/ nautical; Winchalsea/ pin shall see*. Here the rhymes seem somehow more amusing because of the unstressed endings and the use of phrases: the kind of rhyme that is found in Byron's *Don Juan*. It is not inconceivable that finding a rhyme word for many of his place-names gave Lear inspiration for the "plot", like *Tartary* and *artery; Greenwich* and *spinach; Cromer* and *Homer; Vesuvius* and *Vitruvius*. For *Apulia, peculiar* is an obvious but also very appropriate rhyme. As Ede (1987: 52) aptly states, the fate of the characters seems often to depend upon "chance linguistic encounters of rhyme and rhythm": grammetrics and text-world intertwined. With varying degrees of absurdity, it is the "fates" of these characters to which I return in the next section.

Text-world(s) and the absurd

It is a moot point whether it is appropriate to talk about Lear's "text-world" in the singular. After all, there are over two hundred verses, each consisting of one story, self-contained, unrelated to the others. In one sense, therefore, Lear's verses present a "textual universe" or "macro-text-world", of which the individual poems are a part ("micro-text-worlds"). In what follows, however, I am for the most part describing the typical properties and features of the whole set of verses, rather than any one individual verse. Moreover, their uniformity of formal patterning reinforces an impression of global cohesion, rather like the stanzas of one poem, even though there is no progression or development of argument, only a random sequence of actions. As Tigges (1987: 40) aptly states: "The Old Men and Young Ladies from all over the world are *chained* in a chorus of absurd behaviour" (my italics).

In an important sense there is certainly presented to us a definite coherent world, teeming with life, in which characters live and move about and one which appears to be derived from real world geography. Readers can envisage a terrestrial globe dotted with real places: primarily of the British Isles and Europe, but also parts of Asia. North and South America are noted infrequently (Quebec,

Peru), as is Africa (The Nile, The Cape), and no Australasia. Nineteenth-century adult readers would be familiar with many of the places typically visited on the "Grand Tour" or which they themselves had visited, if, like Lear himself, they were restless travellers. Lear's exotic settings distinguish his verses from those of his 1820's predecessors'. Child readers of the period would have fun trying to find the places in their school atlases. They could travel in their imagination beyond the confines of the nursery or schoolroom: the world their oyster. Not all place-names can be found in the average gazetteer, however: Lear teases us, for example, with *Anerley, Port Grigor, West Dumpet* and *Ickley*; and the more exotic-sounding *Boulak, Buda* and *El Hems*. A crucial question remains: where do the illustrations for each of the two hundred verses stand in relation to this text-world? Fore-grounded by their position at the head of each text in most editions they are integral to our understanding: I therefore regard them as an ancillary visual text-world, an "imageworld", like a "satellite" or "moon".

Gavins (2007:12) asserts, following Ryan (1991), that readers start with the assumption that textual worlds have an identity with the actual world: the "prin-ciple of minimal departure". But Lear plays with this, as other fantasy writers do. The apparent real world settings lull the reader into a false sense of security. They provide a point of departure and remorselessly encourage a sense of "normal-ity", which will soon be thwarted. Indeed, the very first lines tease us again. Place appears to be specified in the majority of the verses, although for some this is not the case, as in (3) above: the Old Man exists in limbo. For all the verses, how-ever, without exception, the time of the actions described is certainly vague. But it is this "chronotope" in Bakhtin's terms (Holquist [ed] 1981), this configuration of time and space in the first line, which particularly characterises Lear's verses and the limerick genre as a whole as we have come to know it. "There was an Old Man of Kilkenny" in (4) above tells us only, by the deictic marker of the verb *was* that the Old Man once lived (past tense); but without that explicit adverb marker *once*, albeit itself vague, of the typical fairy-tale chronotope: "Once upon a time there was / lived...". Nonetheless, from our knowledge of fairy-tales, we might subcon-sciously be primed for something unusual to happen. Nineteenth-century readers would not know if the Old Man of Kilkenny and all the other protagonists was a contemporary of theirs, or in the historical past. Lear's drawings, of course, show the fashions of the day; but the overall effect of the minimal information is to sug-gest that these characters are not peculiar to any one period of time: their stories and foibles are universal.

Despite the specificity of any place-name, minimalism pervades the general topography, because of the constraints of the verse form. There is a paucity of markers: outdoors there might be a hill or grove or ditch; indoors a table, stool or stove. In a few verses and drawings there is a moon, but only once a sun, in the text alone for "The Old Man of Corfu". The sea features frequently, often as a symbol of the means of escape; and trees also, for sitting on, or rushing up and down upon. The fleshing out of the landscape must be done by the reader of the text and by the viewer of the illustrations. Rhetorically, the minimalist technique evokes the figure of synecdoche. Just as in the theatre a tree conventionally evokes a forest, so in Lear's verses, within their economy of five lines, a boat will imply the existence of a river or the sea, a stile a field. So too in the drawings: economy is the key. Very few show the detail of a horizon or any background at all. Usually there is just a blank space above a horizontal line indicating the place or "stage" of the action. Even a "field of blue clover", itself a rare description, has only two tiny squiggles that only vaguely suggest a plant or two. The Old Man of Spithead opens a window: we must infer that he is indoors, and again that is all we see in the drawing: just the window. There are a few doors in the verses, but again we must infer a house; all we see in the illustration is the door, and with comic effect for the Young Lady of Norway, who looks as if she is wearing it. With synecdoche as the prevailing trope there is no room for metaphor in Lear's verses. The style of minimalist drawing suggests the spontaneity of a sketch or caricature (Prickett 2005: 119) or cartoon (Byrom 1977, *passim*). It is a free-hand style that would appeal to child readers of all periods, for it is close to what their own style of drawing or doodling might be. Indeed, Strachey (1888: 359) believes that Lear is "pretend[ing] to emulate the awkward scrawls of the schoolboy on his slate". Equally this is far removed from the richly detailed style of his own celebrated paintings and drawings elsewhere. It is this vibrant sketchiness which distinguishes Lear's illustrations from those of his 1820's predecessors, realistic and infrequently amusing.

Ultimately the properties of the settings are not for show: within the five-line frames they must be interwoven with the main characters and be significant for their stories. There is nothing unrealistic, however, about this background; on the contrary it is against this background that the protagonists are foregrounded, who will, with their behaviour, prove to be the locus of the absurd. Without exception they all appear in the very first line in subject position as the unifying "theme" of all the verses.

In the *BN* we read that half of the protagonists are "Old Men", and we can see from either the text or the drawings that one third of them are "Old Persons" who are also male: hence overall about three-quarters are old men. Only one "Old Person" is female. There are only three "Old Ladies", one "Young Girl", two "Young Persons" who are female, and nineteen "Young Ladies". In *MN* the proportions are reversed: there are more "Old Persons" than "Old Men", but again overall three-quarters are old men. "Old Ladies" are infrequent; "Young Persons" are also female; and there is a smaller number of "Young Ladies". Clearly there is a semantic gap: there are no young men in Lear's verses. There is also something of an obsession with old age. (Lear himself was only thirty years old in 1842.) The scarcity of old women and young ladies may well reflect a wish on his part to dissociate himself from the "Young Ladies" and "Old Women" of *AA15YL* and *H16WOW*; but certainly the favouring of an older generation helped his themes and a variety of comic and emotive effects. Lear appears both to recognise and value the eccentricities of old age and also to appreciate some of the conventional constraints felt on freedom of action and expression: felt also indeed by young women. From the second line the stage is set as we shall see for the creative sub-version of conventional expectations of behaviour and activity in two hundred different ways, with differing degrees of absurdity. While eccentrics can appear in any period and at any life-stage, so that we might not be too surprised at a character's dress being covered in darns, due allowance, however, must be made for possible differences of pre-conceptions or perceptions between nineteenth-century and present-day readers, especially about the appearance or behaviour of "Old Persons". The Old Man of the Hague who build a balloon to examine the moon would not appear so "deluded" today as he is judged, in this age of space exploration, and when in 2021 the oldest woman to go into space was eighty-two. The older generation today live longer than their nineteenth-century counter-parts usually and have healthier life-styles, so can be glider pilots at ninety-nine or wing-walkers at ninety-five. Conversely, however, it is not usual today, but highly probable in the mid-nineteenth century, for someone to have "twenty-five sons and one 'darter'" like the Old Person of Sparta; or "twenty sons" (the Old Man of Apulia): no hyperbole then (see below). Lear himself was one of twenty-one children.

However, it is not only that Lear disrupts predominant social schemas or stereotypes, but also, importantly, that he disrupts the prototypical norms and limits of what it is to be human, and so creates a world of pure fantasy. This again distinguishes him from his 1820s predecessors. One man is too stout to get out of a fish-kettle; another is "as thin as a lathe, if not thinner". Long noses feature promi-nently, visually and textually: one is "like a Trumpet"; another "finished off in a Tassell"; another "grew out of sight". There is a nose so long it could reach the toes; another so long that "most" birds could sit on it. The Old Man in a Barge has such "an exceedingly large" nose that it can support a light at night when he is fishing: inspiring perhaps Lear's later poem *The Dong with a Luminous Nose* (1876).

The sense of the absurd is heightened by hyperbole, a key rhetorical figure in Lear's stylistic repertoire, and complemented by the visual exaggeration of the drawings, which become caricatures. One Young Lady's hair curls up a tree and all over the sea; the Old Man's beard in verse (3) cited in Section 2 above is large enough to shelter not just one bird but "Two Owls and a Hen/ Four Larks and a

Wren". Even one bird nesting in a beard seems far-fetched: the remorseless meticulous cataloguing redoubles the absurd effect. Hyperbole works with expressions of abnormal size to create even a surreal effect, and so curiously evokes the dream-world of Lewis Carroll's *Alice* books. The Old Man of Coblenz, with his "immense" legs, could walk "with one prance/ from Turkey to France". One person has a head "as small as a button"; the Old Man of Leghorn is "the smallest that ever was born" and is eaten by a puppy; so too the Old Man of Ancona. I return to further implications below.

Hyperbole is also the appropriate figure to characterise the descriptions of the protagonists' prodigious appetites for food and drink (often with disastrous results). There is a Rabelaisian, Gargantuan sense of excess. Food and drink feature in about one-fifth of the verses in each of *BN* and *FN*. One person feeds on eighteen rabbits; another eats thousands of figs. Strange combinations of foodstuffs give rise to ordinarily incongruous collocations: onions and honey in (4) cited above in Section 2; roast spiders and chutney; bustard and mustard; pickled onions and mice; lobsters and spice.

This relish for (over-) eating is but one contribution to the prevailing sense of freedom, for characters to do what they like, rebelling against the conventions of expected conduct, with behaviour in consequence frequently stretched to the point of absurdity. Predominantly they are the active agents or "actors" of intransitive verbs of frantic movement, in habitual or completed actions; but not infrequently they do absolutely nothing. One chooses to lie on his back with his head in a sack; another, to sit on a rail with his head in a pail. Weirder behaviour is to walk on stilts wreathed with lilies and daffodils; or to stand on one leg to read Homer. To walk on the tips of one's toes seems harmless enough, even running up a tree or going by slow train to Weedon. But spinning on one's nose and chin seems really odd; and rushing down the crater at Etna physically impossible. Transitive verb clauses provoke a similar range of readerly reactions or judgments. Throwing apples and pears (object) at people's heads might be viewed as anti-social; composing a small treatise in a ditch as worthily eccentric; but boiling eggs in shoes a sign of oddity. Freedom of action is not without its cost, however. In about one-third of all the verses in both *BN* and *MN* the characters are the "sufferers" or victims of the actions: whether bored by a buzzing bee, disturbed by crows, or, more dramatically, choked by a muffin or burned by a Barbary ape. I refer to the issue of victim-hood in the next section, in relation to the characters' interaction (or not) with the people around them; but here I would stress that there is no strong moral lesson to be drawn, as in the "cautionary" tales for children so popular well in to the nineteenth century (see further the concluding section). The Young Lady of Norway, squeezed flat by a door, says "calmly", "'What of that?'". In the story of the Old Man of Nepaul, who splits quite in two after a fall from his horse, "strong glue" puts him back together, like the fantasy characters of a Victorian pantomime, Edwardian silent film or a modern cartoon. Overall, the random juxtaposition of the verses with their varied plots works to mitigate a sense of tragedy; as does also the unvarying framework of the outrageous rhymes and the jigging rhythms (see also Ede 1987: 60).

Nonetheless, the depictions of absurdity have the potential to arouse a wider range of emotions in the reader than smiling or laughing. Lear stretches the notion of the absurd to a disturbing limit. To lie on one's back with one's head in a bucket, or to sit on a rail with one's head in a pail: is this simply eccentricity or alienation from the outside world. The story of the Old Man of Cape Horn is by no means ambiguous:

(5)   ...Who wished he had never been born.
      So he sat in a chair,
      Till he died of despair,
      That dolorous Man of Cape Horn.

One of the most striking of such verses concerns the "Young Lady in White"

(6)   ...Who looked out at the depths of the Night;
      But the birds of the air
      Filled her heart with despair,
      And oppressed that Young Lady in White.

No reason is given for her despair, and in the illustration she appears to have aged considerably, floating like a ghost over her window-sill. This is a kind of emotional "meaninglessness" quite distinct from linguistic: life has no purpose. But it will be the twentieth century before Absurdism is used as a term to describe such irrational feelings, especially those represented in literary form (see further Simpson 1998, Gavins 2013). Lecercle (1994: 204) notes how there is no adjective meaning "nonsensical" in French: *insense** means "demented, out of one's senses". Lear's eccentrics display disturbing emotions close to madness.

If Lear stretches the idea of the absurd to an extreme in one direction, in another he stretches it to the surreal; and again he anticipates later literary and artistic movements, while at the same time creatively extending the range of the genre far beyond that of his predecessors. I am using the term "surreal" here in the sense of bizarre and dream-like or hallucinatory. In this final part of this section I am applying it to a large group of verses, about one-third of each of BN and *MN*, which concern the interactions of the main characters with birds and animals, special kinds of "actors" in the stories. The animals serve as a catalyst for a wide range of emotive effects from the comically ludicrous to the darkly disturbing, as readers' mental images of normal real-world attributes and scripts of behaviour are disrupted to varying degrees. As elsewhere, the illustrations make an important contribution to the overall effects.

There is a distinct polarization in text and image depictions between "pleasant" and "unpleasant", the comically ludicrous and the stuff of nightmares. Music and dance play a significant role in conveying a sense of harmony, as persons play jigs to pigs (a favourite animal) or sing songs to a frog or sing to ducks and pigs: eccentric, but acceptable behaviour in the real world. Another set of verses , however, introduce a new dimension, reminiscent of fantasy or fairy-tale, as characters dance a quadrille with a raven; dance with a cat and make tea in a hat; and waltz with a bluebottle fly in the moonlight. Here there is a shift from plausible to the implausible in real world terms with the surreal incongruity in size, emphasised in the illustrations: humans shrink and animals grow bigger. Child readers today are used to jokes which exploit incongruity of size for their comic effect: "How does an elephant get down from a tree? It sits on a leaf and waits till autumn" (Wales 1985, 1987). The same kind of incongruity is seen in the set of verses which describe persons riding away on a hare; riding on a tortoise's back to Karmak; riding on a pig; going up to town on a fly; or going out to sea on a goose. The close harmony between Man and Creature is explicitly indicated in verses like

(7)   There was an Old Man with an owl
       Who continued to bother and howl;
       He sate on a rail
       And imbibed bitter ale,
       Which refreshed that Old Man and his owl.

In the illustration the features of the large owl sitting companiably on the rail are mirrored exactly in the Old Man's eyes, nose and coat tail, as in the story of the Old Person of Crowle "Who lived in the Nest of an Owl". Close harmony is now, as Byrom (1977: 133f) also notes, actual metamorphosis: of creature to human, and of human to creature. In a surreal flight of fancy in the illustrations to several verses persons and creatures greatly resemble each other; and occasionally in the text the resemblance is noted: so the Old Man of Dunblane "greatly resembled a crane".

Visual metamorphosis, however, and incongruities of size can have a more unsettling effect on the reader. They serve to underline and indeed emphasise the more unpleasant relationships between humans and animals, which can result in deep-seated phobias. A person might be "bored" by a buzzing bee, but what if the bee is huge, with a face like his own. What if a Grasshopper jumps on an Old Person's back and chirps in his ear that is as big in the illustration as he is. The Old Man of Quebec's head is strangely contorted as he promises to "slay" the Kafkaesque beetle that appears to meld with his back and jacket.

Lear's representation of the protagonists' relations with the animal world is more complex than it might be supposed, on a spectrum of empathy and antipathy. In the next section I discuss the Persons' social interactions (and indeed lack of them) with a particular group of human actors, their neighbours. Lear's treatment is more nuanced than has generally been considered by critics.

Dialogue, subversion and the "collective voice"

The role of music and dance in the portrayal of a surreal relationship between Person and animal reminds us that Lear's text-world is as much a world of sound as it is of action: of harps, flutes and gongs and screaming owls and young ladies of Russia. It is especially a world of talk and dialogue. The Persons are not alone, but interact with others with varying degrees of cooperativeness.

Early Text World Theory, following Werth (1999), describes the use of direct speech as a "sub-world", rather than an example of "world-switch" following Gavins (2007) later. For the purpose of my argument here I would prefer "sub-world" in so far as it suggests a sub-ordinate or embedded layer of textual meaning with corresponding emotive effects. With the prefix *sub-* it also hints possibly at the concept of "sub-version", which I suggest in this section is significant both for Lear's themes and for the humour. My framework for analysis, however, is drawn not from Text World Theory but from Bakhtin (Holquist [ed] 1981) and Grice (1975), as I am focussing on the dynamics of the interchanges as opportunities for rebellion against the "collective voice" of apparent "common sense".

In both *BN* and *MN* talk appears in about one-third of the verses: they are like mini-plays, and this dramatic quality is lacking in his predecessors. Of these, again about one-third in *BN* are apparent monologues, slightly more than *MN* (one-quarter). Persons are prone to talk to themselves when they are obviously alone, reasoning or planning what to do. So the Old Man of the Dargle says he will roll his barrels down the hill and the Old Man of Dubree declares that it is not "proper or nice" to eat mice. A Young Lady makes an elegiac apostrophe: "Farewell to the end of my Nose!" as it grows out of sight. The Old Man in example (3) cited above in Section 2 is clearly upset by the birds' presence: but is he talking to himself or addressing a silent and invisible audience "off-stage", also not present in the illustration. The most dramatic, even uncanny, of this kind of monologue concerns an Old Man, clearly exasperated, who says

(8) "...Well!
      Will *nobody* answer this bell?
      I have pulled day and night,
      Till my hair has grown white
      But nobody answers this bell!"

His anguish is emphasised by the italics in the text. Readers after 1912 might well be reminded of Walter de la Mare's poem *The Listeners:* "'Is there anybody there?', said the Traveller, /Knocking on the moonlit door". A visual audience is certainly present "on-stage" in the illustrations to some of these apparent monologues: e.g. two men for the Old Person of Dean explaining why he only dines on one pea and one bean; so that readers must reassess them as implicit dialogues rather.

In the majority of these mini-dramas, however, the audience also speaks "on-stage" in the text, and labelled tantalizingly vaguely as *They,* known only to the narrator. (There is only one They in *AA15YL:* "*They* made her eat mustard".) Our mental representation might be to endow this *They* with the homophoric reference of "people in general" (as in "*They're* putting up the taxes again"), often authoritative. *They* can often be viewed antagonistically, referring to spoil-sport behaviour, ineptness or even destruction (Wales 1996:60). Some critics of Lear have certainly discussed the They of the verses in a negative way: Hark (1978:113) describes Them as "this nameless mass society"; and Lecercle (1994:107) summarises such views as suggesting a "hostile collective entity, the mob, sticklers for convention and dogma". He himself sees Them as "omnipresent" and "aggressive" (1994:2); and Carpenter (1985:111) as representing "a public world... vindictive and intolerant". In his poem *Edward Lear* (1939) W.H. Auden writes: "The legions of cruel inquisitive 'They' / Were so solid and strong, like dogs" (cited Noakes 1985:203): the Persons as Their victims. But Their representation is more subtle, as we shall see. Critics' presentation of a "mass" or crowd could, however, be influenced by the presence of another kind of social group, representing specific townspeople. Largely featuring in the last line for purposes of rhyme (see above) they do not speak, but are clearly affected *en masse,* for good or ill, by the actions of the Persons, who in turn cannot really escape from their society: "which distressed/ enchanted/ pleased/ perplexed" etc "all the people of Chertsey/ Filey, Bude", etc. My concern here rather is with the functions of the group of actors specifically labelled as *They.*

Grammatically speaking, since They are physically present "on-stage", the pronoun has specific exophoric reference (Wales 1996:44). Moreover, since They are normally visually represented in the drawings above the verses, the pronoun *They* could be said also to have implied anaphoric reference. Interestingly, the figures in the illustrations are not usually presented *en masse,* but in ones or twos: perhaps an example of visual synecdoche again. In *BN* They feature in about half of the mini-plays, nearly three-quarters of those in *MN*; and They predominantly initiate conversations, the Persons preferring not to. They function as a kind of Chorus; or, in Bakhtin's terms (Holquist [ed] 1981) as a "collective voice" representing a consensus of opinion (*communis opinio),* reflecting social values and norms which They clearly see the Persons as violating, and also order as opposed to disorder. "*But they* said…" in the third line is a common prelude to a shift to intrusion or opposition. The question is, however, whether Theirs is always the voice of "common sense", given that *communis opinio* can also hide prejudice and narrow-mindedness (Wales 2022). In some cases the answer is yes. The speech act of sensible warning occurs frequently: that a Person will get fatter; that the Old Man at a casement will fall. They give helpful advice for "soothing remorse"; and ask what the Old Man of Wrekin's shoes are made of, because they are creaking. In other cases, however, and more frequently, They are perhaps too conscious of propriety, of expected social behaviour, and Theirs is the voice of control. They disapprove of the Old Man of Thermopylae boiling eggs in his shoes; and the Old Person of Brill because his frill makes him look like a fish. In other cases They are certainly over-bearing, intrusive, imperious to the point of rudeness. They dislike a Person for walking on his toes: "You stupid Old Man of Melrose!". They tell the Old Person of Loo to go away for no apparent reason. Sometimes Their emotions lead to violent reactions, and one can then understand why critics have viewed Them negatively. They threaten to "thump" the Old Man of Ibreem, who They see as "disgusting" for wanting to scream. The Old Man bumping a gong all day long is clearly "a horrid old bore", but "smash[ing]" him seems an over-reaction. The hysteria of Their response is heightened by the hyperbolic drawing, showing, threateningly and unusually, an infinite regression of figures. This does not suggest the voice of "common sense".

In an interesting set of examples the reader cannot help but interpret Their judgments as just plain wrong, because of the incongruity between these and his or her own conclusions. Since these deductions often occur in the last lines, there is a strong grammatical resemblance to the judgments made by the unreliable narrator discussed in Section 2 above. "'You *invidious* Old Man of Aosta'" seems an inappropriate reaction to his losing a cow; "'You *abstemious* Old Person of Rye'" also, to someone riding to town on a fly; and "'You *luminous* Person of Barnes'" to his clothes full of darns. In "'You *abruptious* Old Man of Thames Ditton'" the adjective is a nonce-word, but it reveals once again Lear's delight in sound- and word-play. In an absurd world, where nonsense stands sense on its head readers should be prepared for real-world or logical veracity to be undercut, and apparent common sense judgments, whether of narrator or Them, to be proved to be unreliable.

Whether the voice of common sense or not, They act as a foil to the colourful eccentric Persons, precisely because they are joyless and humourless. Readers are more inclined to be sympathetic to the Persons, because their interlocutors are so overbearing; and they are more likely to condone their evasive replies or complete lack of verbal cooperation. It is as if they see even speech acts of concern as an affront to their freedom of expression and behaviour, even if this, absurdly, stretches the limits of "normal" humanity, as we have seen above. The Old Man at a casement emphatically denies that he might fall from it ("He replied 'Not at all!'"). The Old Man of Hurst, warned that he will get fatter, answers "What matter?". Marvelling not unreasonably at the Old Person of Blythe cutting up meat with a scythe, They are told "Scythes for ever!". Again, not unreasonably, They ask why the Old Person of Deal walks only on his heel. "He made no reply" in an act of non-cooperation. They ask the Old Person of Ware, who rides on the back of a bear: "Does it trot?". He replies: "Certainly not! / He's a Moppsikon Floppsikon Bear!": and so flouting the Gricean maxims of manner (what does he mean?) and quantity (he is not very informative).

The use here of a nonsensical pair of rhyming words raises interesting questions about the functions of "meaningless" language with no sense discussed in Section 1: functions which, as Lecercle (1994:107) states, echoing Samarin (1969:70), have not often been studied. It is not unusual for Persons to respond to Them with empty interjections, flouting the maxim of quantity ("She replied only 'Whizz!'"); or with onomatopoeic expressions. So, the Old Person of Sestri, when They said "You are wrong!" merely said "Bong!", flouting the maxim of relevance in an oblique expression of apparent disagreement. Here the Persons are subverting the socially acceptable "rules" of polite conversation in a created language that functions almost as an "anti-language" (Stewart 1979:39) and expressing their desire for alienation from the rest of society. In contrast to many present-day child reader perhaps, young Victorian readers, well-schooled or drilled in the proprieties of conversational behaviour, would have clearly relished such creativity of expression in these anarchic characters and the inversion of good manners. But so eccentric are Lear's Persons that they sometimes appear to talk "nonsense" to themselves: technically a kind of glossolalia. The Old Person of Rimini's "O Gimini!" is extra giggles-worthy because Lear has so obviously coined it for the rhyme. The Old Person of Wick says only "Tick-a-Tick, Tick-a-Tick;/ Chickabee, Chickabaw", although there is a listener in the illustration. He has no desire, it would seem, to engage even in "normal" small talk. The Old Man of the Isles, whose face is "pervaded with smiles", sings "High dum diddle" as he plays on his fiddle. This sounds like a ballad refrain: similarly, for the Old Man of Spithead, who leans out of the window, also with a smile on his face, only to say "Fil-jumble, fil-jumble/ Fil-rumble-come-tumble!". Both Persons seem to be expressing the simple joy of being alive in the reduplications that echo the language of the nursery. However, "rumble-come-tumble" might evoke particular connotations to an adult reader, expressing the same impropriety of speech as the Old Man at the station's "lascivious oration", which They rebuke him for. To child readers the use of happy nonsense could possibly be the verbal equivalent of the sound of blowing a raspberry. Bakhtinian polyphony triumphs over the collective voice, and the irrational over the rational.

Conclusion: Lear's books of "nonsense" in context

Warner (1998: 229) notes the presence of reduplication in "nonsense songs" such as ballad refrains, choruses and nursery rhymes in many languages; and how phonetic and prosodic patterns are laid down before semantic understanding. In an age when reading aloud was the norm, the power of orality is not to be under-estimated. Lear himself would "beat out" his rhymes, "reciting them with a thumping rhythm" on his walks with friends (Uglow 2017: 96). Nor should we forget that the experience Victorian child readers had of other kinds of nonsense verse, including nursery rhymes, would have coloured their appreciation of Lear's poems. The "Old Derry Down Derry" on the cover of the first edition of *BN* would have had echoes, lost to modern readers, of an old ballad refrain from touring mummers' plays (Uglow 2017: 153–4). Just before the publication of *BN* a celebrated collection of English nursery rhymes appeared, edited by the Shakespearean scholar J.O. Halliwell. The limerick's anapaestic and iambic rhythms can be heard in some parts of the lines of nursery rhymes ("Here we go round the mulberry bush") and there are echoes of nursery rhymes about Old Women (Mother Hubbard, Dame Trot, the Old Woman who lived in a shoe) in both Lear and his predecessors. One of the "anecdotes and adventures" of the "fifteen young ladies" concerns an obvious imitation of "Little Miss Muffet". Lear's verses have similar basic text-world properties to nursery rhymes: dishes and fishes, pigs and jigs.

Victorian children would also have been both vastly entertained and also horrified by the flights of fancy in fairy tales such as the Grimms' collection (1823): so that the range of emotive effects in Lear's verses, from the comically absurd to the darkly surreal, would have been familiar to them, providing what Warner (1998: 4) calls "an aesthetic thrill". An even darker strain of children's literature had appeared on the continent in 1845, with the publication, also in illustrated verses like Lear's, of Heinrich Hoffmann's *Der Struwwelpeter* ("Shock-headed Peter"). These were cautionary tales, building on the tradition of educational homilies, of the horrific consequences of misbehaviour such as sucking one's thumb or fidgeting at table. Lear's Old Man of the Nile might cut off his thumbs when he sharpened his nails with a file, but this was an accident brushed off lightly, not a story designed to have a moral: Lear remains a champion of what Orwell aptly called in 1945 "amiable lunacy" (2009: 188). The *BN is* much more the precursor of Lewis Carroll's Alice dream-worlds of 1865 and 1871, with their foregrounding of illogicality and subversion of the expected norms of "common sense" likewise. For Prickett (2005: 119), "nonsense" in Lear and Carroll constituted an entire "alternative aesthetic".

Stewart (1979:5) notes how "nonsense" tends to be regarded as appropriate only to those "on the peripheries of early life"; but, on the contrary, adult readers too in the early Victorian period were also used to a strong tradition of oral nonsense, whether in parlour ballads, music-hall or pantomime (see Wales, 2024). London had its own "Nonsense Club", already established in the eighteenth century, and addressed by figures such as Cowper and Hogarth (Strachey 1888:335). Indeed, the *OED* suggests that the word *limerick* comes from the custom at convivial parties for each guest to sing a spontaneous "nonsense-verse", which was followed by a chorus with the words "Will you come up to Limerick" (for other suggestions see Byrom 1977:50–51, 236). In the late nineteenth century the limerick certainly developed as an adult genre rather than one for children, and it is possible that it was part of a sub-culture in origin. In Verdonk's words then (1988:6–7), Lear's poetry can be seen to be "part of a complex social and cultural process".

How the party game developed, if it did at all, into the genre emerging in the 1820s by Richard Scrafton Sharpe and others described above is a mystery. But adult and child readers alike of Lear's *BN* probably had no strong mental image of this type of verse, since the development of the genre was largely due to Lear himself, as I have tried to show. "Nonsense" collocates with poetry for children, and in a favourable sense, only after Lear. Perhaps this is why he is sometimes called the "originator" of the genre (Orwell 2009:203). But what he developed became a generic prototype for others to imitate. Yet in many respects he remains unique. In my analyses I have sought to reveal the sheer range and potency of his ludic verses, through word and sound play, hyperbole, absurdity and surrealism, with emotions displayed from joy to angst, subtle enough to arouse complex emotive responses in the reader. Form and meaning are stretched to their limit and beyond, at an extreme on a "cline of stylistic experimentation" (Gavins 2013:137). I have also tried to show how the illustrations with their innovative style contribute to the building of the text-world and the emotive effects: idiolect combined with *idiopict*. Lear's grammetrical patterns and absurd stories are now deeply ingrained in the mental and cultural images that modern readers have of the genre, and are taken as the norm by which others are judged. Ultimately then, there is an element of unnecessary modesty in Lear's titles *A Book of Nonsense* and *More Nonsense*.

References

Anon. 1820. *A History of Sixteen Wonderful Old Women*. London: Harris & Son.

Attardo, S. 2001. *Humorous Texts: A Semantic and Pragmatic Analysis*. Berlin: Mouton De Gruyter.

Byrom, T. 1977. *Nonsense and Wonder: The Poems and Cartoons of Edward Lear*. New York: E.P. Dutton.

Carpenter, H. 1985. *Secret Gardens: A Study of the Golden Age of Children's Literature*. London; George Allen & Unwin Ltd.

Deleuze, G. 2003. *The Logic of Sense*. London: Continuum.

Ede, L. 1987. An introduction to the nonsense literature of Edward Lear and Lewis Carroll. In *Explorations in the Field of Nonsense*, W. Tigges (ed), 47–60. Amsterdam: Rodopi.

Gavins, J. 2007. *Text World Theory: An Introduction*. Edinburgh: Edinburgh University Press.

Gavins, J. 2013. *Reading the Absurd*. Edinburgh: Edinburgh University Press.

Gavins, J. & Lahey, E. 2016. World building in discourse. In *World Building: Discourse in the Mind*, J. Gavins & E. Lahey (eds), 1–13. London: Bloomsbury.

Grice, P. 1975. Logic and conversation. In *Syntax and Semantics 3: Speech Acts*, P. Cole & J.L. Morgan (eds), 45–54. New York: Academic Press.

Hark, I.R. 1978. Edward Lear: eccentricity and Victorian angst. *Victorian Poetry* 16: 112–122.

Holqvist, M. (ed) *The Dialogic Imagination*. Austin: University of Texas Press

Jackson, H. (ed). 1947. *The Complete Nonsense of Edward Lear*. London: Faber & Faber.

Lear, E. ?1895. *The Book of Nonsense and More Nonsense*. London: Frederick Warne & Co. Ltd.

Lecercle, J.J. 1994. *Philosophy of Nonsense: The Intuitions of Victorian Nonsense Literature*. London: Routledge.

Nash, W. 1985. *The Language of Humour*. London: Longman.

Noakes, V. 1985. *Edward Lear: 1812–1888*. London: Royal Academy of Arts/ Weidenfeld & Nicolson.

Orwell. G. 2009. Nonsense poetry. In *Shooting an Elephant and Other Essays*, G. Orwell (ed), 201–206. London: Penguin.

Prickett, S. 2005. *Victorian Fantasy*. Waco, Texas: Baylor University Press.

Ryan, M-L. 1991. *Possible Worlds, Artificial Intelligence and Narrative Theory*. Indiana, IA: Indiana University Press.

Samarin. W.J. 1969. Forms and functions of nonsense language. *Linguistics* 50: 70–74.

Sharpe, R.S. 1822. *Anecdotes and Adventures of Fifteen Gentlemen*. London: Edward Marshall.

Sharpe, R.S. n.d. *The Adventures of Fifteen Young Ladies*. London: Edward Marshall.

Shires. L.M. 1988. Fantasy, nonsense, parody and the status of the real: the example of Carroll. *Victorian Poetry* 26 (3): 267–283.

Simpson, P. 1998. Odd talk: studying discourses of incongruity. In *Exploring the Language of Drama*, J. Culpeper, M. Short & P. Verdonk (eds), 34–53. London: Routledge.

Simpson, P. 2000. Satirical humour and cultural context. In *Contextual Stylistics: In Honour of Peter Verdonk*, T. Bex, M. Burke & P. Stockwell (eds), 243–266. Amsterdam: Rodopi.

Stewart, S. 1979. *Nonsense: Aspects of Intertextuality in Folklore and Literature*. Baltimore, MD: Johns Hopkins University Press.

Strachey, L. 1888. Nonsense as a fine art. *Quarterly Review* 167: 335–365.

Tigges, W. (ed) 1987. The limerick: the sonnet of nonsense. In *Explorations in the Field of Nonsense*, W. Tigges (ed), 117–133. Amsterdam: Rodopi.

Tuer, A.W. (ed). [1898] 1986. *Stories from Forgotten Children's Books*. London: Bracken Books.

Uglow, J. (2017) *Mr Lear: A Life of Art and Nonsense*. London: Faber & Faber

Verdonk, P. 1988. *How Can We Know the Dancer from the Dance? Some Literary Stylistic Studies of English Poetry*. Amsterdam: Faculty of Letters.

Verdonk, P. (ed) 1993. Introduction. In *Twentieth-century Poetry: From Text to Context*, P. Verdonk (ed), 1–5. London: Routledge.

Verdonk, P. 2005. Painting, poetry, parallelism: ekphrasis, stylistics and cognitive poetics. *Language and Literature* 14(3): 231–244.

Wales, K. 1985. *The Elephant Joke Book*. London: Beaver Books.

Wales, K. 1987. *The Return of the Elephant Joke Book*. London: Beaver Books.

Wales, K. 1996. *Personal Pronouns in Present-day English*. Cambridge: Cambridge University Press.

Wales, K. 2022. Tellers and listeners: deconstructing the collective voice of common opinion In *Middlemarch*. *George Eliot-George Henry Lewes Studies* 74 (1): 39–48.

Wales, K. 2024. Changing tastes: reading the cannibalese of Charles Dickens' *Holiday Romance* and nineteenth-century popular culture. In *Reading Fictional Languages*, I. Noletto, J. Norledge & P. Stockwell (eds), 133–143. Edinburgh: Edinburgh University Press.

Warner, M. 1998. *No Go the Bogeyman: Scaring, Lulling and Making Mock*. London: Chatto & Windus.

Werth, P. 1999. *Text Worlds: Representing Conceptual Space in Discourse*. London; Longman.

CHAPTER 7

Mechanical inelasticity in discourse
A Bergsonian perspective on dialogue, humour and style

Paul Simpson
Liverpool University

This chapter explores the stylistics of humour with a particular focus on dialogue in television situation comedies. Having acknowledged previous stylistic work on verbal humour where the focus has been on structural elements in discourse, the present chapter moves on to balance research in linguistic pragmatics with philosophical investigations into humour. Use is made of French philosopher Henri Bergson's theory of "the comic" and especially of Bergson's characterisation of humour as a kind of rigidity within a mechanical arrangement. The analytic part of the chapter applies this blended pragmatic-philosophical stylistic model to passages of dialogue in popular sitcoms, respectively, *Father Ted* and *Big Bang Theory*. It is argued that the humour impulse in both sitcoms is often engendered by dialogue which can be understood as the linguistic embodiment of Bergsonian "mechanical inelasticity" in both discourse routines and discourse strategies. Adding to the toolkit of discourse stylistics, the chapter offers a new framework of analysis for the understanding of comic dialogue in, and beyond, television sitcoms.

Keywords: *Big Bang Theory*, dialogue, discourse stylistics, *Father Ted*, Henri Bergson, humour, irony, *Le Rire*, mechanical inelasticity, pragmatics, sarcasm, sitcom

Discourse stylistics and verbal humour, revisited

Over two decades ago, in a volume honouring the work of preeminent stylistician Peter Verdonk (Bex et al. 2000), I published a chapter which explored comic dialogue from a contextualised-stylistic perspective (Simpson 2000). Echoing the broad methods in stylistic analysis advanced by Verdonk over many publications (Verdonk 1997: 14; 2002: 18–22, 68–74; 2013: 14–16, 26–28; 2019: 79–80), that

https://doi.org/10.1075/lal.44.07sim

chapter sought to better understand the intersection between language, text and context. In more nuanced terms, Carter defines "contextualised stylistics" as the relationship between "words on the page" and their social, historical and cultural determinants, discussion of which must be framed on the premise that "context" is at once cognitive and sociocultural (Carter 2000: 267–8). My main focus then was on the stylistic and rhetorical composition of verbal play and the chapter argued, with the benefit of hindsight not especially successfully, that a discourse-stylistic profile could be developed to capture the humour impulse in Irish comic dialogue. Focussing principally on the Channel 4 television series *Father Ted*, a number of characteristics of language were identified which included a *reductio ad absurdum* recycling of verbal patterns at the level of exchange structure. The chapter also assessed the manner by which discoursal and generic properties of comic discourse can resurface across time and asked if it is feasible to talk of diachronic, culture-specific verbal humour.

Whereas the stylistic features identified in that chapter might well be at play in the humorous texts analysed, a simple empirical problem remains unresolved: what if these same features are found elsewhere, in texts that bear no "Celtic" connection or inflection? Indeed, Verdonk (2019) has examined verbal play in Anglo-Saxon poetry and, *pace* my comment on the diachronic progression of humour forms, sees the "riddling" patterns of Old English at work in the obviously more contemporary writing of W. H. Auden. The main aim of what follows therefore will be to revisit and fundamentally reconceive the theoretical and analytic basis of the argument presented in Simpson (2000). Although retaining methods of close textual analysis, the approach here will be expanded by taking as its main impetus the work of a particular philosopher, Henri Bergson, whose ideas are rarely invoked in the stylistic analysis of comic discourse. The next section will set out the core tenets of Bergson's model. Thereafter, my analyses begin with a return to *Father Ted*, a series which, as Cronin notes, is not only enduringly popular but also has rich and continued potential for exploring laughter and humour within frameworks of linguistic pragmatics (Cronin 2018: *passim*). In the present study (in comparison to Simpson 2000), the focus will be on a different scene from the programme and will draw upon the enriched and expanded philosophical perspective just sketched. My analysis concludes with a short illustration of how similar humour techniques can be found at work in the popular American sitcom, *Big Bang Theory*.

Overall, it is hoped that the present study can add a new dimension to that loosely-grouped but nonetheless substantial body of work known as "discourse stylistics". Work in discourse stylistics can be traced to Burton's early study of dialogue in plays (Burton 1980), and subsequent notable contributions to our understanding of the language of drama include McIntyre (2006) and Mandala (2016).

Parallel research, where there is the same emphasis on patterns of dialogue, includes Richardson (2010) and Sorlin (2016) on television dialogue, and Piazza et al. (2011), who focus on "telecinematic discourse". Finally, discourse stylistic methods have been brought specifically to the analysis of humour in popular TV sitcoms in work by Bednarek (2012), Korostenskiene and Lieponyte (2019) and, as noted, Cronin (2018). It is hoped that the philosophically-grounded approach adopted here can offer a wider stylistic perspective on the comic element in patterns of dialogue and discourse.

Bergson (1859–1941) and the meaning of the comic

The key work of relevance to the present study, as noted above, is French philosopher Henri Bergson's treatise on humour and comedy. Entitled *Le Rire: Essai sur la signification du comic*, this was the first book on humour to be written by a notable philosopher (Morreall 2020: 1). Originally serialised in three parts in the *Revue de Paris*, Bergson published a collected and substantially revised version in 1900, and by as early as 1920 this book was in its 19th edition. The first English translation of the book, *Laughter: An Essay on the Meaning of the Comic*, appeared in 1911. Endorsed by the philosopher himself, this now venerable translation came from two of Bergson's contemporaries: Cloudesley Brereton and Fred Rothwell. Reference is made here to the 2007 Dodo Press version of this translation, and, for additional clarity where appropriate, supplementary glosses are offered of Bergson's terms in the original French.

Throughout his explication of the humour impulse are the underpinning and quite narrowly circumscribed concepts of *rigidity* and *comic repetition*. For Bergson, the comic spirit has a logic of its own, but it never transcends what is "strictly HUMAN" (2007: 1–3; original capitals here and *passim*). Early in the essay, the definition of rigidity is situated in a contrast between, on the one hand, a sentient and supple human being and, on the other, a mechanical automaton (2007: 7–14). This core juxtaposition ("*le mécanique par opposition au souple*") leads Bergson to coin the phrase *mechanical inelasticity* to describe a condition of humanity that is displayed, paradoxically, as a lack of humanity which has been induced by rigidity and inelasticity. In essence, the humour impulse inheres in the mechanical inelasticity of people in certain situations, where the human becomes robotic and loses freedom of activity ("*l'automatisme par opposition à l'activité libre*"). The comic spirit, it is argued, inheres therefore in the bearing of the automaton in contrast with that of a sentient and supple human, in Bergson's words, as "something mechanical encrusted upon something living" (2007: 25).

Bergson offers numerous illustrations throughout the essay of the principle of mechanical inelasticity at work. Whereas the majority of these are taken from the writings of Cervantes, Molière and Racine, the first "non-literary" example in the essay asks us to imagine a man who, running along the street, stumbles and falls — an act which induces laughter from passers-by (2007: 1–9). The fall, it is argued, derives from rigidity and a lack of elasticity, and this involuntary element is contrasted to the alternative "unfunny" scenario had the man taken the "whim" to suddenly sit down. The same principle applies to the victims of practical jokes who, so the theory goes, are prevented from being able to attend to the "petty occupations" of everyday life. Bergson conceives such a victim as someone whose inkwell has been filled with mud or whose chair has had its bolts loosened by a "mischievous wag". The passing of time may prompt us to reflect on the actual degree of humour embodied by these practical jokes, but the essence of Bergson's idea is that the victim experiences and displays mechanical inelasticity instead of the living "pliableness" of a sentient human being (2007: 5).

Bergson orientates progressively this notion of "*le mécanique*" towards the idea of repetition. He references the "jack-in-the box" toy, much beloved by children of the time, noting not just their surprise at "the little man who springs out of his box" but the repetitive dimension where the coiled spring is being "bent, released and bent again" (2007: 30–33). Comic repetition inheres in the rendering of a person as a machine that works automatically and uniformly, just like the coiled spring which delights in "REPRESSING THE FEELING ANEW". There are no doubt children's toys from the intervening years which induce similar reactions, but laughter at the jack-in-the-box is intrinsic to its mechanical repetition despite us all knowing in every instance its denouement. In sum, for Bergson, a combination of acts and events is comic if it gives the distinct impression of "a MECHANICAL ARRANGEMENT" (Bergson 2007: 31 & *passim*).

Bergson distinguishes rigidity from a concept like ugliness, arguing that the comic impulse is engendered by the "unsprightly" rather than the "unsightly" (2007: 13). At pains to reassure us that physical deformity is *not* a natural stimulus to laughter, there is nevertheless a concerning explanation of the impulse to laugh out loud at people of colour (not Bergson's actual phraseology here) which is rationalised as a reaction akin to seeing a face "daubed over with ink or soot" or a "white man in disguise" (2007: 18). Remarks like this are unfortunately no more than typical of the often casually racist commentary of 19th and 20th century philosophers, especially it seems when they set their sights of the concepts of irony, humour or laughter (Kaiser 2004: 651–3; Morreall 1986; Simpson forthcoming).

Setting aside for now such attitudes, resonant of the cultural epoch in which they were expressed, attention will focus on how other scholars have, in the intervening years, assessed and developed Bergson's work. In this respect, there are two main types of academic assessment, the first of which concerns the position of Bergson's treatise on the comic impulse within the discipline of philosophy. This kind of appraisal seeks to account both for the theoretical antecedents in the century before Bergson as well as his influence on subsequent philosophical inquiry into humour from the 20th century to the present (Pilkington 1976: *passim*; Billig 2005: 119–121; and see further below). The second type of assessment, more obviously relevant to the present study, concerns the efficacy of the Bergsonian model and its adaptability as a model of analysis for exploring real comic discourse. A short survey of some of these accounts follows.

Given the kinds of illustrations offered in the foregoing summary, there might be good reason for assuming *Le Rire* is no more than a treatise on slapstick and similar forms of "base" comedy. True, Bergson covers the "horseplay of the clown" but he is clear that the idea of *le mécanique* extends to much more "refined" comedy (2007: 10). Suggesting a more cognitive understanding of humour, Bergson talks in terms of absent-mindedness as a reflex of inelasticity, embodied by "a certain rigidity of body, mind and character". By contrast, in a more sociological vein, he remarks that laughter's natural environment is society and that inelasticity can be seen as an "inadaptation" to social life, as something that society "would like to get rid of" (2007: 4). Developing this idea, in a study of farce, Bremel acknowledges Bergson when he notes that, in modern forms of the genre, machines have assumed the tasks once entrusted to servants and slaves. In doing so, these machines acquire a kind of "dramatic validity": they stop and start occasionally and often at the most awkward times on their own initiative (Bremel 1982: 30–31). Bremel adds that in silent movies comical characters behave mechanically — so much so that Bergson in *Le Rire* could "have been writing an annunciation of the film farce that would be unleashed a decade or so later." (1982: 30).

Pilkington (1976) assesses the impact of Bergson on major French writers and locates certain aspects of inelasticity in both literary plot and characterisation. Like Bremel above, the focus is however rather on the comic potential of what in the early 20th century was the new technology of machines rather than on humans exhibiting *per se* a mechanical "inadaptation" to social life. Commenting on Proust, for instance, Pilkington observes how Marcel (the narrator and main character of *À La Recherche*) begs a doctor to help his ailing grandmother. The doctor however is obsessed with operating the buttons of a lift in the building, a "maniacal habit" which arguably displays a mechanical response to a situation (Pilkington 1976: 168–169).

In the opening chapter of an influential collection on humour studies (Durant and Miller 1988), Miller classifies Bergson's model as a "biological" theory of humour (Miller 1988: 5–16). Slightly idiosyncratically, Miller casts the idea of inelasticity in terms of the kind of reaction a "herd" has when it observes a reduction in the versatility and flexibility of one of its members. This reaction results in loud respiratory convulsions (laughter, in other words) and Miller suggests this is because a less flexible or versatile individual endangers the biological integrity of the herd as a whole. Miller's application of the Bergsonian framework to the age-old comic scenario of the man who slips on a banana skin is nonetheless worth documenting. Asking himself why the "banana skin man" has become such an emblematic figure in theories of humour, Miller argues that we laugh at him because:

> instead of retaining his versatility, his spontaneity and his flexibility, the man who tumbles is yielding to the force of gravity and is becoming something like a robot. He is becoming an inflexible object, and at that moment he is being reminded [...] to restore himself to a state of vigilant flexibility [...].   (Miller 1988:10)

Following up this observation, Miller is quite right to point out that Bergson's model, like many approaches to the comic impulse, cannot accommodate the whole of the topic of humour analysis. He adds, however, that we would still be wrong "to laugh this theory out of court" (Miller 1988:10).

Perhaps the most comprehensive explication of the Bergsonian model is Billig's excellent appraisal (2005:111–138), to which he devotes a full chapter of his monograph on laughter and ridicule. Billig's study is somewhat at odds with contemporary humour theories because it offers specifically a social critique of humour's "dark side". Billig criticises the "ideological positivists" who see humour and laughter without exception as intrinsically good and fulfilling positive functions such as rapport building and the aversion of socially awkward interactive routines. By contrast, Billig envisions the humour impulse to be principally underpinned by ridicule, and moreover, that Bergson's model has essentially a "cold cruelty at its core" (2005:125). The core tenets of *Le Rire* are not, he continues, innocent or joyful but are instead disciplinary in origin where ridicule functions as a social corrective. Social interaction, it is argued, does not take place in a vacuum, and the laughter of the group of which we must be part simply serves to free us from the customary feelings of social empathy (2005:124–5).

Billig does not reject Bergson's model outright — indeed, he concedes that it is well equipped to account for the universality of humour. While accepting the idea of *le mécanique* in part, Billig's concern is more with the model's ultimately unkind properties, such as ridicule, and the curative function that comes from a fear of mockery. He argues that if communal laughter is caused by the perception of rigidity, this signals society's desire for order and assists us in adapting to a world that demands elasticity. For Bergson laughter is the mechanism of discipline, what Billig calls the "punishment in the classroom of life" (2005:128).

Across the critical and philosophical appraisal of *Le Rire* there is, to my mind, one conspicuous and rather stark omission: nowhere are the core principles of the model aligned with any understanding of language as discourse; nor are these principles situated within any frameworks in stylistics, pragmatics and discourse analysis. Instead, the visual, the physical and the situational take precedence over the linguistic, pushing the dynamic of social interaction to the margins. True, Bergson hints at an application to language late in the essay where he mentions the "plane of speech". Although unelaborated, this intimates perhaps that language can repeat mechanically and that comic rigidity can be detected in social routines (Bergson 2007: 50–2, 65). Similarly, Billig suggests that philosophers should seek to look behind language and that the potential of the model might be tested through a study of the "micro-functions of laughter" within social interaction (2005: 136–7). In response to this notable gap in coverage, the remainder of this chapter offers a discourse-stylistic application of *Le Rire* to passages of comic dialogue which span two very different, but hugely popular television comedies. It is hoped that the idea of *le mécanique* can be seen in variations in the patterns of everyday language and in a way that demonstrates how the humour impulse is often situated in carefully nuanced, and far from crude, creative play with the routines of social interaction.

Inelasticity in discourse: Nerds, geeks and a very sarcastic priest

This section will focus first on the enormously popular Irish situation-comedy *Father Ted*. The following excerpts embody three key moments from a famous episode of the sitcom entitled "Kicking Bishop Brennan up the Arse" (Series 3, Episode 6). Comprising a kind of set-up phase, a central encounter and a denouement, these exchanges are not just a comic interlude but are rather a mainstay of the episode's overall narrative structure. By way of context, the priests of Craggy Island, Fathers Ted, Dougal and Jack, have lost a football match to a team of septuagenarian priests stationed on an equally beleaguered island off the west coast of Ireland. The loss brings with it a forfeit: a member the losing team must kick their Diocesan superior, Bishop Brennan, up "the arse". To this end, so to speak, the Craggy Island priests plan to invite Bishop Brennan to the parish house on the spurious grounds that a saintly likeness of him has mysteriously appeared on a skirting board. The bishop's bending down to see more clearly the image of himself will, it is anticipated, facilitate an opportune moment to deliver the *coup de grâce*. However, just before the Bishop arrives, the audience learns that he will be accompanied by his understudy, the fawning and sycophantic Father Jessop, whose reputation for using sarcasm precedes him.

The first encounter with the two visitors involves an attempt by Father Ted at *phatic communion*; at, in other words, the familiar and routine pleasantries of language that mark the boundaries of social interaction:

```
Father Ted:   hello father jessop (0.5) er (0.5) helping bishop brennan then↑
Father Jessop: no↓::::: {sneers} i'm up in SPACE (.) doing important work for NASA::↓
```

Discouraged by the first exchange, Ted quickly offers a second phatic token:

```
Ted:   nasty day (0.5) {now diffidently} did you come by the new road↑
Jessop: .hhhh no↓:::::: .hhh {raises eyebrows, rolls his eyes while turning to the
        bishop} (.) we went round by SOUTHERN YEMEN ↓ {the bishop smiles approvingly}
```

Punctuated by resounding audience laughter throughout, the pragmatic foundations are now firmly laid in this set-up phase. Glossed in its broadest terms, sarcasm happens when a speaker ironically alludes to or critiques some originating event, belief, anterior utterance or situation (Simpson forthcoming). Although sarcasm may sometimes be positive in tone (Attardo 2000; Dynel 2009:1289), in its predominant mode, the ironic element in sarcasm conveys what researchers refer to as an "asymmetry of affect" and this asymmetry contains the negative evaluation characteristic of most sarcastic utterances (e.g., Clark & Gerrig 1984:122; Colston 1997; Dynel 2014:537–9; Jorgensen 1996; Kreuz & Glucksberg 1989:376). In evidence in these exchanges between the priests is a very strident display of such negative affect, where Jessop's manifestly untrue and literally outlandish ripostes signal clear disapproval of the anterior utterances to which they reply. In this instance, the target of the sarcasm is the assumed obviousness of Ted's two initiating utterances, polite and innocuous inquiries about, respectively, helping the bishop and the route taken to the parochial house. However, the "safe ground" advanced by this phatic communion is rejected, and Jessop's exaggerated sarcasm signals a degree of negative affect which leaves no doubt that he finds Ted's propitiatory remarks insubstantial and jejune.

I describe Jessop's sarcasm as "exaggerated" with some confidence because, in spoken discourse, sarcasm can be supplemented, consolidated and intensified with a set of specific verbal and paralinguistic cues. These "vocal cues of sarcasm", the primary constitution of which has been discussed (and disputed) in the research, is piled on in spade-loads in Jessop's responses, and to the extent that they produce a "hyperbolic" mode of sarcasm (Kreuz and Roberts 1995). Popa-Wyatt argues that this kind of hyperbole in sarcasm reveals a speaker as especially "mocking, scornful and contemptuous" (2020:100–1). Furthermore, the onset of each of Jessop's sarcastic responses is marked by well-known (though again, sometimes debated) prosodic cues: a lowering of pitch, a slower delivery and a louder articulation (Bryant & Fox Tree 2002; Kreuz 2020:125–30; Rockwell 2000). Supplementing these prosodic cues are key paralinguistic features as in the sneers which are marked by the audible intakes of breath at ".hhhh". Consider also the raised eyebrows and the eye-rolling which are, again, attested methods for delivering an ironic retort to a previous utterance. For example, Tabacaru talks of raised eyebrows as a major "gestural trigger" in spoken sarcasm (Tabacaru 2020: 260–61; see also Tabacaru and Lemmens 2014: 12), while Colston focuses specifically of eye-rolling as a key "disapproval cue" in sarcastic "put downs" like this (2020: 217). Finally, the content of Jessop's hyperbolic ripostes makes them a good candidate for what Kapogianni calls "irony via surrealism" (2011). Kapogianni offers the following illustration:

A: Are you going to school tomorrow?
B: No, I am riding my unicorn to Alaska.

(Kapogianni 2011: 51)

Very much in the style of Jessop, the second speaker employs "a strikingly unrealistic, unexpected, and [...] 'surrealistic' response" (Kapogianni 2011: 52ff). Part of the purpose of this strategy, it is argued, is to invent absurd answers which break the conventions of everyday dialogue with the aim of criticizing the use of common questions considered "stupid" or "mundane" by the ironist — indeed, very much the kind of phatic questions posed by Ted. By way of brief digression, it would be interesting to explore further the intersection between, on the one hand, the specific linguistic properties of surrealism (e.g., Stockwell 2017) and, on the other, the kind of cognitive arc that distinguishes surrealistic sarcasm from non-hyperbolic forms. A calibration of these conceptual spheres would make for an interesting future project.

Returning to *Father Ted*, the next key development in the episode involves the arrival of Mrs Doyle, the redoubtable and long-suffering housekeeper who is a stalwart of the series. Opening the exchange with her characteristic hospitality, she moves quickly to her trademark offer to the visitors of a cup of tea (see Cronin 2018: 261). However, Mrs Doyle soon experiences Jessop's "go to" pragmatic strategy:

```
Mrs Doyle (to the visitors): will I make up a bed in the spare room?
Jessop:                      no↓:::↑ (.) we'll sleep outside in a ditch↑
Mrs Doyle:                   {clearly confused} okay::: so::: {now hesitantly} would
                             you (.) like (.) a (.) cup of tea↑
Jessop:                      ↓no:::↑ (.) {slower} we'd rather die of thirst {the
                             bishop smiles approvingly}
Mrs Doyle:                   okay::: so:::
Ted:                         {aside, sotto voce to Mrs Doyle}: uhmm (.) mrs doyle (.)
                             I think father jessop was being a bit er (0.5) sarcastic
Mrs Doyle:                   {to Ted, then Jessop}: WHAT↑ (.) were you being sarcastic
                             father jessop?
Jessop:                      {rolling eyes} ↓no:::↑ >we want to die of thirst<
```

Ted:	{again *sotto voce*} mrs doyle (.) I know it's a bit confusing (.) but just do the <u>opposite</u> of what father jessop says
Mrs Doyle:	okay::: ↓ so::::: ↓ you:: really:: <u>do:::</u> ↓ want a cup of tea?
Jessop:	{exasperated, holds out his hand, while rolling eyes and turning to the bishop} YES↓
Mrs Doyle:	{smiles knowingly, snatches cup of tea away from Jessop's hand, and leaves room to much audience laughter}

This encounter establishes the key pragmatic opposition between Mrs Doyle, the inveterate literalist, and Jessop, whose chronic sarcastic predisposition, with its hyperbole and vocal cues, initially leaves Mrs Doyle dumbfounded. As a victim unaware of the ironic intention, Mrs Doyle is placed in what has been termed the subject position of a "sheep"; this contrasts with the "wolf" who is someone who understands the ironic intention (see Gibbs and Izett 2005; van Mulken et al 2011). Another important subject position in the interaction is the complicit "confederate", embraced on-stage by the bishop who is an interactant who "understands what the ironist is doing and agrees with it" (van Mulken et al 2011: 52). Where the bishop as confederate enjoys the questionable wit of his protégé, Father Ted, by understanding but *not* agreeing, is by imputation a "non-confederate". However, Ted occupies another subject position which seems special to forms of humorous dialogue that play on commonly understood discourse routines. I term the coin *metadiscoursal facilitator* because in this role Ted "talks about talk". He is an enabler in discourse who explains sarcasm and suggests a corrective so that Mrs Doyle, the sheep, can join in on the verbal play, such as it is (and see further below).

In superimposing the Bergsonian model of *le mécanique* onto the foregoing micro-pragmatic analysis, it is easy to see, on a first reading, that the humour impulse is activated primarily the mechanically inelastic the echanically by Mrs Doyle. In the terms of the model, hers is not a rigidity of body, but of mind and character. Her communicative competence lacks a sensitivity to the routines of ordinary social interaction, to the "petty occupations of everyday life" touched upon earlier. After all, it is her "inelasticity" as a conversational strategist which jeopardises the onward flow of the interaction.

This initial reading is, however, a rather naïve one. It is also easy to read these sequences of dialogue as gendered, in the sense that Mrs Doyle, the middle-aged spinster, must have the commonalities of discourse "mansplained" to her in order to become fully interactionally functional. Yet if this were the entire "gag" of the episode, the narrative would become simply a monochrome series of hostile sarcastic "putdowns" — a stasis that would block any further narrative development. However, little in the world of *Father Ted* is what it seems as the third phase of dialogue, where the final interactive blow is delivered, will demonstrate.

Towards the end of the episode another permanent resident of the parochial house, the misanthropic and foul-mouthed Father (Jack) Hackett, has taken a dislike to Jessop such that he has imprisoned the visitor by padlocking him into a soiled underwear hamper. Now cut adrift from his supportive confederate and peering out from a narrow gap in the hamper, Jessop pleads with Mrs Doyle as she happens to pass by:

```
Jessop:    {falsetto, weak} °help° (2.0) °help° (2.0) oh thank god (.) help me
Mrs Doyle: {cheerily} h::whaaat↓ are ye doin in father hackett's underpants ↓hamper
Jessop     {falsetto, weak} °he locked me in here° (.) °dear god° (.) the ↓SME:::LL
Mrs Doyle: are you not (.) terribly uncomfortable in ↓there
Jessop:    >OF COURSE I'M UNCOMFORTABLE< (.) {breathy, urgent} i want to get out
Mrs Doyle: {cheerily} fair enough so: {winks knowingly, turns away and abandons Jessop
           to his fate, to much audience laughter}
```

Reminding us of the figurative trope that sustains the episode, Mrs Doyle has learned from her metadiscoursal facilitator and has adapted a new paradigm. True, she has moved from one kind of rigidly in discourse into another, the entrenched literalism giving way to the default interpretation of a consistent "oppositeness" in the speech of this particular interlocutor. For Jessop, his hubris leads to his downfall. In the central encounter he had begun to waver when his defining linguistic trait went missing for an instant. The cup of tea missed was an early warning that he too needed his rigidity to be consistent: once sarcastic, always sarcastic. Now locked in a hamper of soiled underclothing, the temptation to be sarcastic appears to have dissipated. But it is now too late: Mrs Doyle is entirely at ease with her new interpretative paradigm, her new inelasticity, in effect. Satisfyingly for the audience, Father Jessop has interactively been hoisted with his own petard.

The thrust of this chapter has been to offer a heightened understanding of the humour impulse by drawing on a particular philosophical framework. It is tempting to categorise the foregoing stylistic account of inelasticity in dialogue as a specifically Irish form of humour. However, as noted in the introductory section above, while a pattern in discourse such as this may be common in "Celtic" humour, that is not to say that its privilege of occurrence is circumscribed to this cultural context only. To close this section, then, a short Bergsonian-inflected analysis is offered of a fragment of comic dialogue from the popular series, *Big Bang Theory*, a programme that on the face of it could hardly be more different, stylistically and culturally, from *Father Ted*.

Big Bang Theory (*BBT*) centres on a group of postgraduate students at a university uncannily similar to the California Institute of Technology. Caltech is noted for its research expertise in astrophysics, which happens to be the students' specialist subject. Bednarek has explored this series from a linguistic perspective, using qualitative and corpus methods, and notes the construction of the students' characters through familiar stereotypes about "nerds" and "geeks"

(Bednarek 2012; and see below). Outside this group is their neighbour Penny, who is something of a dramatic foil in that she is grounded, street-wise and, for want of a better word, "normal". The following exchanges come from an episode called "The Bus Pants Utilization" (Series 4, Episode 12). Penny has found Sheldon playing a theremin in the hallway and invites him in for a cocoa. She discovers that he has been ostracised from a research project because of an insult to its leader, Leonard. Although Sheldon may be re-admitted to the group if he apologises, the speech act of apology does not come easily to him, nor, as we will see, does sarcasm. In this scene, filmed in shot-reverse-shot, both characters are sitting side by side, and much to the irritation of Penny, the dialogue is punctuated by single elongated notes from Sheldon's theremin.

```
Penny:    the thing is (.) you're gonna have tuh offer him {i.e. Leonard} a face (.)
          saving (.) way outa this
Sheldon:  how?
Penny     say you're sorry
Sheldon:  ↓oh:: ↓no:: (.) {adopting his mother's southern USA accent} >Mrs Mary Cooper
          didn't raise her no liars<
Penny:    okay::::::: umm (.) howabout this (.) you know how you're always tryna learn
          about sarcasm?
Sheldon:  No:::
Penny:    No:::?
Sheldon:  I was being sarcastic
Penny:    ohhhhh good for ↓you:::↑ (.) so all you havta do here is say sorry to Leonard
          and say it (.) sarcastically. […]
Sheldon:  OF COURSE↓ … […]
Penny:    ahhright (.) c'mon (.) go
Sheldon:  by the way (1.0) thankyou for the (1.0) delic↓ious cocoa
Penny:    {pleased} you're welcome
Sheldon:  wow i'm getting good at this […]
          {later, in Leonard's flat, very slowly} <let me say again how deeply sorry I
          am leonard for my earlier behaviour and how much I respect and admire your
          leadership>
Leonard:  {puzzled} tha::nkyou
Sheldon:  {winks knowingly to a now very irritated Penny}.
```

Here again is a stretch of comic dialogue that delights in the nuance of Bergson's "petty occupations" of everyday of social life. As observed in the extracts earlier, narrative progression is not propelled by actions and events *per se*, but rather by interchanges in and about speech and dialogue itself. To the great amusement of the studio audience (and undoubtedly viewers at home), the episode cannot progress until aspects of inelasticity in speech are overcome, for without this, there is stasis. In what could prove a difficult transition for Sheldon as *le mécanique*, the traditional claim to sincerity in an apology (which he cannot bring himself to offer to Leonard) needs to be rescinded and replaced with the insincerity of the false claim to truth which is embodied in sarcasm.

Luckily for Sheldon, he is enabled by his metadiscoursal facilitator in making this Bergsonian transition from rigidity into the sentient and the supple. Having been thus schooled by Penny, he wastes no time in practicing the newly acquired pragmatic skill on his former mentor. However, as the transcript shows, his "sarcastic" comment on the quality of her "delicious cocoa" (which is followed by self-congratulation) lacks the key vocal cues of sarcasm described earlier, and the utterance's illocutionary status is, understandably, misread by Penny. Having educated some of the "nerdiness" out of her ungrateful interlocutor, Penny, to her growing irritation, has moved from the subject position of facilitator to that of sheep. By contrast, by the time Sheldon offers his *faux* apology to Leonard, many of the "lower-slower-louder" vocal cues of sarcasm are firmly in place.

Further instances of mechanical inelasticity at the level of discourse no doubt abound in *BBT*. Bednarek (2012) comments on the social awkwardness of the program's central characters, a subculture of "geeks" and "nerds". She offers an interesting observation on how viewers of the series perceive and describe these characters; such descriptions range from (implicitly Bergsonian) "funnily abnormal" to "somehow non-human" (2012: 199–200). It may be then that the discourse of nerds and geeks is mechanical inelasticity embodied, though that issue will have to be explored in a future study.

Concluding remarks

In the introduction to this chapter, I referenced some previous work (Simpson 2000) which focussed on comic dialogue, and while the purpose of the present study was to explore fresh material, there is no doubt that the data from the earlier study would easily support a Bergsonian "make-over" with its attendant concepts of inelasticity and comic repetition. The model might also usefully supplement existing stylistic-pragmatic explorations of comic dialogue in television sitcoms like *Modern Family* (Korostenskiene and Lieponyte 2019) or, as just noted, *Big Bang Theory* (Bednarek 2012). Alternatively, the model could complement work in what is conventionally labelled "humorology", such as Khurana's application (2023) of Bergson to Laurence Sterne's novel *The Life and Opinions of Tristram Shandy, Gentleman* (1759). Although Khurana's study does not investigate stylistic-pragmatic routines *per se*, it does use Bergsonian ideas to highlight interconnections in the novel between linguistic slips and bodily functions. These interconnections, it is argued, reveal a coexistence between, on the one hand, the analysis of humour centered on Enlightenment ideas about the functioning of the body and, on the other, the conceptualisation of humour in "the older medicalised understanding of humours as bodily fluids" (Khurana 2023: 92).

In essence, the Bergsonian framework is not so much about the traditional idea of "incongruity" as employed in much work in linguistic humorology; instead, it is about characterisation through metadiscourse and the potential pitfalls of language-use in everyday social situations. The model set out in this chapter, with its core concepts of rigidity, inelasticity and *le mécanique,* alongside their counterparts in suppleness and sentience, can be applied both to discourse routines and discourse strategies. To this extent, this discourse-stylistic adaption seeks to transcend Bergson's "man who falls while running" or the "horseplay of the clown" where the humour impulse inheres solely in physical and situational rigidities.

Billig (2005: 136) sees in *Le Rire* a theoretical downgrading of verbal humour, and one of the purposes of the present chapter has been to reverse this by foregrounding the comic potential of language as discourse. It has attempted to show how the tenets of *Le Rire* can illuminate plot-advancing mechanisms in humour production with an orientation towards the language code. In the same section of his book, Billig also muses on the kind of contemporary comedy genre of which Bergson would have approved (2005: 136). Imagining what a philosopher from 1900 might appreciate from an array of twenty-first century offerings, Billig identifies two "comedies of embarrassment" in the form of Larry David's *Curb your Enthusiasm* and Ricky Gervais's *The Office.* I think that *Father Ted* and *Big Bang Theory* would make for admirable additions to this list.

References

Attardo, S. 2000. Irony as relevant inappropriateness. *Journal of Pragmatics* 32: 793–826.

Bednarek, M. 2012. Constructing "nerdiness": Characterisation in the *Big Bang Theory*. *Multilingua* 31: 199–229.

Bergson, Henri [1900] 2007. *Laughter: An Essay on the Meaning of the Comic.* Trans. Cloudesley Brereton & Fred Rothwell. Wokingham, UK: Dodo Press.

Bex, A., Stockwell, P. Burke (eds.) 2000. *Contextualised Stylistics: In Honour of Peter Verdonk.* Amsterdam: Rodopi.

Billig, M. 2005. *Laugher and Ridicule: Towards a Social Critique of Humour.* London: Sage.

Bremel, A. 1982. *A History of Farce: From Aristophanes to Woody Allen.* NY: Simon and Shuster.

Bryant, G.A. and Fox Tree, J.E. 2002. Recognizing verbal irony in spontaneous speech. *Metaphor and Symbol* 17: 99–119.

Burton, D. 1980. *Dialogue and Discourse* London: RKP.

Carter, R.A. 2000. Afterword. In Bex et al.., 267–268.

Clark, H. and Gerrig, R. 1984. On the pretense theory of irony. *Journal of Experimental Psychology: General* 113: 121–126.

doi Colston, H. 1997. Salting a wound or sugaring a pill: the pragmatic functions of ironic criticism. *Discourse Processes* 23: 25–45.

doi Colston, H. 2020. Eye-rolling, irony and embodiment. In *The Diversity of Irony*. Athanasiadou, A. & Colston, H.L. (eds.), 211–234. Berlin: Walter de Gruyter Mouton.

Cronin, M.E. 2018. *"Feck Off": Exploring the Relationship between Impoliteness, Laughter and Humour in the British-Irish Sitcoms* Father Ted, Black Books *and* The IT Crowd. Unpublished PhD thesis, University of Birmingham.

Durant, J. and Miller, J. (eds.) 1988. *Laughing Matters: A Serious Look at Humour.* Harlow: Longman.

Dynel, M. 2009. *Humorous Garden-Paths: A Pragmatic-Cognitive Study.* Newcastle: Cambridge Scholars Publishing.

doi Dynel, M. 2014. Linguistic approaches to (non)humorous irony. *International Journal of Humor Research* 27(4): 537–550.

Gibbs, R.W. and Izett, C. 2005. Irony as persuasive communication. In *Figurative Language Comprehension: Social and Cultural Influences*, H. Colston & A. Katz (eds.), 131–151. NJ: Lawrence Erlbaum Associates, Inc.

doi Jorgensen, J. 1996. The functions of sarcastic irony in speech. *Journal of Pragmatics* 26: 613–634.

doi Kaiser, M. 2004. A history of "ludicrous". *English Literary History* 71(3): 631–660.

doi Kapogianni, E. 2011. Irony via "surrealism". In *The Pragmatics of Humour across Discourse Domains.* Dynel, M. (ed.), 51–68. Amsterdam: John Benjamins.

doi Khurana, N. 2023. The humorous body: a Bergsonian reading of Laurence Sterne's *The Life and Opinions of Tristram Shandy, Gentleman. The European Journal of Humour Research*, 11(4): 93–103.

Korostenskiene, J. and Lieponyte, A. 2019. Irony, sarcasm and parody in the American sitcom *Modern Family. Israeli Journal for Humor Research* 8(1): 51–85.

doi Kreuz, R.J. 2020. *Irony and Sarcasm: A Biography of Two Troublesome Words.* Cambridge, MA: MIT Press.

Kreuz, R.J. and Glucksberg, S. 1989. How to be sarcastic: The reminder theory of verbal irony. *Journal of Experimental Psychology: General* 118: 347–386.

doi Kreuz, R. and Roberts, R. 1995. Two cues for verbal irony: Hyperbole and the ironic tone of voice. *Metaphor & Symbolic Activity* 10: 21–31.

doi Mandala, S. 2016. *Twentieth-Century Drama as Ordinary Talk: Speaking between the Lines.* London: Routledge.

doi McIntyre, D. 2006. *Point of View in Plays: A Cognitive Stylistic Approach to Viewpoint in Drama and other Text-types.* Amsterdam: John Benjamins.

Miller, J. 1988. Jokes and joking: A serious laughing matter. In Durant and Miller, 5–16.

Morreall, J. 1986. *The Philosophy of Laughter and Humor* NY: State University of New York.

Morreall, J. 2020. Philosophy of humor. *Stanford Encyclopedia of Philosophy.* https://plato .stanford.edu/entries/humor/?utm_campaign=observational%20comedy.&utm_medium =email&utm_source=Revue%20newsletter [last accessed 8 November 2023]

doi Piazza, R., Bednarek, M. and Rossi, F. (eds.) 2011. *Telecinematic Discourse: Approaches to the Language of Films and Television Series.* Amsterdam: John Benjamins.

Pilkington, A.E. 1976. *Bergson and his Influence: A Reassessment.* Cambridge: CUP.

Popa-Wyatt, M. 2020. Hyperbolic figures. In *The Diversity of Irony*, A. Athanasiadou & H.L. Colston (eds.), 91–106. Walter de Gruyter Mouton.

Richardson, K. 2010. *Television Dramatic Dialogue: A Sociolinguistic Study*. Oxford: OUP.

Rockwell, P. 2000. Lower, slower, louder: Vocal cues of sarcasm. *Journal of Psycholinguistic Research*, 29: 483–495.

Simpson, P. 2000. Satirical humour and cultural context: with a note on the curious case of Father Todd Unctuous. In Bex et al.., 243–266.

Simpson, P. forthcoming. *Irony: Pragmatic, Social and Legal Consequences*. London: Bloomsbury.

Sorlin, S. 2016. *Language and Manipulation in House of Cards: A Pragma-Stylistic Perspective*. Palgrave MacMillan.

Stockwell, P. 2017. *The Language of Surrealism* London: Palgrave MacMillan.

Tabacaru, S. 2020. Faces of sarcasm: Exploring raised eyebrows with sarcasm in French political debates. In *The Diversity of Irony*, A. Athanasiadou & H.L. Colston (eds.), 256–277. Walter de Gruyter Mouton.

Tabacaru, S. & Lemmens, M. (2014. Raised eyebrows as gestural triggers in humour: The case of sarcasm and hyper-understanding. *European Journal of Humour Research* 2(2): 11–31.

van Mulken, M., Burgers, C. and van der Plas, B. 2011. Wolves, confederates, and the happy few: The influence of comprehension, agreement, and group membership on the attitude toward irony. *Discourse Processes* 48: 50–68.

Verdonk, P. 1997. *Het bevrijde icoon: Van klassieke retorica naar cognitieve stilistiek*. Amsterdam: Vossiuspers AUP.

Verdonk, P. 2002. *Stylistics*. Oxford: OUP.

Verdonk, P. 2013. *The Stylistics of Poetry: Context, Cognition, Discourse, History*. London: Bloomsbury.

Verdonk, P. 2019. Riddling: The dominant rhetorical device in W.H. Auden's "The Wanderer". In *Style, Rhetoric and Creativity in Language: In Memory of Walter (Bill) Nash (1926–2015)*, Simpson, P. (ed.), 77–84. Amsterdam: Benjamins.

Transcription symbols used

>	Rising tone.
↓	Falling tone.
(.)	A micropause, hearable but too short to measure.
(1.0)	Audible pause measured in seconds.
{rolls eyes}	Description of non-verbal behaviour (e.g. changes in posture).
CAPS	Emphatic stress.
°quietly°	The 'degree' signs enclose hearable quieter speech.
?	Signals stronger 'questioning' intonation irrespective of grammar.
::	Colons show degrees of elongation of the prior sound.
Underlining	Indicates emphasis (including within individual words).
>help me<	Indicates a segment of speeded-up talk.
.hh	Audible inbreath.
hh.	Audible outbreath.

CHAPTER 8

Cognition and the creative interplay of word and image in Apollinaire's "*Il Pleut*"

Joanna Gavins
University of Sheffield

This chapter honours two of Peter Verdonk's long-standing scholarly interests: first, the relationship between word and image in poetry; and second, the cognition of literary style. In his article, "Painting, poetry, parallelism: ekphrasis, stylistics and cognitive poetics", Verdonk states that human beings have "a prevailing desire for some sort of productive interaction between word and image" (2005: 235), before going on to present a characteristically exhaustive, contextually grounded and cognitively informed analysis of the style of William Carlos Williams' poem, "The Dance". While Verdonk's analysis focuses on an ekphrastic text which, as he explains, "is expected to call the image to mind, to conjure it up, as it were" (2005: 235), he also notes that other poetic forms, including shape poetry and concrete poetry, similarly seem to satisfy our preoccupation with vision and language. My own chapter examines one such poem, while aiming to follow the analytical principles of context-sensitivity, rigour, and theoretical experimentation which underpinned Peter's entire scholarly career. In the analysis of Apollinaire's famous text, "*Il Pleut*", which follows, I bring traditional stylistic and literary-critical approaches into dialogue with more recent cognitive accounts of the experience of reading poetry, specifically looking at the cognition of iconicity in poetry at the very beginnings of what would become the concrete movement in the early twentieth century.

Keywords: Apollinaire, calligrams, cognition, concrete poetry, iconicity, "*Il Pleut*", stylistics

Approaching "*Il Pleut*"

Figure 1 shows Guillaume Apollinaire's poem, "*Il Pleut*", which will form the basis of my discussion. The poem was originally published in the avant-garde magazine *SIC* (*Sons, Idées, Couleurs, Forms*) in December 1916 and later formed part of the collection *Calligrammes: poèmes de la paix et da la guerre* (Apollinaire 1918: 62).

https://doi.org/10.1075/lal.44.08gav

Figure 1.

For important reasons, which I will explain in due course, I have translated the text of the poem from the original French myself, as follows:

It is raining

> it is raining the voices of women as if they were dead even in memory
> it is you also who is raining marvellous encounters of my life oh droplets
> and these clouds rear and begin to whinny a whole universe of auricular cities
> listen it is raining while regret and disdain weep an ancient music
> listen to the falling of the bonds that restrain you high and low

While the discussion to come focuses mainly on this English translation, it also refers closely to Apollinaire's version and the relationship between the translated and original text. I will argue that this relationship bears considerably on our cognition of word and image in the poem and that precisely *how* the text is translated is crucial to our understanding of "*Il Pleut*".

Apollinaire was born in Rome in 1880, the son of a Polish émigrée and an unidentified man, thought to be an Italian officer. He spent much of his early life travelling Europe and settled in Paris around the age of 18, where he quickly became a prominent figure in its vibrant avant-garde cultural scene, befriending and supporting artists such as André Derain, Raoul Dufy, and Pablo Picasso. He enlisted in the French army (possibly in order to secure French citizenship) in 1914 and sustained a shrapnel injury to his temple while serving as an infantry-man in 1916. He was discharged from the army and returned to Paris, but never fully recovered from his wound. He died from influenza in 1918, two days before Armistice Day and aged just 38. Despite his short life and writing career, his work had a profound impact on a range of major artistic and literary movements, including Surrealism (a term which he coined in the title of his play *Les mamelles de Tiresias: Drame surrealiste* in 1916), Cubism, Dadaism, and Fauvism. Later in the twentieth century, his poetry was also a major inspiration for the concrete movement, which first emerged in Brazil and Austria in the early 1950s. The roots of this movement can be clearly seen in "*Il Pleut*" which, like many of the poems in *Calligrammes*, combines word and image in its creation of meaning.

From both a literary critical and a traditional stylistic point of view, "*Il Pleut*" can be considered to be a typical example of literary iconicity. Such a perspective would regard the layout of the words of the poem as a formal device which "mimes" the meaning of the text, to use Nänny and Fischer's terminology (1999; see also Nänny 1986, and Nänny and Fischer 2001 for further examples of this approach). Thus, the vertical alignment of the individual letters which form each of the words of the poem, arranged in lines across the page, can be seen to mirror the shape of falling raindrops and to echo the title of the work. From this perspective, the miming of the poem's meaning through its form only comes into being if, as Nänny puts it "the reader moves from content to form" (Nänny 1986:199). Nänny explains:

> it is in the nature of literature to exploit all linguistic and, hence, also all iconic possibilities for aesthetic purposes... Iconic functions of textual elements, however, are no more than latent possibilities. They will only appear if the meaning of the textual passage is compatible with them.   (Nänny 1986:199)

He argues that the latent potential of a sign to function iconically is only fulfilled through a reader's realisation of the connection between form and meaning and that "iconicity exists only as it is perceived" (Nänny 1986:199).

However, while Nänny's statement acknowledges the essential role of reader perception in this process, this approach nevertheless separates the form of a text and its content in a way which is incompatible with more contemporary, cognitive-linguistic understanding of reading and of the cognition of language more generally. As Freeman (2020) points out:

> What is missing from this form-content perspective is the realization that meaning arises partially from the form *of* content and the content *of* form. In other words, symbols are indivisible.   (Freeman 2020:29)

She goes on to argue:

> iconicity is the process by which a product of human cognition, such as language, art, artifact, or institution, may become an icon, material or immaterial, that enables respondents to construct access to and affectively connect with something beyond that product... creating a material artifact, or embodying movement in the body as in dance, is a means by which the processes of imaginative creativity are made manifest in such a way that they become an icon of respondent affective reciprocity between the material and the immaterial.
> (Freeman 2020:37)

From a cognitive-linguistic point of view, then, our *conceptualisation* of language is not distinct from our *perception*, nor is it separate from any other dimension of our embodied being and cognitive activity. In what follows, I will adopt the same view of language as Freeman advocates above, specifically considering poetic creativity to be an expression of embodied experience, which is fully integrated with other aspects of our cognitive capacity.

Visuo-verbal simultaneity

The cognitive-theoretical idea that the process of perceiving an image might be integrated with the process of conceptualising language would no doubt be one that would appeal to Apollinaire himself. Apollinaire argued that readers of his work should conceive of each piece in its totality and "read in a single glance the whole of a poem, just as a conductor reads at once the different notes in a score, and as one sees at once both the pictorial and typographic elements of a poster" (Apollinaire 1991: 796). As Lockerbie (1980) explains, achieving this simultaneity of perception and conception was a specifically modernist and avant-garde objective for the poet:

> Central among [Apollinaire's] aesthetic ideas was the notion that the modern work of art must adequately reflect the global nature of contemporary consciousness. In the conditions of modern life man has achieved totality of awareness: through worldwide communications he is as aware of what is happening in New York as in Paris; through newspapers, radio, cinema his imagination is stimulated by a constantly changing stream of information and ideas; in the streets and cafes his sense are assailed by a kaleidoscopic multiplicity of sights, sounds, and sensations.   (Lockerbie 1980: 3)

According to Lockerbie, then, Apollinaire's attempt to create a synchronous visuo-verbal poetic experience was not only an aesthetic concern but a direct response to contemporary culture and society. Although he repeatedly claimed that he had nothing whatever to say about politics, dismissing it as "*haïssable, mensongère, stérile et néfaste*" (detestable, deceitful, sterile, and injurious) (Apollinaire 1966 [1902]: 712), Adamson points out:

> paradoxically, never was there so relentlessly public a life as Apollinaire's, and no one has ever dedicated more energy to the promotion of art as an answer to the spiritual malaise of modern life. In that sense, his indefatigable production of criticism as well as his unending public performance of self were nothing if not political both in intent and effect.   (Adamson 1999: 33)

Adamson goes on to argue that Apollinaire's apparent apoliticism was "a mask for his deepest conviction... that only through the visionary power of avant-garde art could men and women living in modern mass societies regain their human capacity for the concrete experience of life" (1999: 34).

Since the simultaneity of perception and conception formed such a central principle in Apollinaire's expression of the avant-garde, any approach to the analysis of his poetry which separates form and content would therefore seem all the more erroneous. Instead, what is needed in order to appreciate the cognitive and artistic means through which Apollinaire deployed the "visionary power" of poetry, as Adamson puts it, is an account of how the various conceptual and perceptual dynamics of his work operate in unison in the minds of his readers. We must seek to understand not only how word and image interact, but more crucially how they interdepend.

What is more, there is now empirical evidence available to support Apollinaire's notion that both the visual and verbal elements of his work can be experienced at once and in their totality. Most helpfully, Shingler (2011) presents a discussion of Apollinaire's calligrams in the light of experimental psychological research into the processes underlying reading and picture perception, and the nature of visual attention and awareness. She does so in support of Apollinaire's claims to have created visuo-verbal simultaneity in his work, and also in order to take issue with Foucault's (1983 [1973]) counter assertion that such simultaneity of perception and conception is impossible.

In his discussion of René Magritte's painting, *Ceci n'est pas un pipe*, Foucault described the work as "a calligram [sic] that Magritte has secretly constructed, then carefully unravelled" (Foucault 1983: 20), also pointing out in a footnote that Apollinaire was also one of Magritte's favourite writers. Foucault goes on to insist that text and image cannot be apprehended at the same time and that viewing a calligram as a picture involves attention solely to the global features of the poem, while reading text requires attention solely to a local level of detail. Shingler reports the results of a small empirical study she executed in order to test these claims. Using a high speed video eye tracker, Shingler examined the eye movements of twelve participants as they read a selection of Apollinaire's calligrams for sixty seconds each. She found that these subjects used a variety of different strategies in their viewing and comprehension of the poems, paying attention to varying aspects of the calligrams and in varying orders. Most participants read the titles of the poems first, but then moved their eyes in multiple directions across and around the texts, sometimes prioritising the verbal features of the poems and sometimes attending to its visual aspects with freer scanning movements. Shingler argues that this is evidence that there is no single perceptual model which fits all readers' experiences of the calligrams. Rather, she points out, it is only possible to specify what readers might potentially *be able to do* when encountering these poems.

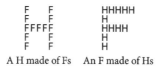

Figure 2.

Shingler goes on to argue that our attention may shift and change during our experience of one of Apollinaire's calligrams and, furthermore, that paying attention to one aspect of a poem in one moment does not necessarily mean that we become completely unaware of its other features. She makes central reference in her argument to the work of experimental psychologist David Navon (1977), whose famous "Navon tasks" attempted to examine the extent to which information presented to subjects at a global level interfered with information presented at a local level. Navon gave his participants images of large letters, made up from patterns of smaller letters in forty-millisecond exposures. Examples of these images are shown in Figure 2. He found that, where information at the global and local level conflicted (e.g. in in a letter F made of smaller Hs, or a letter H made of smaller Fs, as shown in Figure 2), subjects were able to exclude the local level from their attention in order to focus solely on the information supplied at the global level. They could not, by contrast, process local features without being aware of the global whole. Shingler explains:

> On the basis of this, attention may be thought of as a kind of filter: it is selective, but not exclusive. We select some information to come through the filter into our awareness, but other information creeps in too — and global information inevitably finds its way in...   (Shingler 2011: 78)

Shingler presents further supporting evidence from Kennedy's experimental psychological research too (c.f. Kennedy and Murray 1985; Kennedy 2000; Kennedy et al. 2003). She explains that Kennedy's key argument is that readers build up a mental map of a text as they read in working memory. If we use terms from Text World Theory (c.f. Gavins 2007; Werth 1999) to understand this further, we might think of Kennedy's notion of a textual working map as a global-level mental representation, constructed from our experience of the numerous individual text-worlds which result from our dynamic, moment-to-moment comprehension of a text (see Harvey 2024 for a similar argument on the global processing of texts from a text-world perspective). Kennedy's argument, however, is that this mental map is made up not only from verbal information, but visual information too.

Evidence for this can be found in the results of Kennedy and Murray's (1985) experiment, in which subjects were presented with a sentence, then a target word after the sentence (e.g. We bought bread and cheese from the grocer at the end of the street. **bread**). The subjects were then asked to say whether or not the target word was present in the sentence. Kennedy and Murray found that subjects often made a regressive saccade back to the position in the sentence in which the target word had appeared and argued that, given the size of the saccades involved (forty to fifty characters on average), it would be difficult, if not impossible, for the subjects to locate the target word using only their peripheral vision. As Shingler explains, Kennedy and Murray's "spatial coding hypothesis accounts for subjects'" ability to make such large and accurate regressive eye movements by positing that they maintain in working memory a record of the spatial location of words fixated on the first pass through a text, enabling refixation if this is needed" (Shingler 2011: 78). She goes on to argue that Kennedy's research is important for an understanding of visuo-verbal poetry because,

> in highlighting the essential role of visuo-spatial cognition in reading, it presents a challenge to what has perhaps been the dominant trend in the psychology of reading... a tendency to think of written texts as appealing primarily to the ear rather than to the eye, and of reading as "surrogate listening". Countering this view, the spatial coding hypothesis reveals that readers do not focus attention exclusively on one word at a time, or read in a purely linear way opposed to the global awareness required in picture perception; rather, global awareness of the arrangement of text on the page is very much built into the reading process — and this applies even in the case of texts where layout is not a salient feature.
>
> (Shingler 2011: 79)

If we approach *"Il Pleut"* from this perspective, then, it is likely, as it is with all Apollinaire's calligrams, that the reader will be simultaneously aware of and affected by the visual arrangement of the words on the page, as well as the meanings of those words as they read.

From a slightly different cognitive theoretical point of view, Turner (2006) has argued, in a relatively brief mention of *"Il Pleut"*, that the simultaneity of experience the poem achieves can be seen as a typical example of "compression", in Conceptual Integration Theory terms (c.f. Fauconnier and Turner 2003). He argues:

> the lines of poetry fall downward at a slant across the page, in a way that we take as a visual representation of rainfall. The visual image of rain, the representational sketch of that visual image, and the verbal expression are mentally blended. The result is emergent structure: a sketch that can be read; writing that provides a visual representation of rain. Perceiving the view of the rain can be blended with perceiving the writing. Moreover, the reader of the text can be blended with the viewer of the rain. The sound of the rain falling can be blended with the voice of the poem. And so on through a range of evocative potential blendings.
>
> (Turner 2006: 18)

This view is also adopted by Freeman, who sees the "iconic reciprocity" of poetry as resulting from "complex conceptual blending" (2020: 65). Freeman argues that the emergent structure that any blended space ordinarily possesses, in cases of poetic iconicity "is the poem itself" (2020: 74). The end result of the blending process, then, is the experience of visuo-verbal simultaneity that these poems create. In the next section, I will argue that this emergent structure depends not only on the blending of visual perception and the conception of verbal meaning, but more specifically on the dynamic quality of this simultaneous experience.

Experiencing "*Il Pleut*"

It is clear from the experimental evidence discussed in the preceding section that readers are capable of retaining an awareness of the global shape of "*Il Pleut*" at the same time as they are attending to its local features. In particular, Navon's (1977) research would suggest that the arrangement of the poem on the page to look like falling rain is likely to be immediately perceivable for most readers with little interference from the individual letters and words which make up the text. By contrast, when readers do attend to the letters and words of the text, their perception and conception of the verbal elements of the poem are likely to be taking place under an ongoing alertness to its rain-like visual appearance. In short, the rain will continue to be present in our consciousness and to interfere with our reading process, even when our visual attention shifts to a more detailed discernment of linguistic meaning.

What is more, Shingler's (2011) pilot study of readers' eye movements around Apollinaire's calligrams found that the majority of participants focused first on a poem's title, before following a more diverse set of visual pathways. In "*Il Pleut*", the likelihood that the title will form a primary point of attention for readers is increased by the much larger, bold type this part of the poem takes, as well as its incongruous position at the top right of the page, away from the rest of the text. From a specifically cognitive-linguistic point of view, the dynamics of a reader's eye movement, from title to text and onwards, is of crucial importance to our understanding of the poem, as are the dynamics of our reading of the rest of the verbal elements of "*Il Pleut*". This is because, as Cognitive Grammar (c.f. Langacker 1987, 1990, 1991, 2008) would argue, the syntactic sequencing of a text is one of the most important foundation stones for its meaning. The order in which our eye travels through the language of the poem, and the order in which its syntax is arranged, structures the construal of the text in the most fundamental way.

In Apollinaire's original French version of the poem, the verb phrase which forms the title, "*Il Pleut*", can be translated into English either as "it rains" or "it is raining", and this phrase is repeated again in the opening of the first line of vertical text. The first thing to note here is that this arrangement of letters vertically on the page immediately slows the reading and comprehension process at the local level. Apollinaire's choice to align the text in this way goes contrary to Western reading practices and thus presents an instant cognitive challenge to readers. The text of "*Il Pleut*" also contains no punctuation and, although there are small spaces between the individual words which make up each vertical line, it is by no means easy to discern where one word stops and another begins, or indeed what each word is. Nevertheless, the repetition of "*Il Pleut*" as the main text of the poem begins can be seen as a kind of emphatic foregrounding technique, ensuring that the theme of rain remains conceptually prominent, from an initial apprehension of the concrete shape of the poem, through the reading of the title, to the movement into the vertical text. In my own translation of the poem, I have chosen to render the title and opening verb phrase as "it is raining", rather than "it rains". French does not have a present continuous tense, so either of these choices is equally possible. However, I feel that "it is raining" in the English present continuous tense lends an immersive persistence to this phrase which is in keeping with the overall conceptual dynamics of the work, which I will discuss further shortly.

The opening of "*Il Pleut*" thus ensures that rain remains profiled and conceptually present, whatever the order in which a reader's eyes may move around the different elements of the poem. This is a markedly different effect from that which Stockwell (2009) argues can be identified in other literary texts, whereby "certain elements in the space distract the reader's attention and others become relatively neglected" (2009:29). Stockwell states that, when this sort of distraction occurs, "A previous attractor can fade from attention simply by lack of maintenance... Alternatively, the attractor can be explicitly negated out of attention and occluded by a replacement figure" (2009:30). Stockwell also argues that an attractor can be maintained or revivified in reader attention through "stylistic invocation or anaphoric co-reference", or "by sustaining the focus or by various non-shift devices" (2009:29). The repetition of the verb phrase, "it is raining", at the start of the vertical text in "*Il Pleut*" can be seen as one such sustaining device, as can the further specific invocations of rain in "it is you who also rains" and "oh droplets" in the second line, and the final repetition of "it is raining" in the fourth line. However, I would argue that our awareness of the rain is retained throughout the entire experience of the poem and not only because of the presence of such textual techniques. Furthermore, I do not consider it to be the case that the rain falls into conceptual neglect, simply because it is not being referred to in the text, or because other figures become profiled. Rather, following Shingler's findings, I would argue that the global shape of the poem continues to interfere with our reading and sustain the presence of the rain as a central cognitive component of our understanding of "*Il Pleut*". This is more than a resonant but backgrounded presence too: it is not merely an echo, but a persistent chord, sounding throughout the verbo-visual simultaneity of the poem and shaping our experience of it primarily and directly.

As the vertical text of "*Il Pleut*" continues, further detail is added to the opening verb phrase "it is raining", as this initial metaphor is developed with the qualification "the voices of women". Again, it is important here how this line is translated, since the sequencing of the syntax affects the poem's construal. In many English translations of Apollinaire's text, "*il pleut des voix de femmes*" is rendered as "it is raining women's voices". In my own translation, however, I have attempted to retain Apollinaire's original syntactic order as closely as possible, since the reader's eye, if following the text vertically, will lead first to "the voices" before these are further specified as being the voices of women. As a result, in "it is raining the voices of women", it is the voices, rather than women, that are syntactically and conceptually profiled and the definite article with which they are introduced adds an assumed familiarity to the description. Despite this, the fact that both the voices and the women are non-specific and plural gives a ghostly quality to their presence in the poem, a ghostliness which is further emphasised by the clause "as if they were dead even in memory" which follows.

From a Text World Theory point of view, this construction creates an epistemic modal-world (Gavins 2007: 110), a hypothetical mental representation which exists remotely from the main text-world of the poem where "it is raining". Interestingly, this modal-world also creates a "cognitive feedback loop", as Lahey (2019) defines it, where information from the remote mental representation directly affects our understanding of the text-world from which it originates. In this case, the epistemic modal-world describes an unrealised situation where the women are dead "even in memory", but this in turn leads to an inference that they are dead in the originating text-world as well. As a consequence, the voices of women which are raining metaphorically around the poetic persona become all the more haunting and disembodied at the close of the first line. It is also possible that this disembodied effect could encourage a further metaphorical interpretation of the presence of "voices" and indeed of "rain" as incarnations of the horrors of trench warfare, from which Apollinaire had only very recently returned before the publication of "*Il Pleut*". It is a small leap to connect the sounds of women's voices, presumably high-pitched, to the sounds of men screaming or groaning, or even to the sound of falling shells. An even smaller leap could plausibly connect the sound and the movement of falling rain to falling bullets.

In the second line of the vertical text of "*Il Pleut*", the first occurrence of a second person address which is repeated several times in the poem appears in the initial verb phrase "it is you also who is raining". Again, I have attempted to stay as close as possible to Apollinaire's original syntactic order here, since once again this order affects the construal of the text and its comprehension. As the eye follows this line down the page, a degree of ambiguity unfolds in a similar manner to how the metaphorical nature of "it is raining the voices of women" emerged letter-by-letter and word-by-word in the first line. At first, the second person pronoun "you" here can be read perfectly grammatically as a having a zero role in a relational state: "it is you". However, the subordinate clause "who is raining", which immediately follows, makes it clear that "you" is in fact the agent in another metaphorical construction. This "you" is closely aligned with "the voices of women" through the use of the adverb "also" and, as a figure, it is similarly linguistically and conceptually under-defined, despite its profiled position in the line. Apollinaire uses the *"vous"* form of the second person in his original text, which can be both a plural address, fitting with the non-specific and plural "voices of women", or a singular formal address. As the line continues, "you" could also be interpreted as referring to "marvellous encounters of my life", another plural noun phrase. According to Herman's (2002) typology of second person pronouns, the "you" in the second line of *"Il Pleut"* might therefore seem at first apprehension to fall into the category of "horizontal address", or address to another member of the fictional world. I would argue, however, that this particular use of the second person pronoun is not confined to the frame of the fiction in this way. Rather, this "you" is "doubly deictic", to use Herman's (2002) terms once more. While it can be read as referring horizontally, either to the "marvellous encounters" of the poetic persona's life, or to "the voices of women", or even to the poetic persona, the global shape of the poem – and specifically the dynamics of reading that shape enforces – can be seen to extend the reference to the real reader of the text in the discourse-world as well. In order to be able to read "it is you also who is raining", our eyes must travel vertically down the page, following the path Apollinaire has defined for the rain-like shape of *"Il Pleut"*. Consequently, we too embody falling rain through our physical bodily movement and the meaning of "it is you also who is raining" becomes double: the "marvellous encounters" and "the voices of women" are raining within the fictional frame, but so are the words on the page in the discourse-world, and so are our eyes as we read. It is in these moments of plurality in *"Il Pleut"* that the lack of punctuation in the text plays its strongest role, since we cannot rely on the disambiguating function of a comma, an upper case letter, a colon, or any other punctuation mark to resolve any referential uncertainty. The letters on the page fall vertically, like rain, one to the next, gradually emerging as words as we read, but remaining diffuse, fluid, and diluting.

The third line of Apollinaire's text begins *"et ces nuages"* and, again, precisely how this noun phrase is translated into English has the potential to affect our experience of the poem. Many English versions render this line as "and those clouds rear and start to whinny a whole universe of auricular cities" (for example, in Greet's translation [Apollinaire 1980]). However, *"ces"* as a demonstrative adjective in French can be translated equally grammatically either as "those" or as "these", with the difference between these two only being clarified with the optional addition of a *-là* (those) or *-ci* (these) suffix to the corresponding noun. Apollinaire does not add such a disambiguating suffix, but in English disambiguation is necessary. In my own translation, I have therefore chosen "these clouds" rather than "those clouds" and this, it could be argued, further encourages an embodied reading of the poem. The proximal deixis of "and these clouds rear and begin to whinny" locates the clouds more closely to the reader's perspective in the text-world, extending and encouraging a doubly-deictic reading of "you" in the second line through into the third. Through this motivated stylistic choice, "you" the reader in the discourse-world are not only addressed by "it is you also who is raining" as you follow the words vertically down the page (a formal address in Apollinaire's original use of "*vous*"), but also continue to be closely aligned to the text-world through the proximal "these" in the next line. The profiling of the clouds also emphasises this proximity: the clouds are strong figures in this construal, represented to seem close to the reader's perspective in the text-world, but also in the discourse-world through the double deixis in the poem.

The fourth line of "*Il Pleut*" begins with another direct address, this time in the form of the imperative verb "listen", which is repeated again at the start of the final line. Text World Theory normally considers these verbs as creating deontic modal-worlds, in which an instruction can be conceptualised as an as-yet-unrealised possibility (see Gavins 2007:98). In the first occurrence of "listen" in "*Il Pleut*", the reader is invited to listen to the rain and also recognise that the rain is occurring at the same time that "disdain and regret weep an ancient music". However, because the imperative verb "listen" is immediately followed by the present tense "it is raining", this emphasises that the rain continues to fall in the text-world, not some distant conceptual space. "Listen it is raining" specifies that it is in the poetic persona's spatio-temporal location that the listening should happen, once again aligning the reader closely with this text-world perspective and returning our attention from the deontic modal-world to its originating conceptual space. Not only does this line use the stylistic device of repetition to remind the reader of the presence of rain in the text-world, but it continues to blur the boundary between text-world and discourse-world by encouraging the reader to implicate themselves in the imaginary world of the poem. At the close of this line, the occurrence of the verb "weep" brings a further reminder of the rain, with "regret and disdain" metaphorically represented as falling water too. It is worth noting here, of course, that in the original French, "*pleurent*" (from the infinitive *pleurer*) has a much more similar spelling to "*pleut*" (from the infinitive *pleuvoir*), creating a more obvious visual connection between weeping and raining.

The final line of "*Il Pleut*", as I have mentioned, repeats the imperative "listen" at its opening. The proximity of this verb to "listen it is raining" for me doubles the effect of the previous line. It once again encourages the reader to project themselves into the text-world, to align their perspective with the poetic persona, and to listen not only for the imaginary sounds of rain and of weeping, but also now of falling bonds. The verb "falling" here is yet another textual echo of the repeated theme of rain in the poem. More importantly, perhaps, it is echoic of the physical downward movement which is not only conceptually represented in the text, but embodied in the global shape of "*Il Pleut*" and in the eye movements we must necessarily make in order to comprehend the verbal elements of the work. In Apollinaire's text, the verb "*tomber*" also immediately follows the imperative "*écoute*", foregrounding the verb and creating momentary ambiguity before the reader learns what or who is falling. It is no accident either, I believe, that Apollinaire chooses to end his text with the further spatial detail "high and low", producing a final textual description of movement from top to bottom. Such descriptions, Talmy (1983, 1996, 2000) has argued, contain a type of implicit movement called "fictive motion" (see also Langacker 1986, 1987). Matlock (2004) provides experimental evidence to show how fictive motion simulates physical movement in the mind during reading, despite its figurative nature. This evidence suggests that metaphorical expression involving motion, which would include the Apollinaire's description of bonds "falling" too, call for a "dynamic representation" (Matlock 2004: 1396) on the part of the reader, which here again echoes the physical movement of rain.

There is a final use of the second person address in this line too, which I would again argue has a doubly deictic function. In my own reading of the text, I interpreted the falling "bonds that restrain you high and low" to be bonds of automatised perception and this closing metaphor to be a metatextual reference to the highly defamiliarising effect of Apollinaire's poem as a whole. In his attempt to create a simultaneous experience in "*Il Pleut*", Apollinaire not only produces a conceptual blend of visual perception and verbal understanding, he forces his readers to adopt a radically different method of vertical reading, the physical demands of which embody the same downward movement of the rain throughout the poem. In order to appreciate the full spectrum of meaning in this work, we must abandon any normative practices of reading we may hold and reshape our understanding of the relationship between word and image and of poetry itself.

Concluding remarks

I have attempted in this chapter to present a discussion of the conceptual effects of Apollinaire's "*Il Pleut*" which follows the principles of cognitively informed, context-sensitive and stylistically detailed analysis which characterised all of Peter Verdonk's published research, as well as his wider appreciation of literary language and visual art. I have also attempted to represent one of the most famous and influential early works of concrete poetry in a translation which remains as true as possible to the poet's original motivated stylistic choices. My reasons for doing this have been not only to honour Apollinaire's creative intentions, but to try to preserve, as well as to demonstrate, the full experiential dimensions of his avant-garde experimentalism. The approach I have taken, both in my translation and my analysis, is underpinned by an understanding of human conceptual processes which adheres to what is known as "the extended mind" theory of cognition (see Clark 2008, Clark and Chalmers 1998).

In the last of my books which I was able to send to Peter Verdonk for his invaluable commentary prior to publication, *Poetry in the Mind: The Cognition of Contemporary Poetic Style* (Gavins 2020), I used the following very helpful summary from Clark (2008) to explain the extended mind and to underline its distinction from a "brainbound" alternative:

> Maximally opposed to BRAINBOUND is a view according to which thinking and cognizing may (at times) depend directly and noninstrumentally upon the ongoing work of the body and/or the extraorganismic environment. Call this model EXTENDED. According to EXTENDED, the actual local operations that realize certain forms of human cognizing include inextricable tangles of feedback, feed-forward, and feed-around loops: loops that promiscuously criss-cross the boundaries of brain, body, and world. The local mechanisms of mind, if this is correct, are not all in the head. Cognition leaks out into body and world.
>
> (Clark 2008: xxvviii)

In my view, Apollinaire's experiments with visuo-verbal simultaneity stand as a model of this view of cognition, as essentially and inextricably dependent both on the wider physical environment and on the nature of our embodied existence in the world. In *Poetry in the Mind*, I made use of the extended mind approach to cognition to analyse the polysensual nature of the performance poetry of Kae Tempest. Apollinaire's poem can be seen as fundamentally polysensual too, albeit in a slightly different way. Where Tempest uses the language of their poetry, their bodily movements, and their voice to shape the perceptions and emotional responses of their audience, Apollinaire makes use of the visual aspects of cognition and attention, as well as the physiological demands of reading to extend the boundaries of "*Il Pleut*" and of his readers' conceptual experience beyond the parameters of text alone. It is useful, at this point, to return to Turner's description of this experience, which I quote again for ease of reference:

> the lines of poetry fall downward at a slant across the page, in a way that we take as a visual representation of rainfall. The visual image of rain, the representational sketch of that visual image, and the verbal expression are mentally blended. The result is emergent structure: a sketch that can be read; writing that provides a visual representation of rain. Perceiving the view of the rain can be blended with perceiving the writing. Moreover, the reader of the text can be blended with the

viewer of the rain. The sound of the rain falling can be blended with the voice of the poem. And so on through a range of evocative potential blendings.

(Turner 2006: 18)

A further "evocative potential blending" which Turner does not list specifically here, but which I have attempted to demonstrate in this chapter is the blending of the reader with the rain itself. Apollinaire does not simply describe falling rain through language. He also does not simply represent it in concrete form. He shapes his poem in such a way that its visual elements, its verbal components, and the reader's physical interaction with both of these enact and embody falling rain throughout. In *"Il Pleut"*, *everything* is raining: "the voices of women", "you", "marvellous encounters of my life", "droplets", "regret and disdain", "the falling bonds that restrain you high and low". Most crucially, the poem itself rains down the page and our eyes, and thus our brains, rain with it. Apollinaire uses stylistic techniques to ensure this enactment and embodiment of falling rain is sustained from our first apprehension of the poem's configuration on the page, to the close of our vertical reading of individual letters and words. The shape of *"Il Pleut"* is does not simply mime the meaning of the text, it enables us to *think through* the text and to use its physical form along with our physiological responses as tools for our extended cognition.

Acknowledgement

I would like to extend my thanks to Dr Wendy Michallat at the University of Sheffield for offering invaluable advice on French translation and early twentieth century French literature during my research for this chapter.

References

Adamson, W. L. 1999. Apollinaire's politics: Modernism, Nationalism, and the public sphere in avant-garde Paris. *Modernism/Modernity* 6(3): 33–56.

Apollinaire, G. 1918. *Calligrammes: poèmes de la paix et da la guerre*. Paris: Mercure de France.

Apollinaire, G. 1966 [1902]. Letter to Karl Boès. In *Oeuvres complètes de Guillaume Apollinaire: Volume 4*, M. Décaudin (ed.). Paris: André Balland & Jacques Lecat.

Apollinaire, G. 1980. *Calligrammes: Poems of War and Peace (1939–1916)* [trans. A. H. Greet]. Berkeley, CA: University of California Press.

Apollinaire, G. 1991. Simultanisme-librettisme. In *Oeuvres en prose completes*, M. Décaudin & P. Caizergues (eds). Paris: Gallimard.

Clark, A. 2008. *Supersizing the Mind: Embodiment, Action, and Cognitive Extension*. Oxford: Oxford University Press.

doi Clark, A. & Chalmers, D. 1998. The extended mind. *Analysis* 58 (1): 7–19.

Fauconnier, G. & Turner, M. 2003. *The Way We Think: Conceptual Blending and the Mind's Hidden Complexities*. New York, NY: Basic Books.

doi Foucault, M. 1983. [1973] *This is Not a Pipe* [trans. J. Harkness]. Berkeley, CA: University of California Press.

doi Freeman, M. H. 2020. *The Poem as Icon: A Study in Aesthetic Cognition*. Oxford: Oxford University Press.

doi Gavins, J. 2007. *Text World Theory: An Introduction*. Edinburgh: Edinburgh University Press.

doi Gavins, J. 2020. *Poetry in the Mind: The Cognition of Contemporary Poetic Style*. Edinburgh: Edinburgh University Press.

Harvey, P. 2024. *Remembering Atwood: Text World Theory and Memories of Narrative Fiction*. PhD dissertation, University of Sheffield.

Herman, D. 2002. *Story Logic: Problems and Possibilities of Narrative*. Lincoln, NE: University of Nebraska Press.

doi Kennedy, A. 2000. Attention allocation in reading: sequential or parallel? In *Reading as a Perceptual Process*, A. Kennedy, R. Radach, D. Heller & J. Pynte (eds), 193–220. Oxford: Elsevier.

doi Kennedy, A., Brooks, R., Flynn, L.-A. & Prophet, C. 2003. The reader's spatial code. In *The Mind's Eye: Cognitive and Applied Aspects of Eye Movement Research*, J. Hyönä, R. Radach & H. Deubel (eds), 193–212. Amsterdam: Elsevier Science.

doi Kennedy, A. & Murray, W. S. 1985. Spatial coordinates and reading: comments on Monk (1985). *Quarterly Journal of Experimental Psychology* 39: 649–56.

doi Lahey, E. 2019. World-building as cognitive feedback loop. In *Experiencing Fictional Worlds*, B. Neurohr & E. Stewart-Shaw (eds), 53–72. Amsterdam: John Benjamins.

doi Langacker, R. W. 1986. Abstract motion. In *Proceedings of the Twelfth Annual Meeting of the Berkeley Linguistics Society*, V. Nikiforidou, M. VanClay, M. Niepokuj, & D. Feder (eds), 455–471. Berkeley, CA: University of California, Berkeley Linguistics Society.

Langacker, R. W. 1987. *Foundations of Cognitive Grammar, Volume 1: Theoretical Prerequisites*. Stanford, CA: Stanford University Press.

Langacker, R. W. 1990. *Concept, Image, and Symbol: The Cognitive Basis of Grammar*. Berlin: Mouton de Gruyter.

Langacker, R. W. 1991. *Foundations of Cognitive Grammar, Volume 2: Descriptive Application*. Stanford, CA: Stanford University Press.

doi Langacker, R. W. 2008. *Cognitive Grammar: A Basic Introduction*. New York: Oxford University Press.

Lockerbie, S. I. 1980. Introduction. In *Calligrammes: Poems of Peace and War (1913–1916)* [trans. A. H. Greet], 1–20. Berkeley, CA: University of California Press.

doi Matlock, T. 2004. Fictive motion as cognitive simulation. *Memory and Cognition* 32: 1389–1400.

doi Nänny, M. 1986. Iconicity in literature. *Word & Image* 2(3): 199–208.

doi Nänny, M. & Fischer, O. 1999. *Form Miming Meaning: Iconicity in Language and Literature* 1. Amsterdam: John Benjamins.

doi Nänny, M. & Fischer, O. 2001. *The Motivated Sign*. Amsterdam: John Benjamins.

Navon, D. 1977. Forest before trees: the precedence of global features in visual perception. *Cognitive Psychology* 9: 353–83.

Shingler, K. 2011. Perceiving text and image in Apollinaire's calligrammes. *Paragraph*, 34(1): 66–85.

Stockwell, P. 2009. The cognitive poetics of literary resonance. *Language and Cognition*, 1(1): 25–44.

Talmy, L. 1983. How language structures space. In *Spatial Orientation: Theory, Research, and Application*, H.L. Pick, Jr. & L.P. Acredolo (eds), 225–282. New York: Plenum.

Talmy, L. 1996. Fictive motion in language and "ception". In *Language and Space*, P. Bloom, M.A. Peterson, L. Nadel, & M.F. Garrett (eds), 211–276. Cambridge, MA: MIT Press.

Talmy, L. 2000. *Toward a Cognitive Semantics: Vol. I. Conceptual Structuring Systems*. Cambridge, MA: MIT Press.

Turner, M. 2006. Compression and representation. *Language and Literature*, 15(1): 17–27.

Verdonk, P. 2005 Painting, poetry, parallelism: ekphrasis, stylistics and cognitive poetics. *Language and Literature*, 14(3): 231–44.

Werth, P.N. 1999. *Text Worlds: Representing Conceptual Space in Discourse*. London: Longman.

CHAPTER 9

Verbal pickles and pickling

A stylistic engagement with Sinéad Morrissey's "Through the Square Window", with help from Philip Larkin and Peter Verdonk

Michael Toolan
Birmingham University

Peter Verdonk championed canonical modern poets from Great Britain and Ireland, and was well aware of how they sometimes composed "in dialogue" with their antecedent peers (Heaney responding to Hardy, for example). Here I speculate on how he might have admired poems by Sinéad Morrissey, even though she appears in one poem to reprimand the great Philip Larkin for his seeming sexism. I offer some (I hope) Verdonkian stylistic commentary on Morrissey's "Through the Square Window", while also suggesting that Verdonk's reminders about context-variability and historical circumstances are important in a charitable reading of Larkin's "Born Yesterday".

Keywords: deixis, Philip Larkin, Sinéad Morrissey, poetry, sexism, stylistics, transitivity

In the rumination that follows, I will attempt a triangulation among three poems, one by Philip Larkin and two by Sinéad Morrissey (but focussing on just one of the latter), while adopting the general approach to stylistic analysis that Peter Verdonk argued for so eloquently. In the course of this verbal *randonnee*, questions of context, sexism, and "real world reference" will arise.

Peter Verdonk championed the stylistic analysis of modern poetry — poems almost invariably from Britain or Ireland and by anthologised poets likely to remain in the canon: Hardy, Owen, Auden, Larkin, Plath, Hughes, and Heaney. My chapter looks at a poem by a contemporary poet whose work I hope Peter would have agreed stands comparison with the aforementioned: Sinéad Morrissey. I will aim to incorporate some of Peter's insights on stylistic analysis (particularly in his monographs *Stylistics* 2002 and *The Stylistics of Poetry: Context,*

https://doi.org/10.1075/lal.44.09too

Cognition, Discourse, History 2013) in a commentary on "Through the Square Window" and how I would try to read and appreciate this poem, stylistically, with others.

Where to begin? Perhaps with one of Peter's literary greats, Philip Larkin, and a poem he wrote in 1954 to celebrate the birth of his close friend Kingsley Amis's third child, Sally. The poem is entitled "Born Yesterday", which may have been literally but fleetingly true at the time of composition, although its idiomatic echoes thereafter can hardly be ignored (someone who says of themselves or someone else that they "weren't born yesterday" intimates that they are not hopelessly naïve about the tricksy ways of the world). It may be worth noting that this is a fairly early Larkin poem, coming before the publication of *High Windows* and *The Whitsun Weddings*. Owing to multiple permissions costs I cannot reproduce the poem in full; it is, however, readily viewable on many internet websites featuring Larkin's poetry, including a YouTube recording of Larkin himself reading it.

Addressing baby Sally in the second person, Larkin's poem begins by explaining he won't wish for her "the usual stuff// About being beautiful", adding that if she should come to enjoy such good fortune "Well, you're a lucky girl". If however she isn't so lucky, Larkin instead wishes she may be ordinary, averagely-talented, without the exceptional gifts that could "pull you off your balance" and cause everything in her life to be undermined. And he ends with this startling and controversial envoi:

> In fact, may you be dull —
> If that is what a skilled,
> Vigilant, flexible,
> Unemphasised, enthralled
> Catching of happiness is called.

Youngish bachelor Larkin's wish that Sally should not be "pulled... off balance" and, if not exceptional, should aim to be dull got Sinéad Morrissey's dander up. Even sixty years later, "dull" is pejorative at the best of times; in addition, dullness as an encapsulation of all that is derivative and uncreative in art echoes through the English literary canon from Alexander Pope. Wishing dullness on Amis *fille* sufficiently provoked Morrissey that she wrote a spirited poem of rejoinder, "On Balance", about Larkin's misogyny and her own young daughter. This begins:

> Even fully-grown, she'd be a girl to you
> You rarely mention women, except to stress
> Our looks or what we cannot do

And concludes:

> I wouldn't let you near
> my brilliant daughter —
> so far, in fact, from *dull,*
> that *radiant, incandescent*
> are as shadows on the landscape
> after staring at the sun.
>
> (Morrissey 2017:11)

In 1983 Larkin re-published his essay "The Pleasure Principle", first published in the less enlightened 1950s, around the time "Born Yesterday" was composed. In this essay he lays down the law as to the writing of a poem:

> It consists of three stages: the first is when a man becomes obsessed with an emotional concept to such a degree that he is compelled to do something about it. What he does is the second stage, namely, construct a verbal device that will reproduce this emotional concept in anyone who cares to read it, anywhere, any time.
>
> (Larkin 1983:80)

The third stage is "successful reading", wherein readers — ideally of all sorts — "recreate" in themselves what the poet felt. All three stages are interdependent and necessary. As Verdonk also notes, Larkin himself later wrote with some scepticism about his "three stages" explanation of poetry-writing: "my working definition defines very little: ... it leaves the precise nature of the verbal pickling unexplained". The phrase "verbal pickling" is lovely, self-deprecating and homely, even if it only partly fits (items consumed after pickling do not taste just as they would have done before the process; pickling is conserving with alteration).

But the phrase in Larkin's fairly orthodox formulations that attracts my attention is the gendered and ageist one: "a man". Reading these lines in 2023, it's hard not to feel that "a man" excludes or disregards women and children as poets. Perhaps this is more objectionable than the uses of "girl" and "dull" in "Born Yesterday" that so offended Morrissey? Still, in any debate over Larkin's sexism outwith and sometimes within his poems, it's worth noting Peter Verdonk's reminder:

> It is an established fact that language in use, that is discourse, is governed by a wide range of contextual factors, which may extend from the phonological, grammatical and semantic context (sometimes designated as the co-text) to broader contexts such as the situation within which the discourse occurs, the identities, beliefs, attitudes of the participants and the relations holding between them. Even more broadly, readers might also take into account any social, psychological, historical or cultural contexts if these prove to have a bearing on the act of communication.
>
> (Verdonk 2013:81)

These cautions as to the diversity and unpredictability of the contexts within which a reader may make sense of a poem are worth bringing to the Morrissey poem I now wish to focus upon, "Through the Square Window".

> In my dream the dead have arrived
> to wash the windows of my house.
> There are no blinds to shut them out with.
>
> The clouds above the Lough are stacked
> like the clouds are stacked above Delft.
> They have the glutted look of clouds over water.
>
> The heads of the dead are huge. I wonder
> if it's my son they're after, his
> effortless breath, his ribbon of years —
>
> but he sleeps on unregarded in his cot,
> inured, it would seem, quite naturally
> to the sluicing and battering and parting back of glass
>
> that delivers this shining exterior.
> One blue boy holds a rag in his teeth
> between panes like a conjuror.
>
> And then, as suddenly as they came, they go.
> And there is a horizon
> from which only the clouds stare in,
>
> the massed canopies of Hazelbank,
> the severed tip of the Strangford Peninsula,
> and a density in the room I find it difficult to breathe in
>
> until I wake, flat on my back with a cork
> in my mouth, stopper-bottled, in fact,
> like a herbalist's cure for dropsy.

To start with the poem's title, we might wonder about the emphasis on the window being square. If Peter were commenting, he might well alert us to some of the connotations of "square": honesty, trueness, a kind of strength and suitedness (lacking in things built "not square" and therefore "out of true", lacking also in those who are not "being square" with us). I don't think (and therefore discount the idea that) Morrissey also has in mind the dated slang meaning, "overly traditionalist, uncool, unadventurous", but there you have the subjective selectivity of text analysis acknowledged.

Formally, it is possible that the title is nodding towards the 12-line not-quite-sonnets of Seamus Heaney, who championed "squarings": poems or sequences of poems, comprising four three-line stanzas. If so, the eight three-line stanzas here would be two squarings; in which case is there a detectable completion after the first twelve lines, some kind of *volta* at the start of the second putative squaring? I would say not, although between them lines 12 and 13 beautifully manage the shift of attention from the speaker's baby boy sleeping peacefully to the young man outside (the "blue boy") working his magic on the window.

I have always proposed that readers of a poem begin, before attempting anything more detailed in the way of analysis or evaluation, with a first reaction as to what the situation depicted in the poem seems to be; what the poem seems to be about.

The situation of this poem seems unambiguously a dream, a dream experienced by the speaker, who sees "the dead" coming to wash the windows of her house. Almost at once the focus shifts from the window and the window-cleaners to the clouds that the speaker looking out through an unscreened window might see. The speaker's sleeping infant son is equally vividly pictured; strictly, we now have a dream within which the dreamer's child lies sleeping. But the detail with which we are told how the cleaner goes about "sluicing and battering and parting back of glass// that delivers this shining exterior" is so expressive and particular that the poem's "dream" context fades — or we adjust what the speaker means by "dream", to be a way of talking about something powerfully imagined. And while the deictic orientation was earlier that of someone within the house, looking out, the description of "this shining exterior" implies an abrupt deictic shift, as if we and the speaker are now regarding the house from outside. These are dream-world sudden shifts, but a core of realism or naturalism is maintained, only dropping away in the final stanza: in stanza 5 one of the window-cleaners is called a "blue boy" working like a magician, while stanzas 6 and 7 return us to the view, now unimpeded by the intruding heads that were there in stanza 3, and that view is quite specific, being of Hazelbank and the Strangford Peninsula. Suddenly we are firmly situated somewhere north of Belfast.

Commentators have noted the watery imagery in the poem: the lough, the clouds, the washing, the dropsy (an archaic name for the condition where someone has puffy or swollen limbs owing to fluid retention). But while these are present, they do not seem agentive in the sense of water being the source of threat (e.g., by drowning) to the speaker or their baby. Rather the lightly-sketched narrative arc is one where the "invading dead" turn out to be transient window-cleaners, so that on their departure the distant horizon discloses "only clouds" and nothing more threatening. But on their first appearance those window-cleaners are undoubtedly threatening, their presence an allusion to the traditional washing of windows when someone in a house dies. As for the reported lack of blinds that might exclude these unwelcome visitors, this may obliquely allude to the final line of Wilfred Owen's "Anthem for Doomed Youth", and the traditional marking of a death in the family: "each slow dusk a drawing-down of blinds".

How might Peter have tackled this poem? Judging by his commentary in his OILS book on Stylistics, he would very likely have sought to identify particular foregrounded verbal features of the poem, linking them to possible effects they might give rise to in readers, on the assumption that the features and indeed the effects have been carefully considered by the writer, that the features were carefully chosen, as part of an artistic design. None of that goes on in a social or cultural vacuum, removed from social and material circumstances, he would have emphasised; rather the whole business is shaped by context, genre, and purposes, and these are constantly evolving. And continually open to debate.

In 2022 the poet Simon Armitage made a series of programmes for BBC Radio 4 exploring Larkin's influence today. Introducing the series, Armitage said he wanted to "road-test" Larkin's poetry at a time when it was sometimes being removed from British secondary education exam board syllabuses, implicitly deemed no longer relevant to contemporary British culture and sensibilities. "Born Yesterday" was one of the ten poems Armitage reconsidered in detail; this included discussing with Sinéad Morrissey her versed objections to it in her own poem, "On Balance". Armitage asks Morrissey if she thinks Larkin would have worded "Born Yesterday" quite the way he did if the poem had been addressed to a newborn boy, and she believes that he would not, and that his attitude to women generally is problematic. Nevertheless she describes many of Larkin's other poems as numinous and transcendent; and even in "On Balance" she recognises the beauty in the final lines of the Larkin poem, noting "your dazzling // final turn from lack // to grudging benediction".

But the sexism, for Morrissey, is clear and inexcusable. As a grown man of thirty-one, Larkin should not have addressed Sally Amis as "lucky girl", since by the time she would have become gifted and beautiful (or not) she would be a woman and should be so addressed. Even if Larkin were to have protested that he was speaking to the baby and not the imagined grown woman (hence the simple present, "you're a lucky girl", rather than the more glaringly objectionable future-reference "Well, you'll be a lucky girl"), the suspicion of sexism would probably remain. After all, we know Larkin had form. It may also be worth noting two famous poems, with their own sexist or gender-marked tendencies, that may have been intertextual influences on Larkin as he composed his poem for Sally. One is Kipling's "If", where the speaker advises a boy to keep a level head in all sorts of trying circumstances, for then "you'll be a Man, my son!". The other is Yeats's "A Prayer for my Daughter" (the latter may be part of the intertextual background of "Through the Square Window", uncannily: it too begins with the speaker fearing the natural world, a howling storm, threatens the safety of his sleeping child in her cradle). Above all Yeats wishes his daughter will be kind and courteous, and free of any type of hatred, that disfigurer of beauty. But his final stanza prays that her bridegroom will bring her to a house "where all's accustomed, ceremonious", in the richest senses of custom and ceremony; this assumed dependence on male agency is surely contentious, but seems to have received little opprobrium.

And did Sally grow up to be dull in that special sense Larkin described, the person who is effortlessly a catcher of happiness? Or did she in time enjoy some of the "usual stuff" that other more orthodox — one might even say dull — well-wishers might have nominated? Sadly, it seems her life moved in a far darker direction. A Wikipedia entry on her reports that she struggled continually with alcoholism and that her writer brother Martin thought her a victim of feminism's incomplete sexual revolution, which, he controversially contended, promised sexual freedom but left the naïve unfit to cope with the consequences. The character of Violet Nearing in his novel *The Pregnant Widow* (published in 2010, but set around 1970) is based on her. Sally suffered a stroke at the age of 40 and died of an infection six years later, in 2000. Unsurprisingly, others have rejected Martin's diagnosis; some have pointed to Kingsley's separation and divorce from Hilary, Sally's mother, in Sally's childhood as more of an influence than something as abstract as feminism. (Kingsley married Elizabeth Jane Howard in 1965, they divorced in 1983, and in an interesting reversal he spent his final years sharing a house with Hilary and her third husband.)

In airing this background, are we still within the ambit of the "context" of Larkin's "Born Yesterday" poem? Context has no sharp or permanent borders. If you google "Sally Amis", one of the hits takes you to the website of the poet and retired Oxford English professor Lucy Newlyn. In 2019 Newlyn posted a poem responding to Larkin's, inflected by what we know of the real Sally Amis. Her poem ends as follows:

> Sally Amis, manic depressive,
> you died of alcohol, at the age of forty-six.
> The blessing of your father's friend,
> full of love and hope,
> was no earthly use to you
> as you lived your sad, promiscuous, addicted life.
> Can we conclude from this
> that unhappiness is catching?

Perhaps the obviously uncanny, even disturbing, element in Morrissey's "Through the Square Window" speaks to Peter Verdonk's suggestion about the essential purpose of reading literature (Verdonk 2002: 12). He argues that because literature does not directly refer to the world but provides a representation of it (the author's richly partial, stance-taking version of the world) "it enables us to satisfy our needs as individuals, to escape, be it ever so briefly, from our humdrum socialized existence, to feel reassured about the disorder and confusion in our minds, and to find a reflection of our conflicting emotions". And he adds that if all this is true, "we might conclude that the function of literature is not socializing but individualizing". Verdonk immediately turns to analysing a Hardy poem, "Neutral tones", which contains the astonishingly modern couplet "The smile on your mouth was the deadest thing// Alive enough to have strength to die". He notes particularly Hardy's personification of inanimates as clause agents and subjects, and the relative absence of humans as clause subject, despite the poem's implicit topic being a couple's relationship. After a solitary "We" subject at the poem's opening, all the discursive weight suggests that the couple are separating, no longer compatible, that their relationship has turned wintry, and undergoing a terminal withdrawal, like the grey leaves and wintry sun surrounding them.

What would Peter Verdonk have said about the transitivity and agency in "Through the Square Window"? I suspect he would have admired the density of activity it reports, the washing and stacking and sluicing (a dynamic verb on almost every line), the continual coming and going of participants, the room Morrissey finds for the uncertainties of modality (the "I wonder if" and "it would seem"), the rich blend of material and relational processes. But perhaps like me he would have paused and puzzled over those ultra-strange final lines, when the nearly-stifled dreamer awakes, to find themselves

> flat on my back with a cork
> in my mouth, stopper-bottled, in fact,
> like a herbalist's cure for dropsy.

This taxes our powers of interpretation, of naturalising, raising minor questions as well as larger ones. Among the former, what purpose does the "in fact" serve, when we know that a purely "factual" or literal interpretation is deeply implausible? And is "stopper-bottled" a well-formed compound? Bottles have bottle-stoppers, sometimes this is indeed a cork, but what can it mean for the speaker's mouth, or anything else, to be stopper-bottled, if this means "bottled by a stopper", just as home-bottled means "bottled at home"? There seems to be multiple moments of semantic slippage here: no kind of bottle, whether real or the human body as a metaphorical bottle-like container, can be a cure for dropsy, as the text seems to imply. Only the bottle's unmentioned contents can.

Would Peter Verdonk have liked "Through the Square Window"? I am certain he would, and by no means only because he must have many a time noticed how the clouds were stacked above Delft, even if he was unfamiliar with the Strangford Lough which the speaker looks out on. A speaker who seems to be situated a few miles north of Belfast, perhaps in Newtownabbey. Why do I speculate in this way, you complain? Because the speaker name-checks Strangford peninsula, the lough, and Hazelbank: they started it! A speaker who is probably a woman, possibly Sinéad herself, but let us presume neither. But a speaker who sees the arriving bodies — heads, especially — as clouds filling their view of the outside world framed by the window. So much like clouds that the word appears four times in the poem. The poem creates a three-way conflation of the faces of the ghostly dead, the window cleaners, and clouds: one of these turns into another unpredictably, as in a dream.

So were Sinéad and her infant son actually visited by real window cleaners; or is this poem something dreamt (up) in the course of a disorienting but vivid nap? It doesn't matter. What I want to remark on now may seem to you to be tangential to the point of irrelevance. But it's the sort of uncanny coincidence that I can't or won't ignore (coincidence being another word for context, which Verdonk always recognised as relevant but infinitely variable and subjective). At the time of composing this essay, I was tasked with installing blackout roller blinds in our guest bedrooms, to placate our infant grandchildren whenever they stayed overnight with us and (according to their parents) could not sleep (day or night) except in total darkness. By contrast in the poem I learn that Sinéad (if it is she) has her baby son asleep beside her in his cot, in a room with no blinds to shield him from cloudy ghosts on the hunt — or from the chance arrival of "radiant, incandescent" sunlight, for that matter. What to conclude? Unfussy parenting, or that Northern Irish babies are made of sterner stuff, or something else?

It is hard, perhaps absurd, to remove entirely the (auto)biographical aspect of much poetry: the conviction, for example, that Larkin is the "I" in "Born Yesterday" and that the poem is about the Amises' new baby daughter. Or that "Through the Square Window" is in the first instance a dream of Morrissey involving her son, the seeming vulnerability of babies, window-cleaners, clouds over Strangford Lough, and so on. Or, of course, that when in another poem Morrissey writes "I wouldn't let you near my brilliant daughter", she is the "I", and "you" is Philip Larkin. Even when a poem's implicit speaker and addressee are all dead (Larkin, Sally Amis, Kingsley Amis), the referential element persists — although it may help to think of this, as Peter Verdonk proposed, as world-representing rather than world-referencing.

Conclusion

In this discussion of *some* of what I *imagine* Peter might have said about "Through the Square Window" and "On Balance" and "Born Yesterday", I have focussed on context, and context might be felt to be peripheral to stylistic analysis, part of the unbounded and unmanageable hinterland that surrounds the thing itself, the thing being the text, and all that's in it, the one object we can hope all readers will have access to, even if they've never heard of Sally Amis or Strangford Lough or Delft. But Peter Verdonk was acutely aware of the significance of context, as reflected in the sub-title of his 2013 book on the stylistics of poetry, where it is named as one of the four strands that are (must be) woven into stylistic analysis — indeed, the first-mentioned element, and one in which at least two of the other three elements, cognition and history, are deeply implicated. The context in which a reader apprehends a poem must be deeply affected by whatever historical understanding they see as relevant, while that reader's mental processing of the poem will be equally deeply shaped by their own culture and identity. As a result, in the assessments of a number of critics (quite possibly reflecting the reactions of many readers), various sociocultural contexts so strongly colour reactions to the alleged misogyny of calling someone "a lucky girl" and praising a special kind of dullness (on the one hand), that the poem as a whole no longer receives a fair hearing. Likewise reactions to the alleged misandry and inattention to co-text that prompts the rejoinder "I wouldn't let you near my brilliant daughter" can trigger a general hostility to Morrissey's work that loses sight of its quality (see, e.g., Robinson 2017 and Healey 2020 for further discussion).

If poetic licence still means anything, it should urge us to invoke context in a spirit of generosity, of reserved judgement. Take that "I wouldn't let you near my brilliant daughter", the she-wolf defending and celebrating her cub as proudly and fiercely as Yeats did his (and as Larkin might have his, had he been so blessed). One context we should be wary of is the overly literal reading. At least one critic has checked the dates and pointed out that Larkin (ob. 1985) was at rest in Cottingham municipal cemetery long before Morrissey (born 1972) is likely to have produced any children, so that literal nearness in this world is entirely moot. Others point out Morrissey is being hypothetical or counterfactual ("wouldn't", not "won't"), so the complaint of unfairness stands.

For my part, I cannot shed the conviction that, a crafter of brilliant lines himself, Larkin would have loved the pithy protective hostility of "I wouldn't let you near my brilliant daughter". He might equally have understood why Morrissey then swerved away from that blunt vernacular to describe her daughter's brilliance in an extended and hard-to-process figure that stands comparison with Larkin's parallel redefinition of "dull" in the unpredictable final lines of "Born Yesterday". In fact Morrissey's final lines are so clearly intended to match Larkin's that I would interpret them as a form of homage to Larkin, notwithstanding the earlier lines' sharp critique.

Acknowledgement

I am most grateful to Carcanet Publishers, for permission to quote from Sinéad Morrissey's collections published by them in 2009 and 2017.

References

Armitage, S. 2022. Larkin Revisited. Released 12 August 2022. URL: https://www.bbc.co.uk/sounds/brand/m0019yy2

Healey, N. 2020. The lustre in dullness: Philip Larkin, Sinéad Morrissey, and Balance. In *Wild Court*, September 2020. URL: https://wildcourt.co.uk/the-lustre-in-dullness-philip-larkin-sinead-morrissey-and-balance/

Larkin, P. 1955. Born Yesterday. In *The Less Deceived*. London: The Marvell Press.

Larkin, P. 1983. The Pleasure Principle. In *Required Writing: Miscellaneous Pieces* 1955–1982. London: Faber.

Morrissey, S. 2009. *Through the Square Window*. Manchester: Carcanet.

Morrissey, S. 2017. *On Balance*. Manchester: Carcanet.

Newlyn, L. 2019. "Sally Amis". URL: https://lucynewlyn.com/sally-amis/

Robinson, S. 2017. Review of *On Balance* by Sinéad Morrissey. *The Scores*, Issue 3, Winter 2017. https://thescores.org.uk/on-balance-by-sinead-morrissey/

Verdonk, P. 2002. *Stylistics*. Oxford: OUP.

Verdonk, P. 2013. *The Stylistics of Poetry: Context, Cognition, Discourse, History*. London: Bloomsbury.

CHAPTER 10

Bob Dylan's world of words
Beginning to map the linguistic terrain

Gerard Steen
University of Amsterdam

This chapter asks how Bob Dylan's lyrics can be analysed as motivated style. It examines the output of Wmatrix for six of Dylan's most appreciated albums across four decades, taking a close look at quantitative patterns of overuse of semantic fields in comparison with a small reference corpus of American English. Findings are discussed in terms of similarities and differences between Dylan's lyrics and published written general American English, both between the two sets of data as a whole and for each album by itself. Questions about motivated style are addressed against the background of general language patterns, register, and style. In this way, the chapter offers a specific picture of how stylistic analysis of Bob Dylan's world of words can be made more precise in future stylistic research.

Keywords: Bob Dylan, language change, lyrics, register, style, language variation, Wmatrix

Peter and Bob, *bien étonnés de se trouver ensemble*

My training as a researcher in language and discourse started in 1976 with what soon became known as "stylistics": in my second year as a bachelor student of English language and literature at VU University Amsterdam, we worked through Geoffrey Leech's *A Linguistic Guide to English Poetry* (1969), and this laid one important part of the foundations of my academic attitude. I did not take this course with Peter Verdonk, because he worked at "the other university", i.e., the University of Amsterdam, but it might just as well have been him who lit that small flame. Paying tribute to that Dutch connection here is a privilege I cherish.

The occasion offers an opportunity to address a long-standing interest: the attempt to come to terms with the lyrics of Bob Dylan in a way that I can connect with my expertise in language and discourse. I was happy to see how this could work for Richard Thomas in his inspiring *Why Dylan Matters* (2017), which is a

https://doi.org/10.1075/lal.44.10ste
© 2025 John Benjamins Publishing Company

truly personal-cum-professional account of the relation between Dylan and the classics (and much more). I am not sure how Peter would have felt about Bob's Nobel Prize for Literature: the total difference in personalities might have surprised Peter about my conjunction of the two of them in this place. But I am convinced that he would have been open to engage with an analysis like this, if only because it also offers a framework for examining some of the most beautiful metaphors in the English language, like:

> I'm going out of my mind,
> Oh, with a pain that stops and starts
> Like a corkscrew to heart
> Ever since we've been apart.   From "You're a big girl now" (*Blood on the tracks*)

With a career spanning over 60 years and 40 studio albums comprising well over 500 songs, there simply is too much to analyse. I will zoom in on six highlights across four decades, from 1965 until 2006. Opinions about Dylan's work vary just as much as its quality, but most adepts would probably favour a number of highlights that are not in dispute (although *The Cambridge Companion to Bob Dylan*, by Dettmer 2009, has a different emphasis). Dylan would not have become Dylan if he had not produced his first three electric albums in 1965 and 1966, of which I take *Highway 61 Revisited* (1965) and *Blonde on Blonde* (1966) as the absolute top. After that, Dylan's career has had a number of remarkable ups and downs, the peaks of which appear at something like ten-year intervals: *Bood on the Tracks* (1975), *Oh Mercy* (1989), *Time out of Mind* (1997), and *Modern Times* (2006). All of these albums represent Dylan at his best, and they are all clear products of deep musical and poetic renewal over four decades.

There is substantial variation between these five moments in time. The two 60s albums are revolutionary and unique in the history of popular music and have reset the agenda for scores of musicians. Ten years later, *Blood on the Tracks* is one of the most beautiful albums about love and its loss that I know. The turn to *Oh Mercy* came after a long period of radical personal and artistic crisis and is a form of fragile liberation that to me was and still is baffling. *Time out of Mind* shows an existential musical engagement with growing older and the end of life that is in stark contrast with the attempt to stay forever young that is currently exhibited by many of Dylan's colleagues. And *Modern Times* seems to wrap this development up in a gesture that may precisely point to the opposite, actually covering all times (cf. Thomas 2017: 242).

These are reductive verbal attempts to capture what is happening on each of these albums. They are not just meant to point to the lyrics, but to the songs and albums as a whole, to the changes in Dylan's physical and personal voice, and what they may have meant to generations of listeners. They point to a great variety of situations and moods, and this is clearly essential for their language use. And as with many great writers, there are problems of text and of performance: lines have been "stolen"; composition processes have been complex; beautiful songs have been left off albums; lyrics have been adjusted in performances; and musical renderings have dramatically varied across the years. In this context I will be pragmatic and use the text versions as they can be obtained from the web site *Bob Dylan Lyrics* (https://www.azlyrics.com/d/dylan.html).

Another side of Bob Dylan is that he can be notoriously flippant as a commentator about his own work. This can make it difficult to be as serious about his words as you would like to be as a linguist, especially when you want to consider his words as "motivated choice". This is another way in which Bob and Peter are each other's opposites. But that is precisely what makes it worth the effort.

The idea that style may be one appropriate way into this variation and its effects seems natural. I here want to emphasize that style is just one perspective, and that it is not meant to be the most important or representative one. This is true of the role of style in any literary (or even non-literary) text, as I am sure Peter would acknowledge. And it is certainly true of an artist like Bob Dylan, as has also been implied by the close study of all of the albums included here by for instance Christopher Ricks in his well-known *Dylan's Visions of Sin* (2004). Style is just one dimension of text and the way it is produced and received in a discourse event (Steen 2011).

The idea that style may be seen as motivated choice is less natural, or at least more problematic. To me, style is how selections and combinations are made from the available repertoire of language structures, functions, and use, and how these selections and combinations exhibit distinct, idiosyncratic patterns that can be related to (and contrasted with) more general patterns of language use. Dylan speaks, writes, and sings in a particular way, and how does this compare with his contemporary colleagues? The point is, however, that all of this is usually based on habits. Yet not all habits, in everyday life or in writing artistic works, are motivated, or, perhaps more pertinently, remain so. For instance, some choices clearly are more deliberate than others, and this raises many issues about local and general motivation (see also Biber and Conrad 2009). I have written about some of these issues in my work on metaphor (e.g., Steen 2023), and the relation between functions, intentions, deliberateness, consciousness, and motivation is much too complex to go into here.

Moreover, to many there is barely a difference between style and content. The works about Dylan that I have seen barely discuss style, spending all the more time on content. There is even one publication about Dylan that proclaims "The form is the message" (Lloyd 2014), a risky title about the work of an artist who is a little sceptical if not cynical about "messages". Lloyd focuses on text and discourse rather than on language use, but he basically conveys an often shared attitude about style and content. When Thomas (2017) writes about Dylan in terms of the classics, or Ricks (2004) in terms of sin, they write about content through language use, and this is where I can connect, not as a "Dylanologist" but as a Dylan linguist.

What I will do, then, is something rather superficial, quite literally so. I will carry out a limited, narrow form of linguistic analysis and look at just one aspect of the surface of Dylan's texts, his use of words. I hence largely ignore many other aspects of style in fiction (Leech & Short 1981), including grammar, verse and text form, and schemes and tropes. I will do this by means of an automatic tool to help me in ordering my first impressions in order to examine how this approach can help in developing a more concrete view of Dylan's style.

In particular, I will count words, word classes, and semantic fields by means of Wmatrix (Rayson 2008). This is a web interface that analyses frequencies of these three phenomena in any specific set of texts and compares their distribution against distributions in another corpus that can be chosen at will and functions as a frame of reference (see https://ucrel.lancs.ac.uk/wmatrix/). This allows the detection of relative overuse in the group of texts under investigation.

Such data can reveal interesting aspects of language variation in and between the five selected points of time (with six albums) in Dylan's career. They might help to demonstrate how Dylan's styles have changed over time. In fact, this is what another corpus-linguistic approach to Dylan's work has hinted at as well: Khalifa (2007) presents an inventory of prominent words and word classes within a much bigger selection of Dylan's work, and has some interesting details that in future work can be easily combined with my data. My study, complemented with Khalifa's (2007), could therefore be a beginning of a map of the linguistic terrain that includes some high-quality artistic texts that have been hugely significant in many ways in modern culture. I hope Peter would have appreciated this too.

Overall approach

I will use *Highway 61 Revisited* as my introduction to the method of analysis. The obvious way to utilize Wmatrix here is by examining the words, word classes, and semantic fields utilized by Dylan in comparison with their regular distribution across American English. Style is not just a matter of *how* things are expressed, for instance grammatically, but also what, exactly, is expressed. Using different aspects of vocabulary to convey states of affairs in some imagined world clearly contributes to building a style.

One way to examine this aspect of style is hence by means of automated analysis and comparison with some reference corpus. Wmatrix includes a small corpus for this purpose, which it describes as follows: "966,609 words from published general written American English, also using the same sampling frame as the LOB and FLOB corpora". The label of the corpus suggests that sampling was focused on or at least completed in 2006. In this section I will use this corpus as a base line against which I will compare Dylan's use of words, word classes, and semantic fields in *Highway 61 Revisited*. This will enable me to become more precise about the approach in the rest of the study.

The most informative way to get started is to examine which semantic fields are overused by Dylan in comparison with the small reference corpus. According to Wmatrix, these are the top ten overused semantic fields for *Highway 61 Revisited*, ordered by magnitude of deviation: Pronouns (Z8); Negative (Z6); Moving, coming and going (M1); Evaluation: Good (A5.1+); Sad (E4.1-); Entire, Maximum (N5.1+); Kin (S4); Time: Present; simultaneous (T1.1.2); Clothes and personal belongings (B5); and Speech: Communicative (Q2.1). This is based on the automated analysis of roughly one million words in the reference corpus of published general written American English versus 3183 words in the album's lyrics. All of my analyses are available from the Open Science Framework site built for this particular study (see https://osf.io/wrfvj/)

Percentages range from a contrast between 18.00 percent "Pronouns" in the Dylan album versus 8.76 percent in the reference corpus, on the one hand, to a contrast between 0.16 percent for "No Knowledge" in the album versus 0.04 percent in the reference corpus, on the other. Absolute numbers are as follows: for pronouns, there are 573 items labelled "Pronouns" (out of 3180 words) in the album versus 84,722 cases (out of approximately one million words) in the reference corpus. For "No Knowledge", there are 5 cases out of 3183 words in the album versus 360 cases out of approximately one million words in the reference corpus. Odds Ratios are also easy to obtain, showing that the chance of a "Pronoun" occurring in the Dylan album is 2.29 times higher than in the reference corpus, and that the chance of a "No Knowledge" item occurring in the Dylan album is 4.22 times higher than in the reference corpus. Variation is great in more than one way.

In all there turn out to be 22 semantic fields that display a statistically significant relation between incidence in the album versus incidence in the reference corpus. This is 22 fields out of a total of 453 distinct fields and sub fields. The other fields also display variation between the two sets of data, but this falls within the limits of chance and is therefore not distinctive of one or the other corpus.

The distributions of the semantic fields correlate with two other sets of results that are also generated by Wmatrix. This is because semantic fields are attached to words, and words are grammatically divided into word classes. Thus, the semantic field "Pronouns" had 573 cases, which showed 148 occurrences of the lexical item *you*, 53 times *I*, 48 times *he*, 37 times *she*, and so on. In total there were 31 different types of personal pronouns, with rather varying distributions of distinct occurrences (tokens). These range from the highest type *you* to the six lowest types that each had just one token only: *mine, himself, yourself, we, neither, everyone*. This distribution of distinct lexical items related to distinct semantic fields is clearly also related to the distribution of specific word classes in *Highway 61 Revisited*, where second person pronoun is 153, and so on. Semantic fields, words, and word classes present different aspects of the same encompassing information about language use, but in different forms of linguistic detail, which each have their own subtle role to play.

What these figures suggest is a way of talking about Dylan's language use and possibly style that comes from a more general approach to all language use. For instance, this analysis suggests that there may be more interest in Dylan's lyrics on this album than in published general writing in the fields (and perhaps topics and themes) of time, movement, people, and their personal belongings and emotions and speech. This figures with some of Dylan's best albums, having titles like *Highway 61 Revisited, Blood on the Tracks, Oh Mercy, Time out of Mind*, and *Modern Times*. It may even look self-evident or trivial.

But who could have predicted that it was precisely *these* fields that are overused in this particular album, and not another selection of the many possible expressions of Dylan's topics and themes, across albums with these specific but different titles? Will it prove to be a constant component of Dylan's style that he overuses all of these concrete motion verbs and speech verbs? How does he express which aspects of emotions (sadness in *Highway*, blood in *Blood on the tracks*) and which aspects of time? For instance, there are the two album titles of *Time out of Mind* and *Modern Times*, while there are 32 occurrences of *time* across all six selected albums. One of them is "time is a jet plane, it moves too fast" (from "You're a big girl now", *Blood on the Tracks*), and another one is "and time is running backwards, And so is the bride" (from "Ring them bells" on *Oh Mercy*). And then there is the chillingly beautiful song "Most of the time" (*Oh Mercy*):

> Most of the time it's well understood
> Most of the time I wouldn't change it if I could
> I can make it all match up
> I can hold my own
> I can deal with the situation right down to the bone
> I can survive and I can endure
> And I don't even think about her
> Most of the time

How should all this be seen in terms of style, and how is it motivated, precisely? This clearly takes us from language use to discourse events, and requires multidimensional analysis.

What is valuable, therefore, is that the Wmatrix analysis shows how Dylan's themes are expressed in specific selections and combinations of words from the generally available language system. The approach also offers a precise way to compare these lyrics with other texts that seem to do the same, something similar, or something different. Is this configuration of data Dylan, or does this also happen in the lyrics of his colleagues Joan Baez and Joni Mitchel, or his contemporaries, Leonard Cohen or Neil Young? The list could be extended ad infinitum.

This is the kind of data that can easily seem overwhelming, confusing, or alienating; they need to be interpreted with close attention to the overall picture, as well as with consideration of relevant detail. But there is nothing strange about this. In fact, this is precisely what most stylisticians consider in informal but highly expert ways when they attempt to establish stylistic profiles for a work, an author, or a school of writing. What quantitative description and statistical analysis have to offer is to make all of the details explicit, related to each other in consistent ways, and evaluated against some norm of chance. There is no human eye that can keep track of the dozens of groups of words in dozens, hundreds, and even thousands of occurrences across hundreds of lyrics in the same way.

Some of these scores do not necessarily say much about Dylan's style. They instead reflect a more general difference between published general written language use, on the one hand, and language use that belongs to the genre of lyrics, on the other. What we have here is in effect a comparison between many instances of a register, or language variety (the reference corpus), which covers many more specific genres, on the one hand, and ten instances of one specific genre (Dylan's songs on this album) and hence its language use, on the other.

Dylan's lyrics instantiate one genre of discourse that is a form of poetic fiction, typically displaying characteristics of story-telling and drama (Biber 1988, 1989; Biber & Conrad 2009). "Published general written" language use comprises the words of many different genres, and probably does not include lyrics. This fact can explain a large part of the higher proportion of some of the top ten deviations in Dylan's semantic fields (and their concomitant lexico-grammatical manifestations): for instance, "Pronouns" are an essential part of the drama that is typically part of fiction in the form of narrated conversation or in the form of dialogue between poet and addressee in lyrical poems. And "Speech: Communicative" involves verbs like *say, talk, speak,* and *mention,* needed for narrating who speaks and says what to whom. In place 20 of the rank ordered overused fields of the album, and still statistically significant, there is the "Discourse Bin", having almost twice as many expressions that are typical of spoken interaction like *all right, right, you know* and so on than in published general writing. It is hence not necessarily the songwriter Dylan and his style that can account for some of these patterns: they are more properly interpreted as largely to be expected in the general variety of language use exhibited by the genre of lyrics. How this relates to "motivation" is not immediately clear.

At the same time, it may still be true that Dylan's language use shows more characteristics of spoken interaction than is usual in pop lyrics in general. We would need another basis of comparison, however, for assessing this particular aspect of his song writing. We would need a large set of written published language that is not general but comes from other such lyrics. This is not available here.

What we can do, however, is this: we can examine how semantic features differ across time in relation to the same reference corpus. We can do this by, firstly, taking all six albums together and see them as a small corpus representing the best of Dylan's work, comparing them against the reference corpus as one whole. We can also, secondly, take each album separately and see how it varies from the reference corpus by itself; this is a series of six comparisons across time, showing variation between the six albums over time. (And we could also, thirdly, do a small series of different comparisons, examining each time whether one album exhibits a specific style that is different than its predecessor. This would always bring out different deviations from one comparison to the next, because the comparison always involves a different pair of albums. But I will leave this for another occasion.)

All in all then, using Wmatrix to get a grasp of just one aspect of Dylan's style in *Highway 61 Revisited* is a rather complex business. This is not because of the program or the statistics, but simply because doing a stylistic profile of even just one part of one author's work or works is a complex undertaking. The following sections present a beginning with how this can be tackled successfully. It should be noted that this is done on the basis of slightly edited texts, in which informal spellings of words that are not recognized by Wmatrix have been adjusted.

Variation in semantic fields: Register and genre

For the overall analysis, the data and their analysis and interpretation are as described above. This time, however, I am looking at all lyrics from the six albums combined, amounting to a mini-corpus of 20,568 words, and comparing them against the Wmatrix reference corpus for published general written American English of almost one million. The output shows that there are no fewer than 59 semantic fields that are significantly overused by Dylan in the lyrics of these six albums combined (see https://osf.io/wrfvj/) when this is compared to published general witing in American English. This is no surprise given what we saw for *Highway 61 Revisited* above.

The biggest overused field is "Pronouns", comprising 3941 words (19.16%, versus 8.76% in the reference corpus, with an Odds Ratio of 2.47). The smallest is a field with just two citations, called "Comparison: Unusual": this represents 0.01% of the data in Dylan, versus less than 0.00% in the reference corpus, with an Odds Ratio of 15.67. "Pronouns" is easy to understand, "Comparison: Unusual" has the following two cases:

> Then he walked up to a <u>stranger</u>
> And he asked him with a grin
> "Could you kindly tell me friend
> What time the show begins?"
>> From "Lily, Rosemary, and the Jack of hearts", *Blood on the Tracks*

> Last night I danced with a <u>stranger</u>
> But she just reminded me you were the one
>> From "Standing in the doorway", *Time out of Mind*

These are two mistakes by the Wmatrix system: it has taken *stranger* as the comparative form of *strange* instead of two instantiations of the noun, which it does do correctly for the third occurrence of *stranger* in the corpus (in "If it keeps on raining, the levee's gonna break", from *Modern Times*). I will attend to this immediately.

An initial, global impression of all of the output displays several features.

1. Problematic aspects as with *stranger* in "Comparison: Unusual" also occur in other fields. For instance, "Evaluation: Good" is hugely dominated by the occurrence of the sentence or discourse adverb *well*, which is not really related to "Evaluation: Good" (114 out of a total of 164 cases; 1 type out of a total of 15 types). The category of "Existing" combines existential *be* with the copula *be* and the auxiliary *be*, which have nothing to do with existing (there are 729 cases in this field in total, with nine other occurrences that do not come from the verb *to be*). And the semantic field "Time: New and Young" is entirely based on *baby* used as a form of address or reference to somebody's beloved, which only has a metaphorical root in time (1 type with 30 cases). There are a few other fields where things sometimes go wrong, too.

2. The following overused fields belong together for another reason: "Pronouns", "Time: Future", "Negative", "Discourse Bin", "Existing", "Likely", and "If"; they all account for lexico-grammatical aspects of language use by means of pronouns, modal verbs ("Time: Future", "Existing", and "Likely"), sentence adverb *no(t)* and conjunction *if*.

3. Fields like "Moving, coming and going", "Weather", "Anatomy and Physiology", "Sad", "The Universe", and "Damaging and Destroying" group together vocabulary in a way that is much more semantically oriented. These fields range from quite varied groups of words, as happens in "Moving, coming, and going", with 144 types and 470 tokens in Dylan, through "Knowledgeable", with 13 types and 164 tokens in Dylan, to even less varied ones, as in "Exclusivizers/Particularizers", which has just three types (*just, only, alone*) covering 147 occurrences in Dylan (117 times *just*, 18 times *only*, and 12 times *alone*, respectively).

Here is how I have managed this diversity of data. First, I have examined all semantic fields for errors of the magnitude that were reported above for the first group. I have reinterpreted "Existing" as belonging to the second, lexical-grammatical group. The role of five other fields in the various comparisons in my opinion is misleading, and correcting the analysis by Wmatrix is not simple to do. This is why I have left them aside.

The second, lexico-grammatical group is important for the determination of the register of our texts (Biber 1988, 1989). Almost all of these lexico-grammatical fields are in the first dozen places in the rank order of 59 overused fields. This demonstrates their magnitude and suggests their ubiquity in overuse. Lexico-grammatically, Dylan's language throughout is indeed closer to spoken interaction and to fiction than to published general writing, which is to be expected. This group deserves closer scrutiny when comparing one album to the next, or when examining Dylan's development over time, which may clearly also contribute to a description of his style; but that is for another study, which may be undertaken against the background of the findings that follow.

The third group of semantic fields is the group that most manifestly reflects variation in text content, and this may substantially contribute to variation in style. It exhibits two specific features that need immediate attention for achieving a more nuanced global picture. The first feature can be introduced by examining the field of "Weather". This has 21 types and 74 occurrences. It is special because the concordance of this field shows that not all types and tokens are equal: there are eight citations of *wind* from the song "Idiot wind" (*Blood on the Tracks*), four citations of *thunder* from "Thunder on the mountain" (*Time out of Mind*), and 11 citations of *raining* from the song "The levee's gonna break" (*Modern Times*). This makes for 23 cases for 3 types that cannot be compared on an equal footing with all other citations, because they involve this overt form of repetition. Types but especially tokens here are due to the typical verse form of songs.

It turns out that this phenomenon of repetition affects 11 semantic fields in our big third group, involving more than a dozen songs. The occurrences in each of these semantic fields are largely due to one or sometimes two songs, so that this field cannot be seen as part of the general style of Bob Dylan; instead, it is more properly seen as part of the specific style of one particular song. For instance, consider the repetition of *stone* (20 incidences out of a total 27, in "Food") and *stoned* (5 occurrences out of 6, in "Excessive Drinking") in the song "Rainy day women #12 & 35" (*Blonde on Blonde*). Their use is basically limited to this song when considering our entire selection of Dylan's lyrics. This clearly is a local phenomenon in the Dylan corpus. This is even more so because of the ironic opposition between the two uses:

> Well, they'll stone you when you're tryin' to be so good
> They'll stone you just like they said they would
> They'll stone you when you're trying to go home
> Then they'll stone you when you're there all alone
> > But I would not feel so all alone
> > Everybody must get stoned

A similar pattern can be found for the semantic field of "Selfish", where the type *conceit* has 13 occurrences out of a total of 22, simply because of the repetition of the title phrase *the disease of conceit* (*Oh Mercy*).

Things can get complex here. Thus, the word *broken* explains practically half (35 out of 78 occurrences) of the size of the semantic field "Damaging and destroying". This is because of its relentless repetition in the song "Everything is broken" (*Oh Mercy*). Here is the opening of the song:

> Broken lines, broken strings
> Broken threads, broken springs
> Broken idols, broken heads the line
> People sleeping in broken beds
> Ain't no use jiving, ain't no use joking
> Everything is broken

There are 21 other forms of the verb *break* than the past participle. This includes 11 times the line "If it keeps on raining, the levee's gonna break" (*Modern Times*). However, the other types in this field of "Damaging and destroying" exhibit a seemingly fair enough range of items that are each represented by just one or two tokens. This suggests that the one song "Everything is broken" was not coincidental and entirely unique but, instead, one powerful expression of a persisting concern of Dylan's with the theme of damage and destruction.

Yet closer inspection shows that this is incorrect. Separate analysis of each of the six albums shows that "Damaging and destroying" is overused only in *Oh Mercy* and in *Modern Times*, clearly because of the two songs mentioned just now. Its use is not significantly greater than chance in *Blonde on Blonde* and in *Time out of Mind*, and it is absent from *Highway 61 Revisited* and from *Blood on the*

Tracks. I therefore eventually consider "Damaging and destroying" to be more like the one-song case than to be of general concern across all albums.

A similar question arises for the field "Sad", where the word *sad* itself occurs 15 times in "Sad eyed lady of the lowlands" (*Blonde on Blonde*), and *desolation* ten times in "Desolation Row" (*Highway 61 Revisited*). There remain 53 other tokens from this field, divided over 23 types, and these turn out to be overused and spread over the other songs and almost all albums. This is different than with "Damaging and destroying". Indeed, the only album where the use of "Sad" is not significantly more than expected is precisely *Blood on the Tracks*: this is supposed to be one of the saddest albums Dylan ever released because of the supposed connection of the lyrics with Dylan's loss of his marriage with Sara Lowndes. Our finding about lack of overuse of "Sad" here, whereas it is constantly overused in all other albums, raises interesting questions about how that sadness in *Blood on the Tracks* does get expressed. It also raises the question whether that sadness indeed is the dominant feeling, or whether it is for instance anger that may be more important (e.g., in "Idiot wind").

Another case is *world* in the field "Universe", which occurs 11 times in the repeated line "We live in a political world" (*Oh Mercy*), but is then spread across another 30 occurrences in the rest of the lyrics. This appears to be significant overuse in the last three albums, while it is not significant in *Blood on the Tracks,* absent from *Blonde on Blonde,* and non-significant in *Highway 61 Revisited.* These are data that may point to a more general interest on the part of Dylan that may be growing over time. The style in one song, then, can be more focused on hammering a message home with just one word, whereas elsewhere there can be related, systematic stylistic variation. It suggests that my study here is indeed just a first step.

The second special feature in the big third group is the fact that there is another sub group, which is quantitatively just as important. This sub group is characterized by the feature that a semantic field is represented mostly by just one or two words. For instance, "Exclusivizers/Particularizers" is almost completely about *just* (117 out of 147); "Time: General" is here restricted only to occurrences of *ever* (28 out of 28); half of "Time" is to do with *never* (38/74) and the other half with *time(s)* (35/74); "Sensory: Taste" largely figures *sweet* (14 out of 16), but exclusively in a metaphorical sense, which might have to shift it to the field of emotions; "Lack of food" exclusively comprises five occurrences of *hungry* and one of *hunger*; and "Psychological actions, states and processes" is based on 12 times *mind*, one time *minds*, and one time *trance*. Depending on where one draws the line, this set includes about a dozen of semantic fields in the third big group that are based on just one or two words. This may constitute important details in describing Dylan's language use and style, especially because of their frequent role as intensifiers, creating more urgency, involvement and passion in many of the lyrics. But these are small and specific functions in comparison with the bigger fields that I will attend to now.

If we ignore for the moment the more particular sets of fields involving repetition or foundation in a single word, it turns out that the remaining core set of about 25 overused semantic fields in our big third group can be ordered quite coherently in relation to each other. Here is a list of the most prominent fields, descending in order of magnitude, numbered for convenience: (1) "Moving, coming and going"; (2) "Weather"; (3) "Anatomy and physiology"; (4) "Sad"; (5) "Universe"; (6) "Knowledgeable"; (7) "Time: Present; simultaneous"; (8) "Location and direction"; (9) "Relationship: Intimacy and sex"; (10) "Music and related activities"; (11) "Sensory: Sight"; (12) "Trying hard"; (13) "Parts of buildings"; (14) "Clothes and personal belongings"; (15) "No knowledge"; (16) "Sensory: Sound"; (17) "Like". This list comprises the first 17 core semantic fields.

Here is a coherent interpretation of what can be seen in the list. Dylan's writing constructs a world of words where people move, come, and go (1) with their bodies (3) in particular clothes (14). This happens in places (8) involving parts of buildings (13) and weather (2) in an encompassing universe (5) in the present time (7). This involves people's feelings that are often sad (4), people's thinking including knowing (6) and forgetting (15), people's sensing of seeing (11) and hearing (16), and their social activities like music (10) and efforts of trying hard (12), especially in their relationships with others in terms of love (9) and affection (17). The first cluster is the concrete individual, the second cluster is their concrete and more encompassing environment, and the third cluster is their psychological and social experiences. The degree of coherence between all of these aspects within one general scenario is quite natural and almost too good to be true.

This is a linguistic construction of human life by the songwriter that simultaneously highlights some aspects while leaving others in the background. In particular, the focus is on the movements of individuals in their concrete environment with their basic psychological and social experiences in rather general terms. By the present data, what is not highlighted (according to Wmatrix) is Arts and crafts (C), Food (F), Government and politics (G), Money (I), Life and living things (L), Numbers (N), Substances and materials (O), Education (P), Linguistic actions, states, and processes (Q), and Science and technology (Y). Dylan could have overused any or many of these semantic fields to talk about the world that he sings in his songs, and he has done so on occasion, but he has not as a general rule. Instead, he has chosen two fields from "Emotions" (Sad; Like), two from "Motion" (Moving, coming and going; Location and direction), two from "World" (Weather; the Universe), and no fewer than five from "Psychological states and processes" (Knowledgeable; Sensory: Sight; Trying hard; No knowledge; Sensory: Sound). A little lower down the list of significantly overused general semantic fields we also see more occurrences of other sub fields having to do with time.

The above picture is Dylan's semantic signature in comparison with published general written American English. Richard Thomas' *Why Dylan Matters* has many quotations from the songs that could be linked to this and explained by this more general pattern of semantics, but there is no more space here to go into this in detail. Instead, here is how Thomas summarizes his own view of Dylan's writing towards the end of his book: "Much of his genius has been to capture the pain of separation in space and time. That is the essence of folk music and of the blues, in which memory of the past is what helps create song" (2017:248). Separation means moving, coming and going, into converging and diverging locations and directions, at various points of time, between lovers who are sad and damaged or destroyed, who know, do not know, and forget or do not forget, all the time trying hard to keep going, somehow.

This is all part of the tradition of music Dylan is part of, as is made over-explicit in his songs in many ways. If we look at the overused semantic fields, they concern what can be seen and heard, but this then needs interpretation. It reminds me of the way Hemingway writes, one of Dylan's great examples, as becomes clear from his Nobel lecture, where he also says: "We can only see the surface of things. We can interpret what lies below any way we see fit" (quoted in Thomas, 2017:315). In the next section I will exploit this structure to point out what variation and possibly change there is in its development from one album to the next.

From variation to change

The findings in the previous section constitute an abstraction across six albums, which were chosen to represent the best of Dylan in 40 studio albums across 40 years. This has turned out to yield a neat semantic picture of Bob Dylan's language use, with the first 17 fields of the core fields cohering in one understandable scenario. But it also works as if there has not been any variation or change in this work across the four decades between 1965 and 2006. It is a picture that people might use when they discuss Dylan as an artist in contrast with other, more or less comparable artists. It works as an image of Dylan's language use against even bigger abstractions, including the register of published general written American English and the genre of the lyric in modern popular music.

But it is also possible to use Wmatrix to provide a little more detail to this global image and get a little closer to historical reality. We can do separate analyses of each of the six albums in comparison with the reference corpus — as we already saw for *Highway 61 Revisited* above. This involves doing six distinct comparisons which each display a particular configuration of the bigger picture that emerged from all of the albums together just now, and to which each album contributes in its own way. Focusing on the semantic fields relating to the profile constructed above, there should therefore be considerable overlap between this analysis and the previous findings; however, since that was an abstraction, it may also be expected that there are substantial differences.

In other words, in this section I will explore another set of questions. Which semantic fields featuring in the big picture above can be found in which album in which way? Can we perhaps observe a pattern of development across the decades, some semantic fields becoming less prominent over time while others begin to take more space in Dylan's semantic universe? How can these patterns be interpreted?

We already know that all six albums combined in one corpus have 59 overused fields. But it appears that the total number of distinct fields overused in all six separate analyses together adds up to 80 (see https://osf.io/wrfvj/). On average each separate album has 24 semantic fields that are overused in comparison with the reference corpus. These include the four fields that I have classified as flawed and the seven lexico-grammatical fields that are the basis of the big register differences.

Of the 80 overused fields, there are only two that are overused in all six albums, "Pronouns" and "Moving, coming and going", and one is overused in five ("Negative"). In fact, the bulk of the 80 overused fields in these six analyses is unique to a particular album. There are 47 fields that are overused in only one album each. There are another 12 that are overused in just two albums. This does not mean that these fields were absent from the other albums (although this is possible too): these 47 plus 12 fields were overused in one album and sometimes two, but elsewhere they were often part of what may be expected of the language of the lyrics in comparison with the language of the reference corpus. It appears that the spread of the more content-related overused semantic fields, which make up the basis of the semantic profile constructed at the end of the previous section, is a little idiosyncratic.

Table 1 shows how each album performs in the use of the 17 crucial semantic fields building the semantic profile discussed in the last section. These fields are ranked in their order of magnitude emerging from the global analysis of all six Dylan albums combined, discussed in Section 4. Table 1 shows what position each of these semantic fields has in the rank order of overused fields for each individual album in the separate analyses. When a field is not overused, the table says "n.s.", for not significant. When the field is absent from an album, no position is indicated.

Table 1. Positions within the rank order for each album of the 17 top semantic fields of overuse in entire Dylan corpus in comparison with American English corpus; I = "Individual", E = "Environment", PSE = "Psychological and Social Experience"

Semantic field	Dimension	Highway	Blonde	Blood	Mercy	Time	Modern	Total
Moving, coming and going	I	3	9	17	26	2	3	6
Weather	E	–	n.s.	3	23	8	5	4
Anatomy and physiology	I	n.s.	19	5	20	12	11	5
Sad	PSE	5	6	n.s.	14	25	17	5
The universe	E	n.s.	–	n.s.	3	18	10	3
Knowledgeable	PSE	n.s.	14	6	n.s.	16	n.s.	3
Time: Present; simultaneous	E	8	15	–	18	n.s.	25	4
Location and direction	E	n.s.	21	14	25	n.s.	n.s.	3
Relationship: Intimacy& sex	PSE	–	n.s.	n.s.	n.s.	5	n.s.	1
Music and related activities	PSE	13	7	n.s.	n.s.	–	n.s.	2
Sensory: Sight	PSE	n.s.	20	19	22	n.s.	n.s.	3
Trying hard	PSE	n.s.	22	–	n.s.	7	n.s.	2
Parts of buildings	E	n.s.	18	15	n.s.	22	–	3
Clothes and pers belongings	I	9	17	n.s.	n.s.	–	n.s.	2
No knowledge	PSE	22	n.s.	n.s.	n.s.	n.s.	22	2
Sensory: Sound	PSE	–	n.s.	n.s.	23	17	n.s.	2
Like	PSE	–	n.s.	9	–	n.s.	19	2
Total		*6*	*11*	*8*	*10*	*10*	*9*	

Thus, in the second row, for "Weather", we see absence for the first album, use that is not significantly greater than in the reference corpus for the second album, while the other four exhibit overuse of "Weather" to the extent that it ended up in position 3 for *Blood on the Tracks*, 23 for *Oh Mercy*, 8 for *Time out of* Mind, and 5 for *Modern Times*. In this way, variation can be observed between all albums or groups of albums in several ways.

First of all, five albums converge on selecting on almost ten semantic fields from our above list of 17. *Highway 61 Revisited* has a rather lower number, six. Since this album was written in the same time as *Blonde on Blonde*, this cannot be a period effect. In fact, *Highway* is the album with the least properties of the general profile detailed above, while *Blonde on Blonde* is its opposite and has the highest number. In a sense, they are each other's complements. Whether the difference is big enough to set the albums somewhat apart from the others in this way is a question for further research.

Overall, the 17 top fields that are overused in my complete Dylan corpus jointly explain a lot of what is happening in each of the albums separately too (even though each selection of almost ten fields for overuse is different). The picture of overused fields per album explains how the albums are constant but still quite different, emphasizing distinct details from the same scenario, as may be seen from the following overview:

> *Highway 61 Revisited* constructs a world of words where people move, come, and go (1) in particular clothes (14). This happens in the present time (7). This involves people's feelings that are often sad (4), people's thinking including forgetting (15), and their social activities like music (10).

> *Blonde on Blonde* constructs a world of words where people move, come, and go (1) with their bodies (3) in particular clothes (14). This happens in places (8) involving parts of buildings (13) in the present time (7). This involves people's feelings that are often sad (4), people's thinking including knowing (6), people's sensing of seeing (11), and their social activities like music (10).

> *Blood on the Tracks:* people move, come, and go (1) with their bodies (3). This happens in places (8) involving parts of buildings (13) and weather (2). This involves people's thinking including knowing (6), people's sensing of seeing (11), especially in their relationships with others in terms affection (17).

> *Oh Mercy:* people move, come, and go (1) with their bodies (3). This happens in places (8) involving weather (2) in an encompassing universe (5) in the present time (7). This involves people's feelings that are often sad (4), and people's sensing of seeing (11) and hearing (16).

> *Time out of Mind:* people move, come, and go (1) with their bodies (3). This happens involving parts of buildings (13) and weather (2) in an encompassing universe (5). This involves people's feelings that are often sad (4), people's thinking including forgetting (15), people's sensing of hearing (16), and their social efforts of trying hard (12), especially in their relationships with others in terms of love (9).

Modern Times: people move, come, and go (1) with their bodies (3). This happens involving weather (2) in an encompassing universe (5) in the present time (7). This involves people's feelings that are often sad (4), people's thinking including forgetting (15), especially in their relationships with others in terms of affection (17).

Against this backbone, other semantic fields that are locally overused stand out and fill out the semantic profile of a specific album in one way or another. For instance, in our first look at *Highway 61 Revisited* in Section 2 we saw that there was overuse of "Kin" and "Speech: Communicative", and these may be responsible of part of the specific style of the album.

Secondly, the frequency of overuse of each semantic field across the six albums becomes less great as we go down from the top. "Moving, coming and going" is the only field that is overused by all six albums. From here, we go down through sets of five, four, or three albums overusing a semantic field to eventually pairs of albums doing so. This is the reason why it makes sense to construct a semantic core against which the use of other fields fills out different aspects of that core in different configurations per album.

One of these fields is "Music and related activities": it is overused only in *Highway* and in *Blonde on Blonde*. It is noteworthy that Dylan, who is well-known for his concern with different traditions in music, also in his lyrics, made this over-explicit in his two revolutionary albums of the sixties only. After that, he kept this theme at a more regular level. Is this a matter of a change in style?

There is only one semantic field that is overused just once: "Relationships: Intimacy and sex", in *Time out of Mind*. This is a semantic field that is dominated by the word *love*, and it is striking that this word and field are not overused in other albums, too. Moreover, *Time out of Mind* has the reputation of being concerned with ageing and the approach of the end of life, but our finding here suggests that this is intimately linked to memories of love. Dylan is a love poet of the first order, but it appears to be part of his style that this theme is not emphasized by overusing the lexical item *love* or even the related more general semantic field. This may hence need specific stylistic attention, both regarding the general tendency as well as the exception in *Time out of Mind*.

Thirdly, looking at patterns of overuse across albums, we can ask whether there are groupings of selected semantic fields that are overused in early or late work. Overused semantic fields that are limited to early work are "Music and related activities" and "Clothes and personal belongings": these fields are both overused only in the first two albums, *Highway 61 Revisited* and *Blonde on Blonde*, and then become less prominent. Similarly, "Location and direction" and "Sensory: Sight" are overused in three consecutive albums beginning with *Blonde on Blonde*, but do not appear as such in the last two albums (although "Location and direction" is almost significantly overused in *Time out of Mind*). Vice versa, there are four fields that are overused in later works while they did not appear before: these are "Weather" (four last albums), "Anatomy and physiology" (four last albums), "Universe" (three last albums), and "Sensory: Sound" (*Oh Mercy* and *Time out of Mind*). All in all, there are eight out of 16 fields that suggest a period of high and another period of low use. These eight are relatively equally spread in high versus low use across early and late decades. The question arises whether this is a matter of complementation in the use of distinct types of content, one set of fields going up while another goes down.

Fourthly, and finally, another question is how the patterns of overuse relate to the three clusters identified in the previous section within the encompassing semantic profile for all content. In other words, how are semantic fields chosen from the clusters that I labelled "individual", "environment", and "psychological and social experience"? There are three "individual" fields, and almost all albums select two out of three, while *Blonde on Blonde* has all three. The individual looks like a stable starting point for Dylan's world of words in each album.

There are five "environment" fields, and four albums select three. One selects just one (*Highway 61 Revisited*) and one selects four (*Oh Mercy*). It would be interesting to see in further research if this underuse (in *Highway*) or overuse (in *Mercy*) of "environmental" content is a characteristic of the contrast between these two albums as a whole. Perhaps *Oh Mercy* is less concerned with the individual and more with people's relation with or dependence on the environment, which may include the world and the universe and even the supernatural.

The "psychological and social experience fields" are nine, and they vary between the selection of three to five fields in different albums. There are two albums with five: *Blonde on Blonde* and *Time out of Mind*. In this context, selecting only three out of nine "experience" fields looks a little meagre in comparison with the selection of on average two out of three "individual" fields and of on average three out of five "environment" fields, and this may again be a perspective from which to examine more closely the nature of the four albums in question (*Highway 61 Revisited, Blood on the Tracks, Oh Mercy,* and *Modern Times*).

Variation in the language of Bob Dylan involves numerous variables. There is variation over time, per album, per song, and this variation can be observed in the overuse or lack of it in a number of core dimensions of his semantics, having to do with the depiction of individuals, their environment, and their psychological and social experiences. Each of these dimensions is realized by distinct semantic fields which are overused or not as a particular album requires. The classification and terminology of Wmatrix has revealed a number of patterns in the data that can form the basis for further analysis and interpretation. More research is needed to bring all this together in more encompassing configurations that can be linked to other research.

Style as motivated choice

Stylistic analysis is all about comparing proportions of the distribution of language categories in a particular body of work and then interpreting their functions. This even applies to analyses of single cases and the function of their incidence in a line, a sentence, or a paragraph. This is because single cases do or do not stand out against backgrounds of vast amounts of knowledge of language use in discourse events, and this is to do with proportions and interpretation of functions. In this study I have attempted to make explicit one small part of these backgrounds, in order to determine a first glimpse of the patterns of language use in a selection of Bob Dylan's lyrics.

I have employed a reference corpus of published written American English to establish a norm of language use against which the lyrics of Dylan could be examined. Such a register is a category that includes the language use of many different genres (Biber 1988, 1989; Biber & Conrad 2009), whereas Dylan's work is a set of texts that are all lyrics exhibiting a variety of language use that is more or less common to all lyrics. The "more or less" is what distinguishes Dylan's language use from his colleagues, but they all share a way of using language that is typical of song writing. This is one register as opposed to many others that can be constructed at will, including "published general writing". The differences between Dylan's language use on the one hand and the reference corpus on the other, revealed by Wmatrix, therefore do not necessarily pertain to style but to register.

Moreover, Dylan's differences from his colleagues can simply be seen as a matter of their individual employment of the register of the modern pop lyric. His long-standing relation with the folk and blues traditions, moreover, makes his use more specific in comparison with other song writers who do not have such an interest. However, that does not mean that Dylan's use of these traditions is his style — again, they are part of the register of all blues and folk songs, and there is variation in that tradition, also in terms of their language use. So the question begins to emerge where register ends and style begins.

In how far this type of choice is motivated is a moot point. Language use involves making choices, but these may be completely unconscious or *ad hoc* ones. Different text versions over time point to more conscious decisions, just like *verbatim* quotations from other works, and these would presumably be more explicitly motivated, but motivated by what, exactly? The point of my exploration has been to emphasize that there are numerous dimensions of discourse that are involved in the details of language use, and it may be quite hard to track their relationships. At the same time it is clear that choices within the constraints of a register can become increasingly prominent in either overuse or underuse depending on their quantity or degree of deviation. This is one foundation of style.

A set of semantic fields like this is language use. Even if it helps to express, it does not capture what is happening at the level of text content (fiction), text type (narrative), and text form (lyric) which can be identified in a genre-regulated discourse event (writing, performing, or listening to a song). Discourse is another level of analysis than language use (Steen 2003, 2011, 2023). This is not just illustrated by the argument in Thomas but also in other works on Dylan such as Ricks (2004).

Yet language use does offer a starting point for appreciating Dylan's verbal picture of the world. It also offers a starting point for measuring how this picture of the world has varied and perhaps even changed over time, different selections of overuse of semantic fields creating different emphases per album against perhaps a background of a relatively constant concern with "the pain of separation in space and time". This interaction between linguistic and discourse analysis may be developed, tested, refined, and applied in many different ways, but then it first needs to get validated a little better than can happen here.

References

Biber, D. 1988. *Variation Across Speech and Writing*. Cambridge: Cambridge University Press.

Biber, D. 1989. A typology of English texts. *Linguistics*, 27(1), 3–43.

Biber, D., & Conrad, S. 2009. *Register, Genre, and Style*. Cambridge: Cambridge University Press.

Dettmer, K. J. H. 2009. *The Cambridge Companion to Bob Dylan*. Cambridge: Cambridge University Press.

Khalifa, J.-C. 2007. A semantic and syntactic journey through the Dylan corpus. *Oral Tradition*, 2(1), 162–174.

Leech, G. N. 1969. *A Linguistic Guide to English Poetry*. London, New York: Longman.

Leech, G. N., & Short, M. H. 1981. *Style in Fiction: A Linguistic Introduction to English Fictional Prose*. London, New York: Longman.

Lloyd, B. 2014. The form is the message: Bob Dylan and the 1960s. *Rock Music Studies*, 1(1), 58–76.

Rayson, P. 2008. From key words to key semantic domains. *International Journal of Corpus Linguistics*, 13 (4), 519–549.

Ricks, C. 2004. *Dylan's Visions of Sin*. London: Canongate books.

Steen, G. J. 2003. "Love stories": cognitive scenarios in love poetry. In J. Gavins, & G. J. Steen (Eds.), *Cognitive Poetics in Practice*, 67–82. London: Routledge.

Steen, G. 2011. Genre between the humanities and the sciences. In M. Callies, W. R. Keller, & A. Lohöfer (Eds.), *Bi-Directionality in the Cognitive Sciences: Avenues, Challenges, and Limitations*, 21–42. Amsterdam: John Benjamins.

Steen, G. J. 2023. *Slowing Metaphor Down: Elaborating Deliberate Metaphor Theory.* Amsterdam: John Benjamins.

Thomas, R. F. 2017. *Why Dylan Matters.* London: William Collins.

Afterword

Sonia Zyngier

"Painting is silent poetry, and poetry painting that speaks"
(Attributed to Simonides in Plutarch's *Moralia*)

It was a fresh and clear spring day when John Benjamins editor Kees Vaes and Peter Verdonk met to discuss the idea of launching a series on language and literature. If, for a moment, we revisit that morning on April 29th, 1999, we might witness Peter's firm defence of this new book series in his usual calm and gentle tone. The initial title was to be *Literature and Discourse* and, in line with *Language and Literature,* the journal already being published by Sage, it would aim at publishing books and monographs on linguistic methods bringing to light different aspects of literature and other discourses. It would comprehend discourse analysis, experimental psychology, psycholinguistics, computational linguistics, cognitive poetics, sociolinguistics, rhetoric, and philosophy. To bring the project to life, Peter established partnership with Gerard Steen and Willie van Peer and launched *Linguistic Approaches to Literature,* a long lasting and productive series. The first volume, a collection of essays at the interface of linguistics, literary studies and cognitive science, inaugurated the series more than twenty years ago (Semino & Culpeper 2002). In over 20 years, the editorial responsibilities have shifted hands but the series continues sound and steady, now counting with over 40 volumes, with still more in line.

In the same year the series was inaugurated, Verdonk published *Stylistics* (2002). One of the strengths of this introductory book, according to Studer (2002), was the concision and flexibility of the chapters, followed by further reading, which he considered "an intelligent way of organising a complex field such as stylistics, [allowing] the reader to pick and choose what s/he finds interesting or relevant". A practical guide to stylistics, this publication offered a broad overview of the area. In 2013, Verdonk published a more complex book, *Stylistics of Poetry* (2013), a selection of his papers written throughout thirty years of work. Both these volumes are seminal to the area of stylistics and a must in the bibliography of courses which focus on the interface between language and literature.

The series project is only one of the many examples of the generosity, positive thinking, and constructive criticism that have characterized Verdonk's career.

https://doi.org/10.1075/lal.44.11zyn

Always looking on the bright side, ready to contribute wherever he could, he was a dedicated mentor and a devoted friend to many. When his colleague and close friend Bill Nash passed away, he proposed a commemorative collection by eminent stylisticians celebrating Nash's work (Simpson 2019). Although he contributed with one of the chapters in the volume (Verdonk 2019), he preferred to invite Paul Simpson to edit the book, writing quite modestly "Please find enclosed my hesitant attempt at such a proposal which looks a lot more assertive than it is intended to be". According to Statham's review, this volume "engages with a wide range of themes and topics and employs traditional as well as new and continuously emerging approaches in stylistics and its cognate disciplines" (Statham 2020: 454). The same can be said of the present volume. Here, his long-time colleagues contribute with many different branches of stylistics, including textual analysis of poems which are at the core of many of Verdonk's works.

Upon his retirement, he was granted the title of Professor Emeritus of the University of Amsterdam and was presented with a collection of essays in his honour (Bex et al 2000). Carter's words in his "Afterword" of this *Festschrift* can apply to the present book:

> This volume is an appropriate testimony to Peter Verdonk. Its range of problem-solving analytical practices, descriptive frameworks and innovative theorizations serves as a tribute to a scholar who has never ceased to face the awkward problems of his field. Throughout his distinguished career Peter has never lost faith in his recognition that literature is made from, indeed is fundamentally constituted by language and that, complex though this articulatory medium is, its exploration can do much to illuminate and make accessible some of the main ways in which literature works as a human artefact.   (Carter 2000: 267)

It is befitting that a book in honour of Peter Verdonk's memory should be published in the selfsame series he launched and was a staunch supporter of. The depth and scope of each chapter in the present volume pay a due homage and provide an array of perspectives, methods and tools for stylistic analysis. Whether intentionally or not, they express an experiential dimension, namely a feeling of grief for the loss of a cherished friend. Burke introduces the volume by offering a chronological and heartfelt view of Verdonk's career and contributions. Burke's opening is followed by Stockwell's analysis of John Donne's *Meditation XVII*. Here Stockwell argues that style and context are inseparable and that historical contextualization is part of linguistic knowledge. The chapter closes much in the spirit of Verdonk's humour with a witty turn of phrase. In the second chapter, Emmott explores how readers create a representation of a deceased character in Penelope Lively's novel *The Photograph* from the recollection of main and minor bereaved characters. She shows how "the writing style for bereavement memories is sometimes under-specified and fragmented and the episodic memories may be decontextualized" (p. 43). Arguing that Verdonk's rigorous stylistic approach could benefit from a more general framework, Jeffries then provides a detailed analysis of the stylistic choices in Wilfred Owen's war poem "*Dulce et Decorum Est*" to illustrate how analytical framework applied to ideology in political language and news reporting can also work as a general model of textual meaning which may also explain literary and aesthetic effects. Short also emphasizes the strength of the concept of style as motivated choice and offers a detailed stylistic account of "Orange Drums, Tyrone, 1966" by one of Verdonk's favourite poets, Seamus Heaney. Following a similar path, and inspired by Verdonk's analysis of Auden's "*Musée des Beaux Arts*", McIntyre traces parallels with the music hall "Swansong", and, going beyond the language of the text, explores the conative function of the latter. Through his detailed stylistic analysis, he demonstrates how this dark song frustrates expected humour and ends by producing a bittersweet feeling. The title of Chapter 5 ("Where owls nest in beards") is a kind and thoughtful tribute to Peter Verdonk, as explained in an endnote. Only those who knew him well were aware that he was a keen collector of owls. Here Wales analyses the 200 illustrated "limericks" in Edward Lear's books of *Nonsense* and presents evidence, as Stockwell did, that form and meaning cannot be dissociated. The surreal textual world provided by Lear, she argues, is far from being amusing. Many of the limericks are in fact quite somber. Simpson also pays his tribute to Verdonk's keen sense of humour with a chapter on dialogue, humour, and style, where he offers a stylistic framework for understanding the comic element in patterns of dialogue and discourse in an Irish TV comedy. In Chapter 8, Gavins chooses Apollinaire's poem "Il Pleut" to discuss the cognition of iconicity in poetry. In the context of this book, associations to "*il pleure*" are not to be shrugged off. Gavins points out that "It is worth noting here, of course, that in the original French, "*pleurent*" (from the infinitive *pleurer*) has a much more similar spelling to "*pleut*" (from the infinitive *pleuvoir*), creating a more obvious visual connection between weeping and raining" (p. 144). In fact, borrowing her words, the experience of reading this book brings to the reader the "persistent chord" of bereavement which shapes our reading experience of this volume. Speculating on how Peter Verdonk would have analysed two poems by Morrissey and one by Larkin, Toolan also brings up representations of death, albeit tangentially. His point is to build an argument for the strength of contextualized stylistics. Verdonk's concept of "style as motivated choice" is then resumed in the final chapter by Steen, who views it in the light of corpus data derived from the lyrics of Bob Dylan's most representative six albums. Here again the first lines from a Dylan song Steen mentions echo loss: "Oh, with a pain that stops and starts/Like a corkscrew to heart/Ever since we've been apart", from *Blood on the Tracks.* (p. 162). All in all, the experience of reading this volume translates both Peter Verdonk's deep knowledge and the feeling of loss experienced by his friends and colleagues. Indeed, a motivated choice.

Curiously enough, Peter's professional career actually started in international maritime law (for more details, see McIntyre 2013: 5), where he probably realized the value of writing in a clear, concise and direct style. His interest in language and literature, however, led him to pursue an academic career at the University of Amsterdam in the 1970s. Actually, it was by chance that in 1981 he came across an advertisement in the *Times Literary Supplement* announcing a conference at the University of East Anglia organized by Roger Fowler (for more details, see McIntyre, 2013: 5). This first conference turned into a lifetime commitment. He was among the first members to join the Poetics and Linguistics Association (PALA), the stimulating atmosphere of which he acknowledged as a source of inspiration.

Although most of his work centred on the stylistic analysis of poems, Peter never drifted away from literary education. Thus, besides his scholarly contributions, his enthusiasm and natural talent as an educator reflected in the many seminars held at the Department of English Language and Literature at the University of Amsterdam. Through these seminars and the countless lectures he delivered at different conferences, PALA included, generations of stylisticians bloomed and sharpened their skills in textual analysis. More specifically, on one occasion, willing to contribute to pedagogical applications, Peter joined the first Special Interest Group (PEDSIG) during the 1997 PALA conference held in Nottingham, UK, where he provided substantial subsidy to the project carried out by Clark and Zyngier (2003). The aim of this group was to find out whether there was any consensus regarding the practice of stylistics in both L1 and L2 and to arrive at a working definition for pedagogical stylistics. Seven questionnaires from teachers from five different countries contributed to this pilot project. Among the initial findings was that improving students' linguistic sensibilities had to include the way pragmatic and cognitive elements work within quite specific social and cultural contexts.

At that time, defining the areas of action was still being chiselled (Zyngier 2006; Carter 2007; Hall 2014; 2022). Some years later, McIntyre (2011) provided a terminological distinction between pedagogical stylistics and a pedagogy of stylistics, that is, "the application of stylistic techniques in teaching" (p.114), and pedagogical stylistics which investigates the effects of the applications of specific techniques or methods. According to Zyngier and Fialho (2016), it would by now be more appropriate to refer to pedagogical stylistics as the area which studies the language of learning literature (the language of instructions, of students' productions, students' responses etc.). In this sense, pedagogical stylistics should be seen in terms of how scientific methods of research and the empirical data derived from practice, both from qualitative and qualitative perspectives, resulting in evidence-based practice.

Since then, educational settings have undergone many changes, not to mention the growth of online learning as an aftermath of the Covid-19 pandemic. In many places, the teacher's role has definitely shifted from that of a lecturer to that of a mediator (Freire 1973). In addition, the world is being impacted by AI generative programs such as ChatGPT, among others, which have apparently been challenging human creativity. AI programs can now produce essays, poems, lyrics, etc. to the extent that questions on the validity and artistic value of these artificially-generated texts have become imperative. If we could ask Peter, he would probably argue that stylistics provides perspectives and tools which help students see through these texts and sort the wheat from the chaff. Stylistics tools definitely enable readers to assess texts and bring out their ideological inclinations, their biases, and their quality.

Moving from artificially created texts, another area where pedagogical stylistics still needs to be developed involves applying stylistics to languages other than English. Since the 1970s stylistics contributed greatly to speakers of English and of English as an additional language (Brumfit & Carter 1986). Teacher training programs, course books and syllabi have been specially designed to sensitize learners to the workings of language (Carter & Nash 1990; Toolan 1998; Simpson 2014; among many). Peter's edited books (1993; Verdonk & Weber 1995; Culpeper et al 1998; Sell & Verdonk 1994) remain essential to these students and some of the questions he has asked throughout his career are still relevant to pedagogical stylistics (see also Burke et al 2012): why may poems be difficult to read and interpret? Why do students tend to resist them? How can they be aware of the author's verbal artistry and the effect language produces on the reader? What role does stylistics play to students of additional languages other than English? In a globalized world, learning how to see through different languages and cultures may be quite relevant. Some efforts from a stylistics perspective were made many years ago by the OULIPO group in France. Some actions may be taking place in other languages and cultures but teacher training programmes and stylistics courses in languages other than English still have a long way to go.

Reading and interpreting texts in languages other than the original also have consequences teachers and translators should be aware of. As Chesnokova & Zyngier (2022) noted, translators' linguistic options create different contexts which influence students' reading experience and this must be taken into consideration in selecting texts for a course.

Room should also be made to stylistics in courses beyond Language and Literature. For instance, much research has been done on doctor-patient dialogues, interactions in the business place, or in the world of forensics. However, few if any courses are offered to students of these areas on the effect of language choices and the cultural and social implications of their language interactions. More than ever, these courses are needed for those willing, for instance, to engage in psychoanalysis, where patients express themselves through language. What are the actual words they use? How does the therapist interpret them? What happens when the therapist reports what the patient has said? What are the implications? These are questions professional qualification courses should contemplate.

Today, much work is being carried out in the areas of cognition and embodiment to investigate how readers experience literature (see Burke 2010; Stockwell 2022; van Peer & Chenokova 2022) and students will benefit when the results of these investigations make their way into the classroom (for instance, Giovanelli & Harrison 2022). These few examples of where pedagogical stylistics can go illustrate how the field has moved beyond reading and interpreting poems by looking at meaningful structures. Contextualized stylistics has become essential to the various settings in which there is a need to communicate through language, be it visual or verbal (for instance, Douthwaite et al 2017).

Everything we do, say, feel, see is embedded in language. Pedagogical stylisticians need to promote an environment whereby learners become aware of how language works in the various contexts and for what purposes. Teachers need to be prepared to face the challenge of being multipliers. Theories will continue to change, educational approaches as well. However, stylisticians will continue to look at language, its constant shifts and adaptations, its structure, its use in all kinds of situations, and all kinds of effects it achieves. In this sense, Peter Verdonk's publications will continue as fundamental guideposts to stylistics. As a scholar and colleague, he will always be remembered for his humanity and his warmth. The contributors of this volume have been lucky to have shared Peter Verdonk's company and scholarship. His works on stylistics and his example of what it means to be a teacher, a scholar, and a friend will remain. Peter has left us not only a great legacy as scholar, but mostly an example of how one can be both a generous colleague and a kind-hearted friend. Generations of stylisticians will be forever grateful to him.

In his writings and presentations, Peter never forgot to thank his former graduate and postgraduate students for having influenced his thinking on stylistics. But, as he wrote, "in anybody's academic career there is always one person to whom a researcher and writer feels professionally most indebted" (2013: viii). In his case, it was Henry Widdowson; to many, it is and will be Peter Verdonk.

References

Bex, T., Burke, M. & Stockwell, P. (Eds.). 2000. *Contextualized Stylistics: In Honour of Peter Verdonk*. Atlanta: Rodopi.

Brumfit, C. J., & Carter, R. 1986. *Literature and Language Teaching*. Oxford: Oxford University Press.

Burke, M. 2010. Pedagogical issues in stylistics. Special issue. *Language and Literature* 19 (1): 1–128.

Burke, M., Csábi, S., Week, L. & Zerkowitz, J. 2012. (eds.) *Pedagogical Stylistics: Current Trends in Language, Literature and ELT*. London: Continuum.

Carter, R. 2000. Afterword. In *Contextualized Stylistics*, T. Bex, M. Burke, & P. Stockwell (eds.), 267–268. Atlanta: Rodopi.

Carter, R. 2007. Literature and language teaching: 1986–2006. *International Journal of Applied Linguistics* 17 (1): 3–13.

Carter, R. & Nash, W. 1990. *Seeing Through Language: A Guide to Styles of English Writing*. Oxford: Blackwell.

Chesnokova, A., & Zyngier, S. 2022. Considerations on the Use of Translated Poems in EFL Settings. In *Pedagogical Stylistics in the 21st Century*, S. Zyngier & G. Watson (eds.), 233–262. London: Palgrave Macmillan.

Clark, U. & Zyngier, S. 2003. Towards a pedagogical stylistics. *Language and Literature* 12 (4): 339–351.

Culpeper, J., Short, M., & Verdonk, P. 1998. *Exploring the Language of Drama: From Text to Context*. London: Routledge.

Douthwaite, J., Virdis, D. F., & Zurru, E. 2017. *The Stylistics of Landscapes, the Landscapes of Stylistics*. Amsterdam: John Benjamins.

Freire, P. 1973. *Pedagogy of the Oppressed*. Harmondswoth: Penguin.

Giovanelli, M. & Harrison, C. 2022. *Cognitive grammar in the classroom: A case study*. In *Pedagogical Stylistics in the 21st Century*. S. Zyngier & G. Watson (eds.), 131–158. London: Palgrave MacMillan.

Hall, G. 2014. Pedagogical Stylistics. In *The Routledge Handbook of Stylistics*, M. Burke (ed.), 239–252. Oxon and New York: Routledge.

Hall, G. 2022. Pedagogical Stylistics since 2007: a baker's dozen. In *Pedagogical Stylistics in the 21st Century*. S. Zyngier & G. Watson (eds.), 3–29. London: Palgrave MacMillan.

McIntyre, D. 2011. The place of stylistics in the English curriculum. In *Teaching Stylistics*, L. Jeffries & D. McIntyre (eds.), 9–29. Basingstoke: Palgrave/English Subject Centre.

McIntyre, D. 2013. Context, cognition, discourse, history: Peter Verdonk's stylistics of poetry. In *The Stylistics of Poetry*, P. Verdonk (ed.), 1–9. London: Bloomsbury.

Sell, R. & Verdonk, P. 1994. *Literature and the New Interdisciplinarity: Poetics, Linguistics, History*. Amsterdam & Atlanta: Rodopi.

Semino, E. & Culpeper, J. 2002. *Cognitive Stylistics: Language and cognition in text analysis*. Amsterdam: John Benjamins.

Simpson, P. 2014. *Stylistics: A Resource Book for Students*. London: Routledge.

Simpson, P. (ed.). 2019. *Style, Rhetoric and Creativity in Language: In Memory of Walter (Bill) Nash (1926–2015)*. Amsterdam: John Benjamins.

doi   Statham, S. 2020. The year's work in stylistics 2019. *Language and Literature* 29 (4): 454–479.

doi   Stockwell, P. 2022. The Principle of Moments. In *Pedagogical Stylistics in the 21st Century*. S. Zyngier & G. Watson (eds.), 107–129. London: Palgrave MacMillan.

Studer, P. 2002. Review: Verdonk (2002) Stylistics. In LINGUIST List 13.3355, T. Langendoen (ed.), < https://linguistlist.org/issues/13/13-3355/> (28 May 2024)

Toolan, M. 1998. *Language in Literature*. London: Routledge.

doi   Van Peer, W. & Chesnokova, A. 2022. *Experiencing Poetry: A Guidebook to Psychopoetics*. London: Bloomsbury Academic.

doi   Verdonk, P. (ed.). 1993. *Twentieth Century Poetry*. London: Routledge.

Verdonk, P. 2002. *Stylistics*. Oxford: Oxford University Press.

Verdonk, P. 2013. *Stylistics of Poetry: Context, cognition, discourse, history*. London: Bloomsbury.

doi   Verdonk, P. 2019. Riddling: the dominant rhetorical device in WH Auden's 'The Wanderer'. In *Style, Rhetoric and Creativity in Language*, P. Simpson (ed.), 77–84. Amsterdam: John Benjamins.

Verdonk, P. & Weber, J.J. (eds.). 1995. *Twentieth Century Fiction: From Text to Context*. London: Routledge.

doi   Zyngier, S. 2006. Stylistics: Pedagogical applications. In *Encyclopedia of Language and Linguistics*, vol. 6, K. Brown (ed.), 226–232. Amsterdam: Elsevier Science.

doi   Zyngier, S. & Fialho, O. 2016. Pedagogical stylistics: charting outcomes. In *The Bloomsbury Companion to Stylistics*, V. Sotirova (ed.), 208–230. London and New York: Bloomsbury.

Zyngier, S. & Watson, G. 2022. *Pedagogical Stylistics in the 21st Century*. London: Palgrave MacMillan.

Index